ALL MEASURES
SHORT OF WAR

ALL MEASURES SHORT OF WAR

THE CONTEST FOR THE
TWENTY-FIRST CENTURY
AND THE FUTURE OF
AMERICAN POWER

With a New Preface

THOMAS J. WRIGHT

Yale UNIVERSITY PRESS

NEW HAVEN & LONDON

Yale University Press books may be purchased in quantity for educational, business, or promotional use. For information, please e-mail sales.press@yale.edu (U.S. office) or sales@yaleup.co.uk (U.K. office).

Set in Meridien and Futura type by IDS Infotech Ltd., Chandigarh, India.
Printed in the United States of America.

Library of Congress Control Number: 2016957906
ISBN 978-0-300-22328-6 (hardcover : alk. paper)
ISBN 978-0-300-24027-6 (pbk.)

A catalogue record for this book is available from the British Library.

10 9 8 7 6 5 4 3 2 1

To my wife, Karen McMonagle

CONTENTS

PREFACE TO THE PAPERBACK EDITION

Inter-state strategic competition, not terrorism, is now the primary concern in U.S. national security.

—U.S. National Defense Strategy, January 2018

Great-power rivalry is a normal and regular occurrence in world history but it is not normal or regular in recent times. The two decades after the fall of the Berlin Wall were an anomalous period of unprecedented international cooperation. There were disagreements and crises, especially in the Middle East, but Russia, China, and other nations seemed to accept the U.S.-led international order. Some non-Western nations even appeared to be converging with it. In the West itself, the order was expanding and deepening and seemed to be thriving.

We grew accustomed to the major powers settling their differences diplomatically even in the bitterest of crises. When Russia objected to the American invasion of Iraq in 2003, it did not intervene militarily on Iraq's behalf; it made its point at the United Nations. Territorial disputes in Europe and Asia seemed unlikely to lead to conflict. We had faith in the power of globalization and technological change to promote peace, prosperity, and mutual understanding.

Over the past decade, rivalry has resurged, and it is intensifying with every passing month. Russia followed up its annexation of Crimea, aggression in Ukraine, and military intervention in Syria with an audacious and covert political intervention in elections in the United States and Europe. China dissolved its political system of shared power in favor of unbridled power for one man in perpetuity, used coercive measures toward seizing control of the South China Sea, and covertly interferes in the domestic affairs of not only its neighbors but also Europe and the United States. After consolidating their position as authoritarian rulers in 2018, both Vladimir Putin and Xi Jinping are likely to be major players on the world stage for the rest of their lives.

After a brief glimmer of hope in the Arab Awakening of 2011, any expectation of democratic reform in the Middle East has been all but extinguished. Iran and the Sunni Arab states are locked in a regional struggle that is sometimes cold and sometimes hot. The Syrian civil war has resulted in the deaths of so many people that international monitoring groups have stopped counting (the last United Nations estimate of 400,000 was in 2016[1]). It has dragged in outside powers, even splitting two NATO allies, Turkey and the United States. Russia has exploited this regional drama, seeking to establish itself as a powerbroker and making the case for realignment.

Meanwhile, the Western powers are unsure about their role as guardians of the liberal order. Donald Trump's election as president on an "America First" platform was widely interpreted as revealing reluctance on the part of the American people to play a leadership role in the world. At the time of writing (May 2018), after a year of relative deference to the national security establishment, President Trump has shaken up his team to give it a much more nationalistic bent and the future of free trade, the non-proliferation regime, the American alliance system, and U.S. backing for democracy and human rights hangs in the balance. France, Germany, and some other European countries responded to Trump's election by dedicating themselves to building Europe up as a coherent actor, but Europe is still deeply divided on migration, economics, and security and is only now beginning to reckon with economic and political challenges posed by China and Russia.

The new era of rivalry is still in its very early stages. While individual elements are visible, the causes, scope, nature, and stakes of the rivalry remain hazy and elusive. This is not unusual. New geopolitical eras are usually unclear at the beginning. After German unification in 1870, it took more than twenty years for the risks to come into focus. After World War I, it took more than a decade for the fragility and vulnerability of the peace to be understood. It took the Soviet Union and the United States until the Cuban Missile Crisis to understand each other's red lines and how to compete in a way that averted Armageddon.

New geopolitical eras also present great risk. We can be blind to the trajectory of threats, just as President Obama failed to understand how far Russia was willing to go in interfering in the American election until its interference was exposed. They also increase the risk of inadvertent escalation and needless conflicts. In the 1960s, the United States intervened in Vietnam because it feared the spread of communism in Southeast Asia when nationalism and anti-colonialism were what really motivated the North Vietnamese. As we grasp for analogies, as we look for the familiar—thinking that this is a new Cold War or looking for an overarching one-size-fits-all narrative—we make mistakes.

All Measures Short of War is an attempt to frame the United States' strategic future in the hope that we can make wise decisions. I finished the hardcover edition in January 2017, a week before Donald Trump was inaugurated as president of the United States. The core arguments of the book remain as valid today as they were then.

I argued that the era of convergence came to an end because Russian and Chinese leaders believe that the liberal international order posed an existential threat to their regimes. As they see it, if liberalism thrives everywhere, authoritarianism is safe nowhere. The Chinese Communist Party has seen the free press expose corruption among its elite. Putin knows that Russians may seek to emulate the successful "color revolution" in Ukraine or elsewhere in their neighborhood. The leaders know that Western governments will always face pressure to back democracy activists overseas at precisely the moment that authoritarians are most vulnerable, regardless of what assurances or cooperative relations existed beforehand. And so, as China rose and Russia regained strength, they began to push back, hard.

The return to rivalry was inevitable, if tragically so. The United States and its allies could not have addressed Chinese and Russian concerns. To have done so would have brought the essence of the liberal order to an end. Accepting restrictions on the flow of information and political activity would have given Moscow and Beijing a veto over democracy in other countries, not just their own. It would have undermined a world system where rules, values, and votes play a leading role and handed the world to a small number of people to carve up.

Russia and China are very different powers and must not be lumped together. Russia is in overall decline whereas China is rising; Russia has little economic power whereas China is an economic powerhouse; Russia relies mainly on hard power and dirty tricks whereas China has multiple tools at its disposal; Putin relishes direct confrontation with the West whereas Xi tries to conceal his opposition. However, both Beijing and Moscow are revisionist. They seek to overturn basic elements of the existing international order and undermine the order's standard-bearers at home.

They each seek an enhanced sphere of influence in their regions at the expense of not only the United States but also its allies. Some may dismiss these ambitions as regional in scope, but it was the success of regional orders in Northeast Asia and Europe after World War II that created the conditions in which global institutions could succeed. Ultimately, aggression and the annexation of territory are much greater challenges to the global order than disputes about voting weights at the International Monetary Fund or debates on whether the Asian Infrastructure Investment Bank is a good idea. If these two regional orders unravel, it will gravely damage the global order more generally.

Russia and China also want to make the wider world safe for their brand of authoritarianism. They feel compelled to weaken certain liberal norms, especially regarding human rights, democracy, and freedom of expression. They seek to accomplish this by interfering in the domestic politics of Western societies, using what a report by the National Endowment for Democracy has called "Sharp Power": they "pierce, penetrate, or perforate the political and information environments in the targeted countries."[2]

General war between the major powers is very unlikely even as tensions rise. Instead, they compete with all measures short of major war—economic war, coercive diplomacy, cyberwarfare, proxy wars, political warfare, covert action, and incremental revisionism. The protagonists, including the Western powers, exploit the linkages and connections that bind all nations. In effect, they are weaponizing integration to achieve their objectives. This is dramatically changing the American experience of globalization by increasing our vulnerability to those with whom we are connected.

What has become clear to me since I finished the hardcover edition was just how transformative this new era of rivalry is likely to be, not just internationally but also at home. In 2017 and early 2018 we learned so much—how Russia used technology to refine its old methods of political interference to disrupt the American election in 2016; how China is using subtler measures to influence democratic societies; how great powers compete in technological innovation; and how the United States is having doubts about the leadership role it has embraced since the late 1940s.

The extent and sophistication of authoritarian operations in Western democracies have been shocking. A senior U.S. official told me in April 2016 that the White House was worried that Putin might interfere in the election. At the time it seemed a remote possibility. Today Russian meddling is one of the most immediate and difficult threats Western democracies face.

Russia goes beyond pursuing specific electoral outcomes and extends its efforts to stoking divisions within the United States and other democracies. It has proven itself to be very innovative in its tactics. On one occasion, a Russian troll farm in St. Petersburg set up separate Facebook pages to organize pro-Islam and anti-Islam actions in Houston on the same day, May 21, 2017. One page, The Heart of Texas, called for a protest at the Islamic Da'wah Center in Houston to "Stop Islamization of Texas." The other page, United Muslims of America, put together a counter rally called "Save Islamic Knowledge."[3]

China is more subtle. It has used political funding, economic influence and coercion, and Confucius institutes to achieve its objectives. It has also sought to acquire large amounts of data on Westerners, particularly Americans. Some of this activity is covert, but Chinese firms do appear to have bought Western firms that contain large amounts of data as assets. China has also expanded its operations in Central Asia, using investment funds through the One Belt One Road initiative to prod smaller states into dependent relationships with China, and has taken advantage of the Trump administration's abandonment of the Trans-Pacific Partnership.

These developments are just some of the early examples of how this new era of rivalry will surprise us. There is no doubt that the surprises will continue.

The character of the Cold War was defined by the nuclear revolution. Terms like "mutual assured destruction," "deterrence," "brinksmanship," "missile defense," and "arms control" became part of the daily lexicon. The Cold War, in turn, shaped global society as humanity learned to live under the shadow of Armageddon.

The character of today's rivalry will also be defined in large part by technological change. And the rivalry will shape, and possibly transform, society as a whole. The major authoritarian powers will harness technology as a means not just to leapfrog over rivals but also to consolidate social control and shape foreign attitudes. These efforts will have far-reaching consequences.

We cannot predict with precision the technologies of the future but we can make an educated guess. Many experts believe that innovation in the field of artificial intelligence (AI)—the advent of more intelligent and autonomous machines—will transform warfare, rivalry, and society in general. The strategist Frank Hoffman has described the AI revolution as the seventh revolution in military affairs, following the use of banking and taxes to finance war, mass mobilization, the first industrial revolution, the armored warfare of World Wars I and II, nuclear weapons, and the information revolution.[4] As my colleague and Brookings president, John Allen, has argued, this revolution will transform how militaries fight.[5]

Other experts have argued that quantum technology could be "even as significant an advance in the 21st century as harnessing electricity was in the 19th."[6] Quantum technology could result in unhackable information networks and the ability to crack existing systems. It may also enable the reliable detection of targets buried deep below ground and in the ocean.

Breakthroughs in one technology may have an even greater impact when paired with breakthroughs in another. They could upend the balance of power upon which the international order rests. The arms races of the twenty-first century will certainly involve new technologies. Adversaries will find ways to harness and deploy these tools for strategic ends. And, just as the Internet began as a military project before transforming society, so too might this technological rivalry spill over into civilian life.

Western democracies are barely beginning to understand the scale and scope of the task ahead. After just a few years, the rivalry between authoritarian and liberal nations has fundamentally shaken confidence in the soundness of our democracies. It has contributed to greater political polarization. It has wreaked havoc on some of the world's largest companies. And it has led to an escalation of tensions overseas. It is not the Cold War, but the societal challenge may prove similar in scope and scale.

Yes, there is some recognition within the foreign-policy community of the change in the strategic environment. By the end of the Obama administration, the United States had imposed sanctions on Russia and laid down red lines in the South China Sea. But Obama's foreign policy also tried to minimize the competitive nature of the relationship in a way that left the United States badly exposed. By the end of Obama's term, Russia had interfered in the U.S. presidential election and China had made significant advances toward controlling the South China Sea. The prospect of rapprochement with Iran and diminished commitment in the Middle East had contributed to the spread of disorder and regional rivalries.

The Trump administration is riven by internal contradictions. Officially, in the 2017 National Security Strategy and in the 2018 National Defense Strategy, it recognized the end of the post–Cold War era of convergence and the return of great-power rivalry.[7] Clearly, President Trump does not agree with this assessment. In his introductory remarks in the National Security Strategy, and in other major speeches dealing with foreign policy, Trump has barely mentioned Russia and China at all. Instead, he has spent most of his time on the threats from immigration, free trade, terrorism, and North Korea.[8] He frequently criticizes America's allies and seeks to reduce America's engagement in each of the three key regions of strategic importance.

President Trump has repeatedly argued for closer cooperation with Putin's Russia, and he has argued that trade is the only real problem in U.S.-China relations. Some of this is rhetoric, but some of it has a significant impact on policy. In testimony to the Senate Armed Services Committee, the head of the National Security Agency, Admiral Michael Rogers, said the Russians "haven't paid a price at least that's sufficient to get them to change their behavior," adding that the White House had declined to give him the authority to disrupt Russian election-hacking operations at their source.[9]

But even if Trump were to grasp the meaning of renewed strategic competition, Americans would still struggle to grasp how the new era of rivalry will profoundly change the fabric of society. During an election, campaign information needs to be digested and processed differently, for example, and the obligations of the private sector need to be reassessed, especially those of companies collecting large amounts of data or pioneering new technologies coveted by foreign powers.

Perhaps most important of all is the need to reconsider, and perhaps reaffirm, America's purpose in the world. After World War II, the United States saw its purpose as creating and leading an international order of like-minded states committed to liberal democracy, market economies, and the rule of law. President Truman and others believed that the American system could survive and prosper only in a hospitable and friendly international context.

Today, President Trump champions America First—the notion that the United States has gotten a raw deal from the international order and must be more selfish in its dealings with other countries. America First appears to fit in with a more nationalistic mood globally, but it comes at a high price.

America's unique advantage since World War II has been that it defines its strategic interests in a way that is compatible with the strategic interests of dozens of other powerful states. In other words, other countries want the United States to succeed. By insisting that the international order be free, open, democratic, and cooperative, the United States offers something that appeals to a wide swath of people across all nations. Yes, for decades the United States shouldered a disproportionate share of the burden of supporting the international order, but this was precisely why other nations accepted its role and treated it differently than the great powers and empires of old were treated.

The United States must recognize this new era of rivalry and prepare for it. If it does not, the cost will not just be an erosion of the U.S. position in the South China Sea or Eastern Europe. The cost will not even just be the end of the liberal international order and a more transactional, nationalistic, and conflict-prone world. Failing to prepare to compete means losing the struggle with authoritarianism. And losing the struggle could well change America itself for the worse. External political interference could become routine. Democracy could weaken. National economies could suffer under a protectionist international system.

Weakness and loss are not inevitable, however. If the United States chooses to compete responsibly, it can succeed. The challenges are real but certainly no more severe than the challenges previous generations have faced. America's allies have just as much at stake in the competition as America does and are keen to join forces to deal with the new challenges. Democracies are collectively stronger than authoritarian states and have fewer structural weakness even if the weaknesses tend to be more visible. The liberal international order is capable of reform and change and remains the only vision of the world that transcends narrow national interests. This is why I am ultimately optimistic about the future.

NOTES

Epigraph: U.S. Department of Defense, *Summary of the 2018 National Defense Strategy,* January 19, 2018, https://www.defense.gov/Portals/1/Documents/pubs/2018-National-Defense-Strategy-Summary.pdf.

1. Megan Specia, "Syria's Death Toll is Lost in the Fog of War," *New York Times,* April 13, 2018, https://www.nytimes.com/2018/04/13/world/middleeast/syria-death-toll.html.

2. Christopher Walker and Jessica Ludwig, "The Meaning of Sharp Power: How Authoritarian States Project Influence," *Foreign Affairs,* November 16, 2016, https://www.foreignaffairs.com/articles/china/2017-11-16/meaning-sharp-power.

3. "Texas Secession Movement: Russia-Linked Facebook Group Asked Us to Participate in Anti-Clinton Rallies," *Business Insider,* September 14, 2017, http://www.businessinsider.com/russia-facebook-group-ads-texas-secession-secede-trump-clinton-2017-9.

4. F. G. Hoffman, "Will War's Nature Change in the Seventh Military Revolution?" *Parameters* 47, no. 4 (Winter 2017/18), https://ssi.armywarcollege.edu/pubs/parameters/issues/Winter_2017-18/5_Hoffman.pdf

5. John Allen and Amir Husain, "On Hyperwar," *Proceedings,* United States Naval Institute, Annapolis, 143, no. 7 (July 2017): 30–37.

6. Michael J. Biercuk and Richard Fontaine, "The Leap into Quantum Technology: A Primer for National Security Professionals," *War on the Rocks,* November 17, 2017, https://warontherocks.com/2017/11/leap-quantum-technology-primer-national-security-professionals/.

7. The White House, *National Security Strategy of the United States of America,* December 2017, https://www.whitehouse.gov/wp-content/uploads/2017/12/NSS-Final-12-18-2017-0905.pdf.

8. Thomas Wright, "Trump Wants Little to Do with His Own Foreign Policy," *The Atlantic,* January 31, 2018, https://www.theatlantic.com/international/archive/2018/01/trump-foreign-policy-russia-china-nato-mcmaster-tillerson-mattis/552002/.

9. Admiral Michael S. Rogers, *Testimony to the Senate Armed Services Committee,* February 27, 2018, https://www.armed-services.senate.gov/hearings/18-02-27-united-states-cyber-command.

PREFACE

This is a book about why the post–Cold War international order has come to an end and what comes next. I started writing it in the spring of 2014, shortly after Russia's invasion and annexation of Crimea. I finished it in December 2016, just after the United States elected Donald Trump as its forty-fifth president, a man who ran against U.S. global leadership on a nationalist platform of "America First." These events—along with the United Kingdom's vote to leave the European Union—were nothing short of astonishing. But they did not come out of the blue.

The past five years saw the end of the era of convergence and the advent of a more nationalist and competitive world. In the two decades after the Cold War, all major powers appeared to be converging toward a liberal international order that promoted cooperation and integration. They all prospered in a globalized economy and shared the same challenges—terrorism, climate change, rogue states, and economic volatility—even if they disagreed from time to time on how to tackle them. Non-Western powers like Russia and China were never going to transform into liberal democracies overnight, but they appeared poised to become "responsible stakeholders" in this liberal order. Geopolitical differences over territory and ideology never disappeared completely, but they seemed to fade into insignificance. Successive American presidents based their national security policies on this pursuit of convergence.

In recent years, instead of convergence we had divergence. Authoritarian leaders in Russia and China worried that the liberal order would undermine their hold on power, and they coveted spheres of influence in their regions. They tolerated the liberal order when they were relatively weak, but as they became more powerful, they acted on those beliefs. Both pursued revisionist strategies to upend the status quo in their regions, albeit by different means. Meanwhile, the Western model of liberal order took a number of punishing blows, particularly with the financial crisis of 2008. Economic integration—whether with the euro, immigration, trade, or finance—was increasingly perceived as a threat to the well-being of Western nations. The political establishment struggled to respond, and populists began their ascent.

By 2016, the world had become much more nationalist and geopolitically competitive. The United States and Russia were locked in an economic war over Ukraine and in a tense standoff in Syria. China was building islands in the South China Sea in an effort to turn it into a Chinese lake. There were doubts over American resolve as the Obama administration sought to reduce its engagement in the Middle East and pulled its punches in Europe and East Asia, sometimes to secure Moscow's and Beijing's cooperation on global issues.

Trump's election will sharply accelerate the trend. For seventy years the United States built and led a liberal international order characterized by alliances, an open economy, multilateral cooperation, democracy, and human rights. Trump has explicitly rejected this strategy. For Trump, the United States should define its interests very narrowly and set aside any concept of the common good. The liberal order has always rested on American power and a willingness to uphold it. Without such power and leadership, it is fragile and vulnerable.

History suggests that instability is at its greatest in the early phases of a new paradigm, especially one involving strategic competition. For example, the early period of the Cold War was prone to crisis, which only abated and became more predictable after the Cuban Missile Crisis of 1962. The reason is clear: at the beginning, no one is quite sure where the red lines are. The protagonists probe and test each other and often overstep the mark. They are, in effect, in a learning process. Later on, clarity descends. They have a better sense of each other's core interests and strategic limits, and they can adapt to a new equilibrium and peaceful, albeit tense, coexistence. As the post–Cold War order comes to an end, ambiguity reigns and instability beckons.

This book's title, *All Measures Short of War*, is taken from President Franklin Delano Roosevelt's policy in 1939–1941 to do everything to help the Allies short of declaring war on Germany. *Measures Short of War* is also the title of an influential lecture given by George F. Kennan, the author of the doctrine of containment, at the National War College in September 1946 about how the United States and the Soviet Union would try to pressure each other. Now, in the coming era, all of the great powers want to avoid a major war with each other. But they will compete fiercely to gain an upper hand in ways short of a major war. They will engage in coercive diplomacy and military build-ups. They may use force against smaller countries and engage in limited proxy wars with each other. They will exploit each other's vulnerabilities in an interdependent world—economically, technologically, and politically. They may even form temporary tactical alliances with rivals to accomplish their short-term objectives.

None of this is to say that a major war is impossible. It could occur inadvertently, through miscalculation or a dramatic change in intentions. Diplomacy will be needed to keep the peace. Indeed, when Roosevelt pursued an "all measures short of war" strategy, war did break out. But the most likely outcome is a prolonged period of high-stakes peacetime competition with all of the old red lines blurred if not erased. This competition will mainly take place in the three regions of greatest strategic importance—Europe, East Asia, and the Middle East. There will be a strong ideological component that pits liberal democracy against authoritarianism.

One of the most important features of this new era of nationalism and competition is that it occurs against a backdrop of unprecedented globalization. The major powers are closely linked with each other economically and technologically. It is widely believed that interdependence promotes cooperation, but in the coming decade it is more likely to be perceived as a source of vulnerability and strategic competition, whether it involves sanctions, cyberwarfare, or other means of coercion. We already saw this play out in Western sanctions on Russia and in Russia's extraordinary interference in the 2016 U.S. election. This weaponization of interdependence is just a glimpse of what is to come. Norms may emerge, but only after a struggle, with actions taken by all sides, in which an equilibrium is formed and adjusted in accordance with the realities of the balance of power.

The United States is ill prepared for a nationalist and geopolitically competitive world. Those who support the liberal order, like President Barack Obama, have been slow to understand the challenges to it from revisionist states, a collapsing Middle East, and rising populism. Those who embrace the shift, like President Trump, seem unaware of the long-term consequences of a more chaotic world. But Americans cannot afford strategic drift.

The good news is that the United States is strong enough to shape the future. It is not in decline, and it has considerable strengths and advantages that it can bring to bear in its foreign policy. But Americans have a strategic choice to make as consequential as the decision to create the liberal order in the late 1940s. The United States can reduce its role in the world and allow a spheres-of-influence system to emerge, one in which revisionist powers like Russia and China share power with the United States in Europe and East Asia. Or the United States can compete responsibly with these powers to revive and uphold the liberal order. Although sharing power in a spheres-of-influence system may appear attractive at first glance, it would fail to accomplish its objectives and would make the world more dangerous. This book makes the argument for a strategy of responsible competition, which entails increasing American engagement in Europe and East Asia and recognition of the competitive nature of our age. Responsible competition is a strategy the Trump administration is unlikely to adopt, but the United States must ultimately embrace it to protect its long-term interests in this new era of great-power competition.

ACKNOWLEDGMENTS

I am deeply grateful to a large number of people for making this book possible. I have been very fortunate to have The Brookings Institution as my intellectual and professional home since December 2011. Brookings is a wonderful place to work and a melting pot of ideas and expertise. Given the broad nature of my topic, I benefited hugely from talking with my colleagues, and their work is widely referenced in the text that follows. In particular, I would like to thank Jeff Bader, Richard Bush, Philippe Le Corre, Shadi Hamid, Tanvi Madan, Will McCants, Theodore Piccone, Steven Pifer, Jonathan Pollack, Bruce Riedel, Javier Solana, Constanze Stelzenmueller, and Harold Trinkunas.

Several of my colleagues read and commented on various drafts of the book and influenced my thinking on particular parts: Fiona Hill on Vladimir Putin and his foreign policy; Tamara Wittes on the Middle East; and Michael O'Hanlon on defense policy. Michael, who is also our director of research, oversaw a smooth review and approval process and provided wise counsel and support.

Bruce Jones was responsible for my joining Brookings in 2011. He has been an incredible colleague and has had an enormous impact on my thinking. Bob Kagan is someone whose work I admired for many years. His grasp of history, strategy, the role of the American public, and the constraints of domestic politics are quite remarkable, and I learned a great deal from him. Martin Indyk, our executive vice president, has always been incredibly supportive of my work. I was very fortunate to spend a week in the Middle East with Martin in the final stages of drafting the book, and many of the ideas we discussed there are reflected here. I would also like to thank the president of Brookings, Strobe Talbott, for his support, both for me as a fellow and for having a project dedicated to international order and strategy at Brookings.

My friend Jeremy Shapiro may not disagree with every word in this book, but it is a safe bet that he disagrees with every second word. Jeremy is the smartest contrarian thinker I know on U.S. foreign policy, and he has made my arguments much sharper, and hopefully more robust, through continuous, collegial, and entertaining disagreements over the past five years, for which I am very grateful. There have even been occasions where he has changed my mind.

My writing of this book coincided with my involvement with another project at Brookings on the same topic. The bipartisan Order from Chaos study group met for eighteen months from mid-2015 until February 2017 and produced a national security strategy for the United States for which I was the lead drafter. I am indebted to the members of that task force—Derek Chollet, Eric Edelman, Michele Flournoy, Stephen Hadley, Kristen Silverberg, and Jake Sullivan, as well as the three other Brookings members, Bruce, Bob, and Martin—for many stimulating conversations.

I owe a particular debt of gratitude to my research assistants who have helped on this book: Laura Daniels, Rob Keane, and

Will Moreland. All three provided invaluable research assistance as well as ensuring that our day-to-day work ran smoothly despite long writing sessions. Will played a crucial role in finalizing the manuscript.

I benefited greatly from advice from friends and colleagues on various ideas in this book. I would like to thank Misha Auslin, William Burke-White, Joshua Busby, Jon Caverley, Zack Cooper, Samuel Charap, Jackie Deal, Abraham Denmark, Daniel Drezner, Heather Hurlburt, Hans Kundnani, Niamh King, Alexander Lennon, Edward Luce, Evan Medeiros, Jonathan Monten, Nirav Patel, Ely Ratner, Iskander Rehman, Kori Schake, Randy Scheunemann, Erin Simpson, Vikram Singh, Matthew Spence, and Ashley Tellis.

A number of people read the manuscript from beginning to end and provided comments and edits, which were indispensable. These are Mathew Burrows, Daniel Blumenthal, Geoff Dyer, Michael Green, Emile Hokayem, Siddharth Mohandas, Natan Sachs, Elizabeth Saunders, Andrew Small, and Torrey Tausig. Two people merit a special mention for reading the draft multiple times and for spending many hours talking through different aspects of it with me—my good friends David Gordon and Andrew Shearer. The book, whatever its flaws, is immeasurably stronger because of their wise counsel and sharp editing skills.

A number of institutions and individuals provided financial support for this project: the Smith Richardson Foundation, the Carnegie Corporation of New York, Danny Abraham, Jonathan Colby, Raj Fernando, Ben Jacobs, Ned Lamont, and Haim Saban. I thank them all for their generous support of the Order from Chaos project at Brookings, of which this is a part. The governments of Denmark, Sweden, and Finland provided support for international consultations that helped inform my research.

A special thanks to my literary agent, Bridget Matzie. Bridget taught me an enormous amount about the publishing process and how to position this book for a general audience. The book would not be what it is without her advice and help. I would also like to thank Jaya Chatterjee and Mary Pasti, my editors at Yale University Press, and Julie Carlson, my manuscript editor, all of whom have been terrific to work with—and very patient!

My greatest debts are to my family. To my parents and my siblings—Peter, Bernard, John, and Catherine—for giving me early experience in world affairs with lively conversations around the dinner table in Dublin. And to the love of my life, my wonderful wife, Karen McMonagle. Karen has been a tremendous source of support throughout, and I am extraordinarily lucky to have her as a partner in life.

1 THE CONVERGENCE MYTH

The most powerful foreign-policy instrument of the 1990s and 2000s was not a weapon or a diplomatic alliance. It was an idea. Like all powerful ideas, this one was simple: as countries embraced globalization, they would become more "responsible" members of the liberal international order and would, over time, liberalize domestically. Foreign-policy experts had faith in it. CEOs preached it. *New York Times* columnists wrote Pulitzer Prize–winning books about it. Presidents made it a core part of their national security strategies. Citizens of other nations believed it, too, including many Russians, Chinese, Indians, and Brazilians. It did not matter whether you were on the left or the right. Almost everyone bought into the basic notion of convergence, even if they were unfamiliar with the term.[1]

Convergence went far beyond the end of history predicted by Francis Fukuyama—Fukuyama noted the absence of ideological alternatives to capitalism but recognized that non-ideological struggles would persist.[2] Convergence meant that major powers would stop treating each other as rivals and begin to work together to tackle common challenges. They would reform their economies to better compete in the global marketplace. They would develop common rules to govern how nations behave internationally. The story of the past quarter century is the rise and fall of this idea of convergence. Its initial success utterly transformed world politics and produced an unprecedented period of peace and cooperation among the great powers. Its collapse over the past five years has left U.S. strategy unmoored, allowed the reemergence of geopolitical competition between the great powers, and raised serious doubts about the future of the liberal international order.

AN UNBALANCED AMERICA

One might ask why the post–Cold War period was unique. What was it about an age of convergence that distinguished it from all other eras in modern history? Yes, the United States was a dominant power, but the period was hardly harmonious. Like other decades in modern times, it was tumultuous. The 1990s and 2000s saw financial crises, genocide, mass atrocities, rogue states, terrorist attacks, and wars. But a fundamental change had occurred. The defining and unique feature of world politics after the Cold War was the absence of balancing against the United States.[3] Balancing is a term of art in political science to describe how a major power will push back against another country that it sees as especially powerful or threatening.[4] It is, in effect, the act of engaging in a geopolitical competition. Balancing can include arming your rival's enemies, building up your own military, creating an alliance to contain your rival, or setting down red lines over which you would go to war. History is replete with examples of balancing. The United States and the Soviet Union balanced against each other throughout the Cold War. The United States balanced against Imperial Japan. Britain, infamously, was slow to balance against Nazi Germany even though it played the role of balancer on the European continent for centuries, intervening on behalf of the weaker power to prevent any one country from controlling all of the European landmass.

The absence of balancing did not mean that other countries always agreed with the United States. They did not. Rather, it meant there were limits to how they would express their opposition. When Russia opposed the United States over Iraq in 2003, it did not arm Saddam Hussein, intervene on his behalf, or place military advisers in Iraq, as it would do in Syria in 2015. It confined itself to a vote in the UN Security Council. Russia also opposed NATO diplomatically but not by invading its neighbors. China pursued a much more restrained and multilateral foreign policy in Asia than it does today. It had claims on the South China Sea but it did not build islands on the scale it does now, it did not coerce its neighbors as it has in recent years, and its relations with the United States were much more relaxed.

There were occasional spasms of anger. In 1999, after the United States bombed Serbia into submission over Kosovo, Russian forces landed in Pristina airport in Kosovo to prevent it from being occupied by the United States. Wesley Clark, commanding general of NATO forces, was furious and gave the order for his troops to attack the Russians, but his deputy, a British general by the name of Michael Jackson, refused to carry it out. "I won't start World War III for you," Jackson told Clark. Another incident occurred on the other side of the world two years later. In April of 2001, two months after George W. Bush took office, a U.S. spy plane crash-landed on Hainan Island, off the coast of China, after colliding with a Chinese fighter jet. The Chinese held the American crew and plane and refused to release them until the United States apologized for spying. For a while, the crisis looked likely to spark a dramatic worsening of U.S.-China relations and accelerate a return to rivalry, but a face-saving solution was reached. These were isolated incidents of geopolitical tension, however, and did not represent a particular strategy of balancing by any power.

There is a widely held view that the world was simpler during the Cold War. But the single most complicating factor in world politics is when a large and prosperous country sees it as its mission to ensure that another country's foreign policy fails. Contrary to widespread belief, world politics became easier and more straightforward after the Cold War. It was a permissive environment for the United States in which there was minimal great-power resistance to its foreign policy. The often vituperative debate on U.S. strategy in the 2000s masked the fact that the costs of failure had radically diminished from the height of the Cold War and that the scope for choice had widened accordingly.

The absence of balancing was an extraordinary revolution in world politics. It created a unique moment in history in which geopolitical competition subsided and countries were more inclined to cooperate with each other.[5] For centuries states had competed and fought. The twentieth century was the bloodiest ever. But the unexpected collapse of the Soviet Union provided the United States and the West with an unprecedented opportunity. The United States could lead all nations into a new era. The major powers would work with each other to tackle shared challenges. States would still compete with each other but over economic investment and trade opportunities, not to enhance their own security at others' expense or to claim more territory.

This was no accident. It was a choice. The United States emerged from the Cold War as an unrivaled superpower—what some referred to as a unipolar power—and sought to do two things.[6] The first was to maintain and extend its military primacy so that the gap between the United States and potential rivals was so large that it would be futile to challenge it. Research by political scientists has shown that this approach was generally effective: the extent of U.S. power meant that potential rivals were discouraged from balancing against the United States.[7] The gap was simply too big. Why embark on a risky strategy when the odds of success were so low? As long as the United States remained vastly more powerful than its potential rivals, others would be strongly discouraged from balancing against it.

The power gap may have been necessary, but it was not sufficient. After all, if the United States had become a threat to other great powers like Europe, China, and Russia, they could have united in a grand coalition to stop Washington in its tracks. But they did not because instead of conquering other major powers, the United States made its second choice. It offered participation in much of the Western liberal order to the rest of the world so that potential rivals could benefit from engaging with the United States.[8]

These choices and the absence of balancing opened the door for a new era of globalization as the United States spread the gospel of markets, deregulation, capital flows, foreign direct investment, and trade. Countries competed for a share of the ever-increasing pie, and they transformed their own economies and systems of government to be more competitive. In *The Lexus and the Olive Tree*, *New York Times* columnist Thomas Friedman captured the zeitgeist of the moment. Globalization, he wrote, "is the system that has now replaced the old Cold War system, and, like that Cold War system, globalization has its own rules and logic that today directly or indirectly influence the politics and economics of virtually every country in the world."[9]

In a 2002 book titled *The Ideas That Conquered the World*, Michael Mandelbaum of Johns Hopkins University argued that the world was dominated by three major ideas: "peace as the preferred basis for relations among countries; democracy as the optimal way to organize political life within them; and the free market as the indispensable vehicle for producing wealth."[10] These ideas provided the basis for a "market centered international order" that "commanded almost universal allegiance not only because every country saw potential benefit in it but also because there was no viable alternative."[11]

Elites and governments the world over would recognize that their interests were best served by converging with the U.S.-led order. Thus China began to open up with incredible success while India, Brazil, and other developing economies experienced enormous societal changes and rapid economic growth. This assumption operated not just for Russia, China, and emerging powers, but also for Western countries, which were already part of the order. The political left would open up to the market and abandon notions of socialism. And this is exactly what happened as a new generation of globally minded center leaders came to power—in the United States with Bill Clinton pursuing a centrist and reform-minded economic policy, in the United Kingdom with Tony Blair, and in Germany with Gerhard Schroeder.

There were also some American strategists who believed that the United States could help the process of convergence along by giving history a little push. The International Monetary Fund thus came to impose strict conditions on how countries, like Russia, must reform their economies. The United States used its foreign economic diplomacy to further the so-called Washington Consensus, which required recipients of development aid and financial assistance to follow certain economic policies, such as fiscal discipline and privatization. On the security front, the United States embraced regime change and humanitarian interventions in order to remove the worst violators of liberal values and replace them with democratic regimes more open to integrating into the international community. There were also more subtle, light-touch strategies—for instance, the United States and Europe helped non-governmental organizations and international institutions work with other countries to aid the transition to market democracy.

It is not so much that geopolitics went away, but rather that the United States had a royal flush that it displayed in front of other players. Russia was a shattered country in the 1990s with no capability to stop NATO expansion or U.S. interventionism. China was very much in the "biding time" phase of its rise. Beijing could privately covet disputed territories in its neighborhood, but it had no viable strategy to confront Washington over them.

Over time, U.S. leaders would identify a third driver of convergence. The major powers faced the same threats—catastrophic terrorism, nuclear proliferation, climate change, pandemic diseases, and economic volatility. These shared threats were so great that they eclipsed traditional security problems like territorial disputes and the threat of war among the great powers. Just as the European powers of the early nineteenth century had joined forces to combat the common threat of revolution, so too would today's great powers work in concert against common threats. This belief existed in the 1990s, but it became an accepted fact after 9/11 and throughout the 2000s as the world struggled to deal with al-Qaeda and as transnational threats became a more pressing concern.

To its architects, the real genius of the convergence strategy was, and in some cases still is, that eventually it would create a global order that could survive the decline of the United States. Historically, order is created by powerful states—it never emerges organically or by accident—and it dies when those states decline. Great Britain and Russia created the Concert of Europe, which collapsed when Germany unified and rose to great-power status. Great Britain built the British Empire, which dissolved after World War II. The United States created the Western liberal order. Normally, the U.S. order would collapse upon the decline of the United States and the rise of a country like China. But some U.S. strategists, scholars, and leaders believed that they were creating an order that would become indispensable to rising powers because it transcended old notions of the national interest. Even after America had declined or reduced its leadership role, non-Western powers would need its rules and institutions to grow economically, to reassure other countries about their power, and to tackle common problems. The survival of the U.S.-led order would eventually become decoupled from American primacy because once non-Western powers had converged with it they would not go back.[12] It was a strategy that had some prospect of success, not least because it objectively promised a better type of world than did those approaches whereby the great powers would struggle and fight with each other at the cost of possibly millions of lives, as well as miss opportunities for mutually beneficial, cooperative ventures.

CONVERGENCE UNDER THREE PRESIDENTS
The notion of convergence pervaded the three post–Cold War U.S. administrations. It was an explicit goal of their strategy and defined the parameters of it.

The Clinton Administration
Bill Clinton became president just after the collapse of the old order. It was not then clear that America would ascend during the 1990s to become the world's unipolar power. Although

several analysts did predict it, the mood was generally pessimistic. Clinton's rival for the Democratic nomination in 1992, Paul Tsongas, had as his slogan, "The Cold War is over and Japan won." The previous administration—of George H. W. Bush—had toyed with the idea of pursuing unipolarity, but it was roundly rejected by the president and his top aides after being floated by several people in the Pentagon, led by Paul Wolfowitz.[13] In the early years of the Clinton presidency, the Clinton administration searched in vain for a foreign-policy doctrine. By the mid-1990s, however, it had begun to come into focus. The United States would "enlarge" Western institutions like NATO, it would promote market democracy in Russia, and it would push the globalization of the international economy.

Clinton's national security adviser, Anthony Lake, outlined the first element of this strategy in a speech at Johns Hopkins University in September 1993: "Throughout the Cold War we contained a global threat to market democracies; now we should seek to enlarge their reach, particularly in places of special significance to us. The successor to a doctrine of containment must be a strategy of enlargement—enlargement of the world's free community of market democracies."[14]

James Steinberg, who served as Clinton's deputy national security adviser, later said that "Clinton was an anti-realist. He didn't see that there had to be inherent competition among nations. The success of some was not threatening to others. It was their failure that was threatening."[15] Clinton's favorite book, which he wove into speeches on his worldview, was Robert Wright's *Nonzero,* which posits that the world is becoming more complex, thus creating greater rewards for cooperation. Clinton did not believe that this would happen automatically or that it was irreversible, but he did think that if democracy and prosperity took root, the world would become a cooperative place.

The signs were good. Russia and the United States were working together and overcame differences on NATO expansion. Clinton would later write, "While not an expert on Russia, I knew one big thing: on the twin issues that had constituted the casus belli of the Cold War—democracy versus dictatorship at home and cooperation versus competition abroad—Yeltsin and I were in principle on the same side."[16] Clinton brought China into the World Trade Organization "in order to continue China's integration into the global economy, and to increase both its acceptance of international rules of law and its willingness to cooperate with the United States and other nations on a whole range of other issues."[17] Of Jiang, Clinton wrote that although he didn't always agree with him, "I became convinced he was changing China as fast as he could, and in the right direction."[18] This did not prevent Clinton from pushing China on economics or human rights, but it did mean that he was optimistic about the future trajectory of relations and China's ultimate role in the order.

In his memoir, Clinton wrote, "The world will continue its forward march from isolation to interdependence to cooperation because there is no other choice."[19] This is not to say that Clinton expected a harmonious world. "The interdependent world," Clinton wrote, "is inherently unstable, full of both opportunity and forces of destruction."[20] A more integrated world would be vulnerable to what he privately called "organized assholes" like al-Qaeda.[21] There would also be rogue states, nuclear proliferation, and financial crises. This was the dark side of globalization. It was this dark side that Americans expected to pose the security threats and challenges of the future, not old-style geopolitical competition. These were issues on which the major powers could find common ground.

The George W. Bush Administration

The George W. Bush administration bought into all three explanations for convergence—American primacy, the international order, and common interests. In a speech at West Point in June 2002, President Bush told the cadets: "America has, and intends to keep, military strengths beyond challenge, thereby making the destabilizing arms races of other eras pointless, and limiting rivalries to trade and other pursuits of peace."[22] This was a radical statement. He was arguing that great-power rivalry occurred as nations became *more* equal in power. The United States would do the world a favor by ensuring that never happened so the great powers could focus on common challenges.

But Bush also believed that the great power peace was rooted in common interests. In the introduction to his first National Security Strategy, he wrote:

> Today, the international community has the best chance since the rise of the nation-state in the seventeenth century to build a world where great powers compete in peace instead of continually prepare for war. Today, the world's great powers find ourselves on the same side—united by common dangers of terrorist violence and chaos. The United States will build on these common interests to promote global security. We are also increasingly united by common values. Russia is in the midst of a hopeful transition, reaching for its democratic future and a partner in the war on terror. Chinese leaders are discovering that economic freedom is the only source of national wealth. In time, they will find that social

and political freedom is the only source of national greatness.[23]

Bush believed that the common threat of terrorism would reduce regional rivalries. There are also echoes of Francis Fukuyama's end-of-history thesis, which predicted that after the fall of communism, liberal democracy was the only viable pathway to modernization.[24] In 2005, the Bush administration's deputy secretary of state, Robert Zoellick, would explicitly articulate the idea that emerging powers could advance their interests within a liberal order. Zoellick said that once it became "a responsible stakeholder, China would be more than just a member—it would work with us to sustain the international system that has enabled its success. Cooperation as stakeholders will not mean the absence of differences—we will have disputes that we need to manage. But that management can take place within a larger framework where the parties recognize a shared interest in sustaining political, economic, and security systems that provide common benefits."[25]

The Zoellick speech was hugely influential and reflected the hope that as China's power continued to rise, China's leaders would exercise it in a manner consistent with the U.S.-led international order. This is not to say that the balance-of-power approach completely disappeared in the Bush administration. That administration sought, as Secretary of State Condoleezza Rice put it, to "change the relationship with . . . [another] emerging power"—India—which had been a goal since the very beginning of the administration in 2001 and was designed as a hedge against a rising China.[26] It negotiated and signed an agreement for civil nuclear energy cooperation with India, which also served to end U.S. isolation of India after its nuclear test in 1998.

It was in the Middle East where the Bush administration most controversially sought to give convergence a push. Bush believed that the Arab world would embrace democracy if it was given the opportunity. Thus, after the terrorist attacks of 9/11, Bush invaded Iraq, in part because he believed Saddam Hussein had weapons of mass destruction, but also because he believed that once Saddam was gone, Iraq, and the region, would work with the United States and the U.S.-led order instead of against it.

The Obama Administration

The Obama administration tried to build on the Bush administration's great-power approach, although with some differences. By the 2008 election, Democratic foreign-policy experts were generally expressing the belief that the United States and the rest of the international community shared the same major threats and challenges, including terrorism, climate change, pandemic disease, instability in the global economy, and nuclear proliferation.[27] States would continue to have their differences—such as China and the United States over Taiwan, or Russia and the United States over Georgia—but these differences would be secondary to what they held in common. Unlike its predecessor, the Obama administration was comfortable with moving away from American primacy as a strategic goal. Senior administration officials began to use the term multipolarity, which they associated with greater cooperation and burden-sharing instead of competition and less cooperation. For instance, Vice President Joseph Biden, speaking in 2009 in Ukraine, which was to become a global flashpoint in the return of power politics, said, "We are trying to build a multi-polar world, in which like-minded nations make common cause of our common challenges—the stronger our partners, the more effective our partnerships."[28]

President Obama's "reset" was a major strategic initiative to bring Russia back into the fold as a partner in the international order. Meeting in London in 2009 during the G20, Obama and Russian President Dmitri Medvedev issued a joint statement declaring that they were "ready to move beyond Cold War mentalities and chart a fresh start in relations between our two countries."[29] Obama also reached out to China in an effort to deepen the bilateral relationship. He supported institutionalizing the G20 at the leaders' level and giving it responsibility for management of the global economy. At the London G20 summit, Obama explained his view on why the United States needed to bring non-Western powers into the fold: "Well, if there's just Roosevelt and Churchill sitting in a room with a brandy, that's a—that's an easier negotiation. But that's not the world we live in, and it shouldn't be the world that we live in."[30]

The Obama administration began with a worldview in which the role of the United States was to lead in solving problems that all major states had in common. The notion that Russia or China or any other major power (with the exception of so-called rogue states like North Korea) would have interests that conflicted directly with those of the United States was anathema. Or if they did have conflicting interests, it was assumed that they paled in comparison to shared interests.

The decision to invade Iraq may have been a disaster, but after the worst of the war was over, the situation did not seem irretrievable. By 2008, the U.S. surge had restored some semblance of stability to Iraq and a government was in place. The election of Barack Obama provided hope that the United States could translate his enormous popularity into influence with ordinary Muslims throughout the Arab world. Obama gave a speech at Cairo University in June 2009 titled "A New Beginning."[31] His intention was to turn the page and encourage political change in the Arab world instead of imposing it through the use of force.[32] The methods may have been different from those of his predecessor, but the assumption was similar: the interests and views of the peoples of the world were converging, and the future was bright.

As Obama described it to Jeffrey Goldberg of the *Atlantic*, "I was hoping that my speech could trigger a discussion, could create space for Muslims to address the real problems they are confronting—problems of governance, and the fact that some currents of Islam have not gone through a reformation that would help people adapt their religious doctrines to modernity. My thought was, I would communicate that the US is not standing in the way of this progress, that we would help, in whatever way possible, to advance the goals of a practical, successful Arab agenda that provided a better life for ordinary people."[33]

The point here is not that these three presidents were necessarily wrong to see the world in this way. Clinton had reason to believe that China and Russia were trending in the right direction. Bush faced a major new threat from terrorism that united nations in a common purpose. And Obama saw an opportunity to increase cooperation after the worst financial crisis since the 1930s. But the expectations of all three went unfulfilled. The world did not continue to integrate so that nations could face shared challenges together, free from old rivalries. Instead, traditional geopolitics reimposed itself on the international system.

Why did the premise of the U.S. strategy turn out to be wrong?

A FALSE DIAGNOSIS

The primary flaw in the idea of convergence was the assumption that all states perceived the liberal international order as benign and that convergence would operate independently of American power. A secondary flaw, which applied in the Middle East, was that it underestimated the power of sectarianism and ethnic divides. There was much about convergence that was bang on the money. American power discouraged balancing and caused states to look for other strategies. Globalization was appealing to many. But the flaws meant that it could not last. And as Herb Stein, an economic adviser to President Nixon, famously put it in what became known as Stein's Law, "What cannot go on forever will stop."

So what was the threat that the Russian and Chinese regimes perceived from the new liberal international order? Now it is often misunderstood as a conventional military threat whereby NATO expansion and U.S. forward positioning and surveillance in East Asia had created a security dilemma with Russia and China. They had not. NATO's military capability in Europe actually plummeted during this time.[34] And East Asian nations were ambivalent about their alliances with the United States prior to 2008. There are two specific risks, however, that the liberal order posed, and poses, to Moscow and Beijing.

The first is the threat that the liberal order would democratize Russia and China. The United States and Europe openly hoped and believed that Russia and China would become liberal democracies as they integrated into the order. There was no intention to forcibly topple Putin or the Chinese Communist Party (CCP), but the success of democratization elsewhere—the so-called color revolutions—led many to predict that the same thing would happen in Russia and eventually in China. While democracy is very probably in the interests of the Russian and Chinese people, it is certainly not seen that way by their governments and it is their governments that get to decide national policy. It was this threat—of democracy and color revolutions—that really lay behind Putin's alarm about NATO and EU expansion. Even if the West wished to reassure Moscow and Beijing on this score, doing so would be impossible, because the threat emanated from the success of the order in other countries—in Eastern Europe in particular—and not from bilateral diplomacy with Russia and China.

American leaders were vocal about their desire to bring about democratic change in Russia and China. For instance, in a speech at Moscow State University in March 2011, Vice President Biden told students that "most Russians want to choose their national and local leaders in competitive elections. They want to be able to assemble freely, and they want to live in a country that fights corruption. That's democracy. They're the ingredients of democracy. So I urge all of you students here: Don't compromise on the basic elements of democracy. You need not make that Faustian bargain."[35]

The Chinese leadership believes that the United States is committed to undermining its regime and supporting a transition to democracy. Most Americans see support for political change in China as aspirational and not something that Beijing should be worried about. But to Beijing, it is an active American policy that includes support for democracy activists in Hong Kong, the use of media organizations like the *New York Times* to expose corruption in China and delegitimize the regime, military assistance for Taiwan, ambiguity about terrorism by Xinjiang separatists, pressure on human rights, support for religious freedom in China, and high-level meetings with the Dalai Lama. Chinese scholar

Wang Jisi observed that Beijing's distrust of the United States is "deeply rooted and in recent years it seems to have deepened." Part of the reason, Wang says, is that "since the very early days of the PRC [People's Republic of China], it has been a constant and strong belief that the US has sinister designs to sabotage the Communist leadership and turn China into its vassal state."[36]

The second way the order threatened the interests of Russia and China was by depriving them of a sphere of influence. Since the Cold War, U.S. policy has been that all countries should be free to decide their type of government and their foreign relations for themselves, without interference by an outside power. Traditionally, great powers acquire a sphere of influence in which they have a say in the domestic politics of their smaller neighbors. The desire for such influence often arises from a sense of insecurity either deeply rooted in history or owing to the nature of the regime—both of which apply to Russia and China. Beijing and Moscow cannot understand why the United States has an unlimited sphere of influence while they are not allowed to expand their influence in East Asia and Eastern Europe, respectively. They dismiss the notion of consent and invitation that is the key feature of U.S. alliances, one that distinguishes these alliances from normal hegemonic or imperial arrangements. Putin hoped to secure more freedom to maneuver in his neighborhood in exchange for supporting the United States in Afghanistan and in the war on terrorism. The fact that this did not, and could not, happen was a contributing factor to his foreign-policy turn.

The United States had no intention of facilitating a Russian or Chinese sphere of influence because it saw no need to concede any ground. Moreover, the countries that would be in such a sphere of influence have their own agency and would strongly resist, thereby potentially destabilizing U.S. alliances and strategic partnerships. After the Cold War, U.S. policymakers believed that playing a role in the U.S.-led order was in the interests of Russia and China and those in either country seeking a return of power politics were anachronistic and counterproductive. From the perspective of the United States, potential challengers like Russia and China as well as emerging powers like Brazil and India could play an increasing role in the international order only to the degree that they accepted the basic legitimacy of the existing arrangement.

The United States also hoped to enlarge the security order to include new countries and envisioned that this expanded order would have purposes other than fighting terrorism. According to this scenario, the seven-country enlargement of NATO in 2004 and the eastward movement of the European Union would create a Europe whole and free. The deepening of U.S. alliances in Asia and the engagement of non-allied countries like India, Indonesia, Vietnam, and Myanmar would strengthen the U.S.-led regional order. Existing alliances would also be deepened where possible to consolidate the U.S. presence in key regions.

But both Russia and China saw these efforts as having the purpose, at least in part, of constraining future opportunities for expansion of their own regional influence. Key pillars of the liberal order—the notion that countries should be able to modernize if they so choose, regardless of where they are located, and the belief that the world should consign spheres of influence to the past—improved life for many nations, but not all regimes saw it that way. When the dissatisfied accumulated enough power to push back, they did. Both China and Russia grew rapidly in the 2000s and thus became more geopolitically capable. Between 2000 and 2010 the Chinese economy grew fivefold, from $1.2 trillion to over $6 trillion; meanwhile the Russian economy expanded from a GDP of $259 billion in 2000 to over $1.5 trillion in 2010 (and more than $2.2 trillion in 2013 before it began to decline).[37] With greater resources, they no longer had to acquiesce.

A separate dynamic operated in the Middle East. There U.S. policymakers mistook popular dissatisfaction with monarchical and authoritarian regimes as a sign that liberal democracy could take root. Unfortunately, the weakness of the state, the lack of safeguards for minority rights, and the sectarian context meant that revolution merely fueled regional disorder, the collapse of state structures, and counter-revolution. This is a subject to which we will return.

THE END OF CONVERGENCE

These strains on the convergence thesis were evident at the turn of the millennium. Bill Clinton suspected that Vladimir Putin was not a committed democrat. On his final visit to Russia as president in June 2000, Clinton dropped in to see Boris Yeltsin, who had retired six months earlier. "Boris," Clinton confided, "you've got democracy in your heart. You've got the trust of the people in your bones. You've got the fire in your belly of a real democrat and a real reformer. I'm not sure Putin has that. Maybe he does. I don't know. You'll have to keep an eye on him."[38]

The strategy of convergence might have otherwise come apart in the early 2000s, but the terrorist attacks of September 11, 2001, and the threat of weapons of mass destruction being used against civilian targets, revived it. The Bush administration prioritized the war on terrorism above all else, and Russia mistakenly believed that if it provided basing rights in Central Asia and generally cooperated in the war, significant U.S. concessions elsewhere would result. For instance, the United States might,

Moscow hoped, withhold support for political change inside Ukraine or give Russia more leeway in its neighborhood. This expectation was based on a flawed assessment of the U.S. position. The United States never envisaged sacrificing its core strategic goals in Europe in exchange for cooperation in the war on terrorism. Indeed, it probably never occurred to U.S. policymakers that such a deal would ever be on the table. As the decade wore on, the contradiction between Russia's expectations of what its support would buy and that support's true value were laid bare. China had fewer illusions about a quid pro quo, but it was happy for the United States to be distracted given that it could have faced a tougher U.S. policy in Asia had the terrorist attacks of September 11 never occurred.

Convergence unraveled in fits and starts. By the beginning of President Obama's second term, the trends were unmistakable. As Robert Kagan presciently wrote in 2008, "the tantalizing glimpse" of a transformed international order was disappearing and the world was becoming "normal" again.[39] Each region had its own dynamic.

Russia

Putin's frustration with the United States grew throughout the 2000s. From his perspective, Russia had helped the United States in Afghanistan but received no quid pro quo in its own neighborhood. Instead, the United States persisted with NATO expansion to the Baltics and partnership agreements with countries on Russia's borders. The United States and European Union backed the 2004 Orange Revolution in Ukraine and were increasingly vocal about democracy promotion. What angered Putin most was the U.S. missile defense project, which would include sites in Eastern Europe. Russia had more than enough missiles to breach these defenses, but the project signaled that this part of Russia's neighborhood was no longer to be considered a sphere of influence. By the mid-2000s, mutual trust was breaking down. Putin was eroding democracy at home and criticizing U.S. policy in Russia's neighborhood. In May 2006, U.S. Vice President Dick Cheney, speaking in Lithuania, admonished Russia, accusing Russian opponents of reform of "seeking to reverse the gains of the last decade."[40]

Putin publicly broke with the West in February 2007 at the Munich Security Conference, an annual gathering of senior officials and experts from either side of the Atlantic. He accused the United States of trying to create a "unipolar world" with "one center of authority, one center of force, one center of decision-making." "It is a world," he said, "in which there is one master, one sovereign. And at the end of the day this is pernicious not only for all those within this system, but also for the sovereign itself because it destroys itself from within." In this new system, Putin warned, "we are witnessing the almost uncontained hyper use of force—military force—in international relations, force that is plunging the world into an abyss of permanent conflicts."[41] Putin's speech marked the moment when the post–Cold War world turned away from cooperation and toward competition. But the turn would not follow a smooth trajectory. Over the next five years Russia oscillated between both postures, until it finally shifted toward rivalry abroad and authoritarianism at home.

Before things got temporarily better, they got much worse. Russia's invasion of Georgia in 2008 sent U.S.-Russian relations into a deep freeze. Casualties in the Georgian War were fairly low. The official numbers provided by the three protagonists—Russia, Georgia, and the separatists—suggest somewhere around eight hundred, although these could be inflated. Nevertheless, as the late Ron Asmus titled his book on the subject, it was "a little war that shook the world."[42] The war demonstrated Russia's determination to prevent the further expansion of NATO and Western influence. It showed that Moscow was willing to use force against another state (the first time it had done so since the Cold War). This was not Kosovo or Iraq where Russia would be satisfied with making statements at the UN Security Council. This time, the objections were backed up with force. This was a watershed event, but it did not appear that way at the time. The Russian invasion lasted only five days, after which Moscow agreed to mediation and a ceasefire. The newly elected U.S. president, Barack Obama, would promise a reset with Russia and held out hope that increased cooperation could ultimately transform the U.S.-Russia relationship for the better. Only over time would it become clear that this was an illusion.

When the Obama administration took office, it undertook the reset with Russia whereby it sought to cooperate on areas of common interest while recognizing that the two countries still had important differences. An underlying condition of the reset was that Putin had left the presidency and Washington was hoping that engaging with Dmitri Medvedev could strengthen his position and edge Russia toward a more normal democratic politics.[43] The reset yielded several successes. The United States and Russia negotiated the New START Treaty, supply routes through Afghanistan, tough sanctions on Iran's nuclear program, accession of Russia to the World Trade Organization (WTO), and even a UN Security Council resolution authorizing the use of force in Libya. NATO expansion was also effectively off the table.

This all changed when Putin came back to the presidency in 2012. Senior U.S. officials at the time have noted that the Russian foreign-policy bureaucracy became notably more hardline upon the announcement of Putin's return, which was months before he actually took office.[44] And yet it took them some time to realize how much Russia had changed. Michael McFaul, then U.S. ambassador to Russia, later said, "We underestimated how big a change that was. I briefed the president with the view that there should be continuity since we assumed Putin played a central role in foreign policy."[45] Putin had seen where the reset was headed and he did not like it. There was no prospect of a new European security architecture, as Russia wanted. The West continued to press for human rights and democracy.

Putin believed that Medvedev was too soft—Medvedev had abstained at the UN Security Council on the West's Libya intervention and he seemed open to liberal reforms at home.[46] As Putin's biographer Stephen Lee Myers put it, "Perhaps it was because he was younger, perhaps because he never served in the security services, or perhaps because of his convivial nature, but Medvedev did not share this bleak distrust of the West, of democracy, of human nature."[47]

If there was even a faint possibility that Putin would continue to cooperate with the West, it evaporated even before he took office. After the 2012 election, hundreds of thousands of Russians took to the streets to protest Putin's return to power. Putin saw the hand of the West everywhere. It was, he believed, an attempted American coup. He became determined to consolidate his control of Russia, and even more paranoid about the West. Looking back, McFaul would say, "Had there been no demonstrations against the regime, the US-Russia relationship might have had a different trajectory." He added, "It was those events that drove how Putin pivoted against the United States."[48] In reality, Putin's pivot was already well under way, and was setting the stage for his actions in Ukraine in 2014.

China

Prior to 2008, China's neighbors were relaxed about its rise. Leading scholars such as David Kang, a professor at the University of California San Diego, argued that East Asian nations were accommodating China instead of balancing against it.[49] China was playing a constructive role in the region, which many contrasted with America's heavy-handed clumsiness during the 1997 East Asian financial crisis. China supported greater regional cooperation and was careful to abide by multilateral rules and norms. In 2006, Joshua Kurlantzick wrote: "Since the late 1990s perceptions of China in Southeast Asia have shifted significantly, so much so that elites and publics in the majority of the ten members of ASEAN now see China as a constructive actor—and potentially the preeminent regional power."[50]

That changed after the financial crisis. China pursued its claims in the South China Sea more assertively, engaged in a major spat with Google over Internet freedom, played an obstructionist role at the climate change negotiations in Copenhagen, sought to balance militarily against the United States in East Asia, pressured its neighbors not to support multilateral negotiations on territorial disputes, and regularly and openly criticized U.S. leadership. Most observers attributed this shift to a Chinese perception that America was in inexorable decline and now was the moment to act more assertively overseas. Chinese officials and experts argue that China was merely responding to the provocative actions of Vietnam, the Philippines, Japan, and others.

These events caught the Obama administration by surprise. Whereas the Bush administration had expressed the hope that China would be a "responsible stakeholder" in the international order, the Obama administration began by treating China as if it was already a responsible stakeholder in that order. It sought to deepen engagement with China multilaterally through the G20, and bilaterally through the Strategic and Economic Dialogue (SED) and a presidential visit to China in November 2009. U.S. officials avoided actions that could aggravate Chinese officials: for instance, the president deferred his meeting with the Dalai Lama in the fall of 2009, and the administration explored changing the policies toward India that threatened to rile China.[51]

By early 2010, this policy had collapsed as the administration and outside observers questioned whether China shared U.S. objectives and was willing to take on the burdens of leadership in the international order. Some observers pointed out that China always had an assertive streak, but as Jeffrey Bader, who served as NSC senior director for Asia from 2009 to 2010, put it, "Beginning about 2008 and continuing into 2010 one could detect a changed quality in the writing of Chinese security analysts and Chinese official statements and in some respects in Chinese behavior. Citing the financial meltdown and subsequent deep recession in the United States in September 2008, some Chinese analysts argued that the United States was in decline or distracted or both."[52]

By 2010, the United States had again shifted gears. The Obama administration played a crucial role in organizing Southeast Asia to push back against China in territorial disputes, it sold arms to Taiwan, it deepened its alliances and partnerships, and it put human rights back on the agenda. These initiatives led to the announcement of the pivot or rebalance toward Asia, which became one of the signature initiatives of the Obama administration. China responded with its own strategic initiatives, particularly in the South China Sea and East China Sea (see Chapter 3). East Asia was becoming a much more competitive place. But Beijing came to understand that there was no place for Chinese nationalist ambition in the U.S. worldview. As Andrew Nathan and Andrew Scobell have described, the various factions within the Chinese foreign-policy decision-making process all agree on one pessimistic conclusion: "as China rises, the US can be expected to resist."[53]

For three decades after China's modernization, Chinese leaders maintained a low-profile foreign policy. Deng Xiaoping understood that an assertive China risked choking off its source of economic growth by provoking its neighbors to unite against it. This was famously expressed in the phrase "tao guang yang hui," which roughly means "develop capabilities but keep a low profile." The leaders who followed Deng largely adhered to this approach. But as Bader, now at the Brookings Institution, notes, the current Chinese president, Xi Jinping, inherited a China unlike any modern Chinese leader.[54] It had developed vast capabilities thanks to over a decade of double-digit economic growth and massive defense-spending increases. As the first Chinese leader in thirty years not anointed by Deng, Xi was not bound by his formula. By the time Xi took office, China was already beginning to flex its muscles.

The Middle East

The story of how convergence came undone in the Middle East is very different from the story of this development in Europe or East Asia. The Islamic Republic of Iran was never a partner of the United States. In fact, successive presidents waged an economic war against Iran and threatened to attack it if it continued with its nuclear program. So unlike China and Russia, Iran did not turn against the United States and the liberal international order. It did not become revisionist. It has been a consistent enemy of the United States and a revisionist power since the Ayatollah's revolution in 1979.

Nevertheless, convergence was a real force in U.S. strategy toward the Middle East. It was just not directed toward Iran. American presidents believed that the Middle East needed to modernize and democratize. They believed that the old Arab monarchies were living on borrowed time, they were creating more problems—Islamic extremism and a disaffected youth—than they were solving, and that in time their citizens would demand change. As we saw earlier, Bush and Obama differed on how this would be achieved. Bush thought that the invasion of Iraq and the demonstration of American power in the heart of the Arab world would set in motion a process of change that would ultimately lead to reform throughout the region. In November 2003, he told the National Endowment for Democracy: "Iraqi democracy will succeed—and that success will send forth the news, from Damascus to Teheran—that freedom can be the future of every nation. The establishment of a free Iraq at the heart of the Middle East will be a watershed event in the global democratic revolution."[55] Obama believed that engaging Muslim communities and turning the page on Bush's war would generate change from below. In the end, both methods failed.

The initial failure of the Bush approach is well known. Freed from Saddam Hussein, Iraqis found themselves without a state structure to fall back on. Democracy became a sectarian head-count with civil war the inevitable result. There was some respite with the surge, but it could not bring about political reconciliation, and Obama ensured its failure by reducing U.S. diplomatic and military engagement with the Iraqi government.

Obama's strategy began with great promise and excitement but it met its first real test with the Iranian Green Movement of 2009. The Obama administration remained silent and uninvolved, partly because it feared that the students would be tainted by association with an old enemy, but also because it worried that an intervention would damage U.S. diplomacy with Tehran. The brutal repression of the revolution was a sign of things to come and a big blow for anyone who had hoped that Iran's vibrant youth movement heralded domestic change and integration into the international order.

The death blow to convergence came with the most hopeful moment in decades. The self-immolation of a fruit vendor in Sidi Bouzid, Tunisia, set in motion a series of incredible events that toppled authoritarian regimes in Tunisia and Egypt and left others reeling. The Arab Spring seemed to offer incontrovertible evidence of the convergence thesis: Arab societies were modernizing and democratizing by choice. They were rejecting a transition of power from one set of monarchs to their kin. Unfortunately, and as we shall see in Chapter 4, the revolution failed because democracy was widely perceived as a thin veil for sectarian majoritarianism and Islamism.

By 2016, the Arab Spring had given way to a regional calamity with four civil wars, the rise of ISIS, a cold war between Tehran and Riyadh, and an emerging authoritarian regime in Turkey. The Obama administration shifted from a strategy that looked forward to transformational reform to one of callous indifference and disengagement. Obama put the crisis down to "millennia old" hatreds and tribalism.[56] After two decades of trying to bring about change, the United States declared, in essence, that the Middle East was beyond saving.

The End of Global Convergence

The return of geopolitics and the collapse of convergence in the Middle East was accompanied by a third development: six weeks after the Russian invasion of Georgia, the United States was rocked by the collapse of Lehman Brothers, which triggered a full-scale global financial crisis. In its first year, the global crash of 2008 was actually worse than the 1929 crash with respect to all the major economic metrics—industrial production, world trade, and equity markets.[57] The United States stood on the brink of a new Great Depression. Even when that fear passed, the recession would prove to be the worst since the 1930s. Meanwhile Europe was plunged into a severe economic crisis of its own that threatened the future of the euro.

For almost two decades, the United States had championed the process of globalization, and especially the deregulation and integration of the world's financial markets. This held the promise of continued high levels of growth and mutual prosperity but it made the global economy more crisis-prone. Indeed, there were major crises during this twenty-year period: in Mexico in 1994, East Asia in 1997, Russia in 1998, the United States in 2008, and Europe in 2009. Today, for the first time since the Cold War, the driving narrative behind the global economy is no longer how to increase the openness of markets and economies. Cornell University professor Jonathan Kirshner has observed that much of the world does not see the crisis as a black swan—that is, a rare and unpredictable event—but as a direct consequence of the particular model of global capitalism that has been pursued.[58] The problems have not been fixed. As University of Chicago professor and former head of India's central bank Raghuram Rajan put it, "There are deep fault lines in the global economy, fault lines that have developed because in an integrated economy and in an integrated world, what is best for the individual actor or institution is not always best for the system."[59] Banks that are too big to fail, financial instruments that are too complicated to understand, asset bubbles, and interconnectedness all but ensure continued volatility.

Moreover, the global economy is increasingly perceived as a threat to national economic success, not its driver. Over the past five years, Western democracies have become much more protectionist and nationalist in their economic outlook. Many voters see migration, international trade, and finance as threats to their livelihood. This sentiment caught the political establishment by surprise and culminated in the populist shocks of 2016—Britain's vote to leave the European Union and Donald Trump's victory in the U.S. presidential election.

WHAT WILL HAPPEN NEXT?

It is tempting to argue that convergence failed, that successive U.S. administrations were foolish, and that the United States and the world are worse off for having tried it. Indeed, some of the champions of convergence in the 1990s and 2000s have turned on it with all the zeal of converts. In a book titled *Mission Failure,* Michael Mandelbaum castigated the central thesis of his earlier work *The Ideas That Conquered the World.* The United States, he argued, used its power to interfere in the internal affairs of other countries, economically and politically, to disastrous effect.[60] Such a conclusion is tempting, but wrong. Convergence was a strategy with a reasonable chance of success. More than that, it partially succeeded. Much of the world gravitated to the U.S.-led liberal international order. India, most of Southeast Asia, Brazil, and most of Eastern Europe liberalized economically and politically and engaged with the West.

Despite these successes, the failures count. Russia and China are now actively balancing against the United States and its allies.

The Middle East seems locked in a deadly downward spiral that threatens the European Union. Security competition between major powers has returned. The U.S.-led liberal order is under pressure from multiple directions. Meanwhile, the effect of these changes is only beginning to be felt in the global economy. The new era of great power rivalry will be as transformative to world politics as its absence was in the 1990s and 2000s.

We seem to be in the initial phase of a new era of geopolitical competition that may, if history is any guide, last for decades. But we do not have a good understanding of what this era will look like. What are Russia's and China's objectives and how do they intend to achieve them? How do we explain the differences between them and do they pose a real challenge to the United States? How important is the Middle East to this competition? What does the reemergence of great-power rivalry mean in an age of globalization? And what can and should the United States do in response?

The title of this book, *All Measures Short of War,* comes from U.S. strategy in the early years of World War II, when President Roosevelt sought to help Britain in every way he could without actually fighting Germany. Today's great powers will compete vigorously with each other in order to shape, transform, or undermine the world order, but they all hope and intend to avoid a major war. The risk and cost are simply too great and the potential benefit too small. Of course, war could still occur inadvertently. Perhaps a leader will take a chance, thinking he or she can keep any war limited, but miscalculate. Or a leader may misunderstand the intentions of another and overreact. But as the United States, China, Russia, and several others engage in geopolitical competition with their rivals, they will do so with the intention of winning in peacetime. They will use their military to establish positions of strength; they will employ the tools of diplomatic coercion; they will seek to win the hearts and minds of other nations; they will ruthlessly exploit each other's weaknesses; they will use economic leverage for geopolitical ends; and they may countenance the use of force against third parties or even fight each other in proxy wars.

The reemergence of great-power rivalry poses immense challenges to the United States. There are no easy answers or painless strategies. World politics is becoming more complicated and zero-sum. It will be filled with dilemmas and tough choices. The purpose of this book is to explain why great-power rivalry has returned, how to think about it, and how the United States can respond.

THE IMPORTANCE OF REGIONS

A useful starting point in navigating this world is to look closely at an apparent contradiction in Russian and Chinese behavior. Moscow and Beijing are more cooperative on global issues—including nonproliferation, counter-terrorism, and the global economy—than on regional problems like Ukraine and the South China Sea. Generally, too, the crises that dominate the news cycle tend to be regional while the broad global trends, such as economic development and infant mortality, are often positive. For some scholars and policymakers, this apparent contradiction suggests that talk of a geopolitical challenge is overblown. In their view, only if we see a rival peer competitor with a distinctive global ideology, like the Soviet Union or Nazi Germany, can we say that we are entering into a truly geopolitical era.

But there is another way of looking at global order and geopolitical risk. The most important piece of the liberal order is not the United Nations or international financial institutions, important as they are. It is healthy regional orders. America's greatest success after World War II was to create a system in Western Europe and Northeast Asia that brought an end to German and Japanese imperialism and provided the basis for shared prosperity. If those regional orders fall apart, so will the global order. For example, a war between China and Japan—the world's second and third largest economies—would have massive repercussions for the global economy. A Russian incursion into the Baltics would raise the risk of nuclear war between the world's two largest nuclear powers. And the general deterioration of order in Europe or East Asia—whether it is from economic crises or rising insecurity—can have a global impact.

It is for this reason that Russian and Chinese activities in their neighborhood are more indicative of their approach to the international order than their explicit policy on global issues, although those are also important. Ultimately, a country's willingness to honor the norm against territorial conquest is much more important than its compliance to the dispute settlement mechanism of the World Trade Organization or voting weights at the International Monetary Fund. And it should come as no surprise that China and Russia are regionally focused—after all, major powers are usually primarily concerned with their immediate environment rather than abstract notions of global leadership. So how are the world's regions faring?

2 EUROPE'S MULTIPLE CRISES

Of all of the threats and challenges that have shaken the international order over the past five years, it is the disorder in Europe that may be most shocking. True, the unraveling of the Middle East has killed many more people and China's rise may be the more difficult problem in the long term, but nothing quite matches Europe for a reversal of fortune. In the mid-2000s Europe seemed well positioned for the twenty-first century. As American reliance on hard power ran into trouble in Iraq, Europeans felt vindicated in their skepticism of U.S. foreign policy. In 2003, the European Union produced its first National Security Strategy. It began: "Europe has never been so prosperous, so secure nor so free."[1] Leading foreign-policy experts wrote books about how Europe would rule the world in the twenty-first century or how the European Union was the world's second superpower.[2] When the financial crisis broke in 2008, it was widely viewed in Europe as the inevitable consequence of unbridled American capitalism and deregulation, to which the social democratic European model compared very favorably.

Americans regarded Europe as a region where the business of history was finished. The threats of the twentieth century—fascism, communism, and belligerent nationalism—had been dealt with, and European countries had transcended the nation-state to create a postmodern system that eschewed violence and was seeking an exemption slip from the normal challenges of world politics. Europeans would not do much to help the United States in the world's trouble spots, but they would not require much attention either. Europe would be a postmodern haven from the trials and tribulations of the twenty-first century. This zeitgeist was perfectly captured by Richard Haass, president of the Council on Foreign Relations, in June 2011 in an article titled "Why Europe No Longer Matters": "Europe's own notable successes are an important reason that transatlantic ties will matter less in the future. The current Eurozone financial crisis should not obscure the historic accomplishment that was the building of an integrated Europe over the past half-century. The continent is largely whole and free and stable. Europe, the principal arena of much 20th-century geopolitical competition, will be spared such a role in the new century— and this is a good thing."[3]

President Obama evidently agreed. He effectively canceled the 2010 EU-U.S. summit, the first time an American president had done so. He had an "unromantic" view of the transatlantic relationship and was focused elsewhere.[4] The message was clear—Europe could and should take care of itself.

Today, the very existence of the European Union is in doubt. Most attention focuses on the return of Russian nationalism, but Europe's general strategic situation has deteriorated rapidly over the past five years. The European Union faced its worst-ever integration crisis over the euro. Then the order in its east (with Russia) fell apart, followed swiftly by the order to its south in the Middle East. Britain voted to leave the European Union. And then, America's seventy-year commitment to the transatlantic alliance was thrown into doubt by Donald Trump's election as U.S. president.

The effects of these events have been dramatic and extensive. The euro crisis has weakened the political center and sapped the public's appetite for European integration. Russia's revisionism has destroyed any hope of a Europe whole, free, and at peace. The refugee challenge and terror threat have overwhelmed national governments' efforts. Brexit has put the European Union on the brink of a breakup. And Trump's election raised questions about the credibility of the NATO alliance and U.S. support for European integration. The pileup of crises has also led to terrifying negative synergies. Russian actions in Syria have exacerbated the refugee flows. Economic stagnation and rising populism have created the political climate in which the British voted to leave the European Union while providing fertile ground for political interference by Moscow in Europe's domestic politics.

It is an ugly picture. A weakened European Union teeters on the brink of dissolution and faces a deeply insecure, revisionist, and dangerous Russia while the United States reconsiders its role. But to understand the dynamic, we must first go back to the moment when cracks began to appear in the European Union.

European integration may well be the greatest political accomplishment of the twentieth century. Out of the rubble of war, European statesmen, with the support of the United States, pooled their sovereignty and created a functioning political and economic union that transcended the modern state system. The European Union is difficult for non-Europeans to understand. It is imperfect and incomplete, and its story is one of incremental steps toward union, often prompted by the crisis of the day. Each generation of leaders, from the 1950s on, moved the ball a little further down the field. Sometimes the European Union can seem hopelessly dysfunctional, and member states often assert their own interests to the detriment of the common good. But the European Union exerts enormous influence over the daily lives of European citizens. It has also been a powerful force for spreading and consolidating liberal democracy—first in Western Europe, then in Central Europe and to the east. By 2008, European integration remained incomplete, but much had been achieved. Europe had a single market and customs union, a common currency, populations that could move freely among member nations, rules for how to handle refugees, and a foreign-policy chief. Few people would have guessed the European Union was on the eve of a series of interlocking crises that would rock its foundations to the point of fracture.

THE EUROCRISIS

After the Cold War, French President François Mitterrand encouraged the German chancellor, Helmut Kohl, to embark on a bold step of integration to reassure Europe and the wider world that a reunited Germany would be firmly anchored in the European Union. The result was monetary union. Fiscal union (a common taxation and spending system) and a banking union (whereby bank debts would be shared by all member states, not just the country where the bank was headquartered) were judged to be too politically difficult. Europe's leaders believed that they were necessary—Kohl said that monetary union would remain "a castle in the air" without political union—but they were confident these steps would follow in time.[5]

Many economists pointed out the dangers of monetary union without a fiscal and banking union, but for much of its first decade, the euro looked like a tremendous success. It soared past the dollar in value. In the 2008 James Bond movie *Quantum of Solace*, one villain, a corrupt Bolivian general, demanded his bribe in euros since the dollar was not what it used to be. But beneath the surface all was not well. The member states of the European Union had vastly different growth rates. Some countries, like Ireland and Spain, were growing at over 5 percent a year. Others, like Germany, were stagnant. But there is only one interest rate in a monetary union, and in the European Union it was set to suit Germany. The result was predictable and predicted—cheap interest rates were like rocket fuel to already fast-growing economies and drove asset bubbles, especially in property.

When the music stopped after the collapse of Lehman Brothers in 2008, the German finance minister, Peer Steinbrück, said the financial crisis was "above all an American problem" and that the United States would "lose its superpower status in the global financial system."[6] This reflected a widespread view in continental Europe that its economic and financial system was in far better shape than the "unregulated" Anglo-American model. This view could not have been more mistaken. The crisis would exact a greater toll in Europe for two reasons: Europe lacked the necessary institutions to cope with the crisis, and Germany insisted on imposing austerity on the Eurozone with catastrophic consequences.

The massive property crashes in Spain, Ireland, and Portugal, along with poor public finances in Greece, made some national banks bust overnight with their governments not far behind. The markets took notice and charged much greater rates for loans to the periphery than to the so-called core (countries like Germany that were judged to be economically sound). The rate spread— the term to describe the range between the price of a loan to

Germany and to the periphery countries—fluctuated widely. During the Eurocrisis, the peak yield for ten-year bonds was just over 3 percent for Germany, 14.76 percent for Ireland, 17.36 percent for Portugal, and a prohibitive 46.8 percent for Greece.[7]

Thus the financial crisis very quickly became a Eurocrisis. Europe was divided in two. The Eurozone core believed that the crisis was a Lutheran morality tale. They had behaved morally by not spending more than they had, while the periphery countries had spent like there was no tomorrow. Now that the periphery was bust, it was manifestly unfair that well-behaved countries should pick up the bill. Indeed, such charity could be dangerous by encouraging repeated bad behavior in the future. By this line of thinking, the sinners should be punished and made to mend their ways. As German Chancellor Angela Merkel told French President Nicolas Sarkozy, "Chacun sa merde" (To each his own shit).[8]

The view from the Eurozone periphery—Ireland, Portugal, and Spain—was very different. They believed that low interest rates in the 2000s, which were a function of a single currency tailored for Germany and other large economies, had led banks in the core to lend enormous amounts to the periphery, where investors sought a higher return. When the crisis struck, and the asset bubble burst, the core banks were thus partially to blame and all European banks were at risk—not just those on the periphery but also those in core countries including Germany, Belgium, and Austria. The German government disagreed with this view, insisting that the periphery governments pick up the entire bill. They also sought to punish the periphery for their mistakes by insisting that the European Central Bank provide them with punitive loans with interest rates far beyond what the International Monetary Fund recommended. This step was salt in the wound for the Spanish, Irish, Greeks, and Portuguese, who believed they were being forced to bail out Germany and its allies for mistakes the core banks had made.

This divide defined European politics for five years. Ever so gradually, Germany supported new institutions to prevent future crises and ease the current one. This included steps toward a limited banking union, new powers for the European Central Bank to backstop the Euro, and fairer bailouts. But the German government also insisted on harsh austerity measures that stymied growth and resulted in a prolonged period of deflation and stagnation. Some austerity was required, but there were no offsetting policies to create growth. Moreover, there was to be no mutualization of debt and the banking union remained incomplete. Leading economists warned that these missing elements would cripple institution building, making the institutional backstops insufficient to prevent or deal with a future crisis. But the leaders pointed out the unforgiving politics they faced at home. The suspicion of "Europe" was so high that European voters would never agree to transfer the most sensitive fiscal and financial powers (taxation and mutualization of debt) to a central authority.

Much of the frustration had to do with protracted stagnation and no end in sight. What made the politics particularly toxic is that the German economic model has no real plan for growth. The Germans believed that their own experience with structural reform in the early 2000s was a model for others to follow even though the analogy was badly flawed.[9] German Finance Minister Wolfgang Schäuble has made it clear that he opposed any increase in the nominal levels of German debt even if the interest rates were effectively negative.[10] This is a logic that no private-sector businessperson would think rational—after all, if you can borrow money for free and invest it for a modest return, you come out better off. The German model envisages all EU member states running current account surpluses, meaning that they would save more than they spend. But if everyone did this, the result would be another Great Depression.

The fact that the Eurozone survived intact is little cause for comfort. Early in the crisis, economists recognized that it would be irrational for a state to leave the Eurozone even if it was suffering badly inside it.[11] Any advance notice, or even expectation, of an exit would cause a massive bank run, leading to the collapse of the departing country's banking system. If the government managed to conduct the process entirely in secret or was able to establish capital controls in advance of any such expectation, those with savings in national banks would be devastated as the new currency plummeted in value. The country would have to default on its debts because it would remain denominated in euros. As a consequence, it could be locked out of international financial markets for years to come. Businesses would also fall victim to the devaluation and would likely owe money to foreign suppliers. Many would go bankrupt, thereby deepening the recession. Because all of these consequences would be attributed to the government's decision to leave the euro, this is a political risk no leader would voluntarily take. Even the Cypriot government in 2012 and the Greek government in 2015 proved unwilling to leave the euro despite powerful economic and political incentives to do so.[12]

The Eurocrisis delegitimized Europe in the eyes of many of its citizens. They felt trapped in an economic straightjacket that was nevertheless suicidal to take off. It also left Europeans marooned in an extended lost decade that is worse than the stagnation Japan had dealt with in the 1990s and 2000s. As financier George Soros put it: "The European Union was meant to be a voluntary association of equals but the euro crisis turned it into a relationship between debtors and creditors where the debtors have difficulties in meeting their obligations and the creditors set the conditions that the debtors have to meet. That relationship is neither voluntary nor equal."[13] As one former senior European official put it, the European Union used to be a win-win proposition but the euro made it win-lose, which fundamentally changed the politics.[14] As we shall see, Europe's lost decade exhausted the political capital of the pro-EU camp and empowered populists and nationalists. When other crises hit, the defenses of the European Union would be stripped bare.

RUSSIA'S QUEST FOR REVENGE

As Europe was suffering through its economic crisis, Vladimir Putin had problems of his own. In 2011 and 2012, tens of thousands of Russians took to the streets to protest his return to the presidency. The drop in commodity prices had undermined his ability to deliver economic growth.[15] And the West was continuing its push to expand its borders, this time by means of association agreements with Ukraine and Moldova. As Putin saw it, the international situation was as bad, if not worse, as it had been in 2007 when he made his Munich speech. The reset had been a ruse for the United States to get what it wanted from Moscow while Russia's core interests were ignored. The situation was, he believed, untenable.

Putin would later tell a group of journalists that talks with the West were a waste of time. He had hoped to broker a compromise on thorny issues like NATO or EU enlargement but "all we heard was the same reply, like a broken record: every nation has the right to determine the security system it wants to live in and this has nothing to do with you."[16] Putin's frustration was not with his American or European interlocutors per se but with basic principles of the liberal international order. The West would not suppress democracy in Russia's neighboring countries to make an autocrat feel more secure. Nor would it cede a country to Russia's sphere of influence without the consent of the people affected. Compromises of the sort that Putin envisaged represented a very different type of international order.

For most leaders, sovereignty means that every country in the world has certain rights. But that is not Putin's definition. Putin equates sovereignty with autonomy, which means being able to provide for your own security and welfare without becoming tethered to allies or relying on larger nations.[17] Thus there are only a handful of truly sovereign nations in the world. The United States is sovereign. China is sovereign. Russia is once again sovereign. And that's about it. Many other nations have outsourced their security to the United States. Some of these, like France, the United Kingdom, and Japan—could reclaim their sovereignty if they wished. The rest could not even if they so desired. They are too small to take care of themselves. Putin does not understand why Russia, a sovereign nation in this sense, ought to be treated on a par with states like Estonia, Latvia, and even Poland. Surely, he believes, Russia ought to have a special role, one at a level equal to that of the United States and a handful of other large states.

In this sense, the European security architecture offends him: it elevates the influence of the smallest members. Russia's only formal role is as one of fifty-four members in the Organization for Security and Cooperation in Europe (OSCE). It is excluded from NATO and the European Union, where tiny states have a seat at the table. Russia had proposed a new regional security architecture to replace NATO but it was immediately dismissed out of hand by the West, which recognized it for what it was—an effort to undermine the principle of sovereign equality.[18]

Russia's long-term goal is to bring about a transformation in the European security order so it more closely accords with Russia's notion of a hierarchy of sovereign states. It has no interest in further legitimizing NATO or allowing it to consolidate its current membership even if it did not expand further. Russia wants to be consulted, and to have a veto, over all major decisions for European security, including over NATO—which it would like to see disbanded—and over EU expansion. Ultimately, Putin would like to see the European Union reduced to a customs union incapable of projecting a unified diplomatic power. Globally, Russia sees the UN Security Council as the ideal forum for managing peace and security. The structure of the council, whereby five nations are given a permanent seat with a veto, means that no decisions can ever be made without Moscow's approval.

In the aftermath of the Ukraine crisis, many people criticized the European Union for not foreseeing and forestalling Putin's reaction. While it is true that the European Union should have recognized Putin's true position, the break between Putin's Russia and the West was all but inevitable. He would challenge the status quo. It was just a matter of time. Preparations were well under way.

In late 2012, Putin appointed Valery Gerasimov, formerly a tank commander who had fought in the Chechen War, as the new chief of the Russian general (army) staff and tasked him with revising the country's defense and mobilization plans. Shortly after taking on his new role, Gerasimov gave a speech to the general meeting of the Military Sciences Academy where representatives of the government and the leadership of the armed forces of the Russian Federation were in attendance. Gerasimov's theme was the nature of modern warfare. He told the audience that Russians should not continue to expect that threats will come in the traditional form of an invading force:

> In the twenty-first century we can observe a trend of blurring of the differences between the states of war and peace. War is not declared, and once begun, it does not follow familiar patterns. Experience of armed conflicts, including those associated with the so-called color revolutions in North Africa and the Middle East, have confirmed that a thoroughly prosperous state can in a matter of months and even days turn into an arena of fierce armed struggle, fall victim to foreign intervention, and be plunged into the abyss of chaos and humanitarian disaster, and civil war. Of course, the easiest thing of all is simply to say that the events of the "Arab spring" are not a war, so there's nothing here for us, the military, to study. But perhaps it's the opposite: maybe it is precisely these events that represent the typical war of the twenty-first century.[19]

This new type of war requires a more holistic approach to fighting than does one involving conventional military force. As Gerasimov explains, "The emphasis in the methods of confrontation being employed is shifting toward widespread use of political, economic, information, humanitarian, and other non-military measures, implemented by means of engagement of the protest potential of the population. All this is supplemented by covert military measures, including implementation of measures of information struggle and the operations of special forces. Overt use of force, often under the guise of peacekeeping and crisis management, occurs only at a certain stage, primarily to achieve definitive success in the conflict."[20]

Gerasimov was telling Putin what he believed: the West was already at war with Russia—or more accurately his regime—and had been for some time. It was an unconventional or irregular war. But this did not make it any less dangerous. Russia could respond to a conventional invasion with nuclear weapons but it had fewer defenses against this type of subversion. Russia, Gerasimov concluded, "should not copy other people's experience and try to catch up to the leading countries. Rather we should try to overtake them and ourselves be in the lead."[21] There are signs that Russian forces were doing exactly that. As four senior U.S. Army officers told the U.S. Senate in testimony on Russia's military challenge, "It is clear that while our army was engaged in Afghanistan and Iraq, Russia studied US capabilities and vulnerabilities and embarked on an ambitious and largely successful modernization program."[22]

Putin put Gerasimov's advice into effect in Ukraine in 2014. He saw the European Union's Association Agreement with Kiev as the latest manifestation of the external threat to Russia. When he pressured Kiev to pull out of the accession agreement, there were massive protests that toppled the government. Putin was then faced with a dilemma. He could watch as Ukraine was "lost" to Russia forever, or he could act. And act he did. Russia's swift military action stunned those Western observers who had dismissed Russia as a third-rate power in decline. These observers had focused on poorly trained conscripts and rusting naval vessels but missed a concerted effort to strengthen Russia's deployable power in specific areas, especially in highly trained special forces. This began after the invasion of Georgia in 2008 when the Kremlin was surprised with how poorly its forces performed. Moscow had the military cut the number of conscripts, improve training, streamline command and control, and purchase new equipment.[23] In Crimea, it deployed special forces to create the illusion of a popular revolt against Kiev and gain control. The

United States and the European Union were stunned but expected Putin to maintain deniability and a distance. He surprised the West again, however, by announcing that he was annexing Crimea. It was the first such act in Europe since World War II.

Russia's invasion of Crimea has been referred to in terms implying novelty—the Gerasimov Doctrine, hybrid war, special war, little green men, and grey zone warfare. But in truth it is not new and such labels can be misleading.[24] Military powers have long made use of fifth-column organizations composed of their ethnic minorities in neighboring states. They have also used infiltration, political subversion, and aggressive intelligence operations. The United States, the Soviet Union, France, Great Britain, Israel, Hezbollah, and many others have used these tactics. It would be wrong to suggest that this is Putin's innovation. But it is equally wrong to dismiss it as old hat. The fact that Russia is using such tactics in post–Cold War Europe is in fact new. NATO has not had to cope with such provocations for some time. And this type of calibrated aggression poses special challenges.

Putin took the opportunity afforded to him by his operation in Crimea to press his case against the United States and its liberal order. In a speech on March 18, 2014, announcing the annexation of Crimea, Putin said:

> After the dissolution of bipolarity on the planet, we no longer have stability. Key international institutions are not getting any stronger; on the contrary, in many cases, they are sadly degrading. Our western partners, led by the United States of America, prefer not to be guided by international law in their practical policies, but by the rule of the gun. They have come to believe in their exclusivity and exceptionalism, that they can decide the destinies of the world, that only they can ever

be right. They act as they please: here and there, they use force against sovereign states, building coalitions based on the principle "If you are not with us, you are against us." To make this aggression look legitimate, they force the necessary resolutions from international organizations, and if for some reason this does not work, they simply ignore the UN Security Council and the UN overall.[25]

For Putin, the United States had destabilized the Middle East and unleashed new generations of Islamist terrorists. It was holding international institutions hostage for its strategic ambition. It had brought the global economy to the brink of ruin. Putin would make this argument repeatedly in the years that followed. He sought to rally the non-Western world to his cause. As Fiona Hill and Clifford Gaddy observed, "Putin made it a priority to seek out and associate with countries that wanted to chip away at the unipolar system and dilute the influence of the United States regionally and globally."[26] And he had some success. He persuaded the other BRICS nations (Brazil, India, China, and South Africa) to abstain on a UN General Assembly resolution condemning the annexation. Although Russia had been expelled from the G8, Putin attended the BRICS summit in Rio in July 2014 and was greeted as a friend with nary a word of criticism leveled against him.

As we shall see in Chapter 5, the European Union and the United States would retaliate against Putin with sanctions. The sanctions were imposed shortly before a dramatic drop in the price of oil, which magnified the impact of the sanctions on the Russian economy. Putin is nothing if not a retribution-oriented player. For Putin, the sanctions were further confirmation of a declaration of war. From that point forward, he would take every opportunity to weaken the European Union. He would use internal subversion, covert funding of anti-EU political parties, and information warfare. The stage was set for a protracted period of conflict during which Putin would use all the means at his disposal, including force, to advance his agenda.

Putin did not neglect more conventional forms of hard power. In fact, he saw hard power as his key advantage against the European Union, which was a soft-power superpower with little stomach for real combat. Thus Russia has massively increased its probing of Western defenses, such as buzzing NATO ships and flying over NATO airspace. Russia has also invested in its nuclear forces for the past decade—especially by building smaller and more usable nuclear weapons—to offset NATO's conventional superiority. It has adopted the "escalate to deescalate doctrine," which envisages the early use of nuclear weapons in a limited war to demonstrate Russia's superior willpower and to compel NATO to back down.[27] Russia has also carried out massive military exercises that involve the first use of tactical nuclear weapons.[28] These high-risk policies are a marked departure from the fragile stability provided by mutual assured destruction during the Cold War.

Meanwhile, Russia has slid into authoritarianism and increasingly into dictatorship. The Russian government has cracked down on the media, brought criminal charges against investigative reporters, and launched a major propaganda campaign. Putin's government also has suppressed political opposition, with leading opponents of the regime killed under mysterious circumstances in Russia and even abroad, or imprisoned on trumped-up charges. Throughout the Russian government, power has become increasingly centralized and corruption has become pervasive. Immigrants, ethnic minorities, and the LGBT community all face discrimination and widespread harassment.

Putin also has a political strategy to weaken democracy and advance authoritarianism overseas. He is oddly embraced by fellow strongmen the world over—including Abdel el-Fattah al-Sisi of Egypt and Turkey's Recep Tayyip Erdoğan before the two had a falling out over Syria—as the de facto leader of a counter-revolutionary alliance against American-style liberal democracy. He has cast himself as the protector of traditional values against a decadent West. As we shall see later in this chapter, he is covertly funding far-right populists throughout the European Union, including the National Front in France, and is stoking the flames of nationalism and xenophobia. And he has pioneered the use of innovative cyber attacks, such as the selective hacking of American political actors in 2016 to influence the course of Western elections.

Putin understands that to advance his agenda in Europe he needs new friends and partners. He has sought to diversify Russia's foreign relations away from the West and build ties with other nations. He has worked with the BRICS, he has tried to build a partnership with Beijing, and he has explored openings to Japan and several other countries. These initiatives have not compensated for the loss in wealth from economic war with the West, and have not been without their difficulties, but they have nevertheless helped reduce pressure on Russia and advance Putin's agenda.

The unmistakable fact is that the European Union now faces a troublesome, well-resourced, revisionist power on its border. Putin's Russia may appear locked into a long-term economic decline, borne out of its inability to reform and modernize and its poor demographic outlook, but it will not go quietly. The combination of acute domestic insecurity, an external soft-power threat, and an exposed underbelly has produced a nationalist and aggressive Russia that is determined to use its hard power to revise the European security order.[29]

Some argue that Russia's trajectory of decline and Putin's own insecurity show that these are not long-term threats but a continuation of Russian imperialism's association with Russian insecurity. As Henry Kissinger writes, as far back as the seventeenth century, prior to the modern state system, "Russia's failure to dominate its surroundings . . . had exposed it to the Mongol invasions and plunged it into its nightmarish 'Time of troubles.'" Indeed, when asked to define Russia's foreign policy, a mid-seventeenth-century minister to Czar Alexei answered, "expanding the state in every direction."[30] In the second half of the eighteenth century, Catherine the Great saw authoritarian rule as the only means of holding together the vast Russian state; any other form of government, in her view, would lead to "its entire ruin."[31] In May 1944, as the Soviet Union began to plan to dominate Eastern Europe once the war ended, George Kennan wrote, "Behind Russia's stubborn expansion lies only the age-old sense of insecurity of a sedentary people reared on an exposed plain in the neighborhood of fierce nomadic peoples."[32]

Putin's challenge to the European order has ebbed and flowed. By the summer of 2015, it seemed to be ebbing. Europe appeared to have come to grips with the Ukraine crisis, at least in the short term. The unified front on sanctions held together. Europe also dodged an economic bullet in June 2015 when it averted a Greek exit from the Eurozone. The deal reached was flawed and exacerbated many of the fault lines in the European project, but catastrophe was avoided. So European leaders could have been forgiven for allowing themselves to think the worst was over. But it was still to come. The third shoe was about to drop, and drop hard.

THE DISINTEGRATION OF SYRIA

By the summer of 2015, the Syrian civil war had raged on for over four years with more than 200,000 dead (the figure now well exceeds 400,000).[33] Europe had had to cope with the return of foreign fighters and some refugee flows but these challenges had never topped the political agenda. In July and August, however, the refugee flow began to pick up. Violence and disorder escalated, making a normal life impossible. Some destinations— Lebanon, Jordan—began to tighten their borders, while others, like Libya, became more dangerous. Consequently, refugees ventured west and across the Mediterranean. Europe tried to stop the flow, especially at sea. They ceased search and rescue operations, in the hope that migrants would be deterred by the dangers of the journey. But most were not. Thousands died.

Few noticed this crisis until September 2, when the body of a three-year-old Syrian boy named Aylan Kurdi washed up on a Turkish beach near Bodrum. He was one of twelve people who had died after a boat of refugees capsized on its way from Turkey to the Greek island of Kos. Aylan was discovered face down in the sand, dressed in a red t-shirt and blue shorts, as the waves lapped around his head. The powerful picture shocked the world. His death caused a change in public opinion. Western governments suddenly found themselves under great pressure to do more. In the United States, even Donald Trump, then in the throes of his presidential campaign, said the situation was "so horrible on a humanitarian basis" that he would consider letting Syrian refugees in to the country (Trump would reverse himself within a couple of weeks).[34] Aylan would be one of 3,770 refugees who died at sea in 2015.[35]

The day after Aylan's image captured the world's attention, Merkel gave a speech at Bern University that would help secure her position as *Time Magazine*'s Person of the Year. She promised that Germany would take in Syrian refugees and dispense with the normal legal requirements. Merkel's catchphrase "Wir schaffen das" (We can manage this) would become famous in Germany and define her approach. Refugees interpreted her speech as a green light and turned up in Germany in unprecedented numbers. By November, Germany was receiving 10,000 refugees a day. The number for 2015 would reach 800,000—four times the figure for 2014—with another million expected in 2016 if the rules did not change.[36]

The refugee crisis would quickly dominate European politics. It was not obvious why. After all, the Syrian refugee flows are large but not unprecedented. The flows from the Balkans, Rwanda, and Somalia in the 1990s were greater. So why is this a crisis when previous flows were manageable? One reason is that the Balkan refugees were more widely dispersed—many went outside of Europe and those who came to the European Union settled in a number of countries. But there is another, more important factor. The 2015 refugee crisis came at a moment when the European Union was gravely weakened from the Eurocrisis and from its renewed rivalry with Russia. The institutions of the European Union had reached breaking point. Domestic politics had taken a turn for the worse, with populists well situated to take advantage of a new crisis. And Europe had to deal with unhelpful external actors, especially Russia and Turkey, both of which tried to exploit Europe's vulnerabilities for their own ends.

It did not help that European institutions were woefully inadequate to handle the challenge. The EU member countries had abolished many of their internal borders—by means of the Schengen Agreement—but they had not established common external border controls. Refugees to the European Union were governed by the Dublin Convention, which stated that refugees were the responsibility of the EU state in which they first arrived. The Dublin Convention was utterly overwhelmed by the Syrian crisis. States on Europe's southern border—Greece, Hungary, and Romania—were unable to cope with hundreds of thousands of asylum seekers. There were calls to reform the system so that all European countries would share the burden fairly, but this effort failed for one simple reason: no leader could afford politically to bail out the others. German diplomats would admit privately that they stopped asking for EU burden sharing because they knew there was no chance it would happen and worried that it would undermine public support for European integration.[37]

The refugee crisis underscored that costs—whether banking debt or the burdens of taking in refugees—are nationalized in the European Union. There is no solidarity. The state that gets left holding the can has to keep it. In this context it could come as no surprise that governments began to act unilaterally to stem the flow to their states. In early 2016, the Danish government announced that refugees would have to give up their possessions or savings in exchange for state assistance. The world was outraged, especially since Denmark is usually held up as a model of social democracy, but the government achieved its objective—namely, to send a message that Denmark is not an attractive destination.

The refugee crisis was bad enough by November 2015, but it soon became much worse as it merged with another element of the collapse of the southern order—terrorism. Europe was already on edge. The year 2015 had gotten off to a bloody start when three armed men invaded the Paris office of the satirical magazine *Charlie Hebdo* and killed eleven people. This was merely prologue for what was to follow.

Shortly after 9:00 p.m. on Friday, November 14, a man wearing a suicide vest tried to enter Stade de France, where French President François Hollande was attending a friendly soccer game between France and Germany. A security guard detected the vest and the man blew himself up outside. A sense of uneasiness descended on the stadium as spectators tweeted the unusual sound. The game continued while the president was rushed out. Meanwhile, two other attacks were unfolding in popular Paris nightlife spots, which were packed with young people out on a Friday night. Shooters opened fire with semi-automatic weapons on Le Carillon bar in the 10th arrondissement, killing fifteen and injuring another fifteen. Three other restaurants and bars—Café Bonne Bière and La Casa Nostra pizzeria, which were beside each other, and La Belle Equipe bar to the south—came under attack, with terrorists killing another twenty-four people there.

The last of these shootings was reported at 9:34 p.m. Six minutes later, three terrorists in their twenties wearing suicide vests entered the Bataclan Theater in the 11th arrondissement where the American band Eagles of Death Metal was playing to a packed house of 1,500. They opened fire on the crowd, killing eighty-nine. By the end of the night, 134 people would be dead. French President François Hollande said, bluntly, that France was at war.

But at war with whom? France's problem has less to do with radical Islam and more to do with what the French scholar Olivier Roy calls the Islamization of radicalization.[38] What Roy means is that France's terrorism problem derives from alienated second- and third-generation young Muslims who feel detached from French society and have fallen in with a radical ideology offering purpose and meaning. Their radicalization process is similar to that experienced by members of the Baader-Meinhof Gang in the 1970s or by other radicals. Most are not particularly pious. For instance, Hasna Aït Boulahcen, a twenty-six-year-old woman who tried to help the mastermind of the Paris attack evade capture, was described as a party girl and recreational drug user until she was radicalized six months earlier. Syria and ISIS gave these alienated and disaffected youths a mission and a purpose.

In Berlin, Merkel was out on a political limb. Days after the Paris attack, German authorities foiled an assault on a German football game in Hanover at which members of the German cabinet, including Merkel, were due to attend. The game was abandoned after credible intelligence of an attack was received. On New Year's Eve, Germany faced another problem when more than a thousand young men of North African and Middle Eastern descent assaulted dozens of women in Cologne. Because they were operating in large groups, police were overwhelmed and it proved very difficult to identify the individuals involved. According to an internal police report, "women, accompanied or not, literally ran a 'gauntlet' through masses of heavily intoxicated men that words cannot describe."[39] In the following days, details were slow to emerge as the media and authorities were reluctant to hype the incident out of concern that it could lead to a backlash against migrants. If this was the strategy, it backfired. Merkel found herself under increasing pressure from all sides.

After the attacks in Paris many Europeans saw Russia, and the Russian September 2015 intervention in Syria, as part of the solution. In fact, it quickly became part of the problem. Russia's pretext was ostensibly about fighting ISIS, but the driving motivation was to protect Assad's regime and deal Russia in to any negotiations about the future of Syria. From the European Union's perspective, the Russian move made the refugee crisis much worse. The single most important cause of refugee flows from Syria has been Assad, not ISIS. Russia helped shore up his power and created thousands more refugees every week. In early February 2016, Russian tanks, artillery, and airpower helped lay siege to Aleppo, resulting in over 70,000 people leaving the city with tens of thousands poised to follow. The refugee inflows into Europe actually served Russia's interests and Putin may well have seen the increase in these flows as an added benefit of his intervention in Syria— the refugees made European countries more desperate and more open to working with Russia and to accepting Assad's demands. Meanwhile, Russia played both sides of the fence and exacerbated populist sentiment. The state media hyped up stories of refugee crimes in Western Europe. EU officials suspected that Russian intelligence was directly involved in steering refugees to EU member countries while it also covertly funded and backed anti-immigrant far-right parties including the National Front, Pegida, and the Euroskeptic Alternative for Germany (AfD).[40]

The crisis to Europe's south is not primarily a humanitarian problem although it has a significant humanitarian dimension. It is also not primarily a terror problem although that is an important element of it. Europe's exposure to its southern neighborhood is, at its heart, a geopolitical problem. It is rooted in the collapse of the Middle East regional order. Russia's intervention was one part of that drama. The changing stance of the United States in the Middle East was another. Washington's reluctance to intervene in Syria would greatly complicate Europe's options.

BREXIT

The fourth crisis was the culmination of a decades-old problem that had hitherto been brushed under the carpet. Euroskepticism has deep roots in Britain, especially in the

Conservative Party. Divisions over the European Union contributed to the downfall of Prime Ministers Margaret Thatcher and John Major and bitterly divided Conservatives during their years in opposition. Euroskepticism was also a constant thorn in the side of other European leaders who found their project of integration disrupted, thwarted, and stymied by a recalcitrant Great Britain. Yet the European Union always found a way to muddle through. The euro even seemed to make things easier, at least for a while, because it showed that the rest of the European Union could proceed without Britain.

David Cameron was determined to avoid the fate of his predecessors and sought to put an end to Conservative divisions on Europe. He did so by embracing Euroskepticism. Cameron was a critic of the European Union and a strong opponent of joining the euro. He hoped this would be sufficient, and if the past was any guide it should have been. But the goalposts began to shift during the Eurocrisis. Euroskeptics were no longer campaigning against membership of the euro; they increasingly wanted to leave the European Union altogether. Facing an additional challenge from the UK Independence Party, Cameron tried to head Euroskeptics off at the pass and proposed to hold a referendum on membership if he was elected to a second term. Some people believe that Cameron never intended to have to hold a referendum because he believed he would be the prime minister of a coalition government and that his governing partners, the Liberal Democrats, would insist on abandoning the pledge. In a classic case of being careful what you wish for, Cameron unexpectedly won an outright majority in the general election of 2015 and had no way of avoiding a referendum. He would have to win it.

Cameron's strategy was straightforward but flawed. He accepted the premise that membership in the European Union was a bad deal for Britain but he promised to negotiate better terms that would make membership worthwhile. Everybody knew that the negotiations were designed to provide Cameron with a fig leaf to justify his change of heart. He won some new concessions but was hamstrung by the fact that Britain already had a good deal—it had exemptions from the passport free zone (known as the Schengen zone) and the euro. Cameron trumpeted the negotiations as a great triumph but after hearing the government lambast the European Union for years, many voters were unconvinced. The refugee crisis and concerns about immigration were the primary issues in the campaign and worked in favor of Leave. The weakness of the Labour Party, which normally could be counted on to campaign strongly in favor of EU membership; the hostility of the press; and continued stagnation in the European economy all played a role in the outcome.

The result—a Leave win by 52 percent to 48 percent—was a surprise. Betting markets had estimated a 90 percent chance of a Remain win just before the polls had closed.[41] Most people expected a shift toward Remain out of an abundance of caution, but it was not to be. The result shocked Britain and Europe. Cameron resigned and six weeks of political bloodletting in the Conservative Party followed, which ended with Theresa May becoming prime minister. It quickly became apparent that there was no plan about how Britain could leave the European Union. It was also clear that the European Union's framework for a country to leave was woefully inadequate. Drafters of the Lisbon Treaty provided for a two-year negotiation under Article 50, but the timeline they chose was completely arbitrary and did not allow for parallel negotiations about future relations between the exiting state and the rest of the European Union.

Brexit worsened the crisis of European integration. It showed that a country can leave if it wants to. It made it less likely that the European Union would be able to act as one against Russia, because Britain was a leading voice for tough sanctions. It tilted domestic politics throughout the European Union toward stricter limits on immigration and refugees. It raised the prospect of an economic downturn in Britain and the rest of the European Union. Moreover, it all but guaranteed that Europe's leaders would spend much of the next five years locked in extremely difficult negotiations about the European Union's future.

AMERICA'S DECLINING INTEREST IN EUROPE

Europe has long complained about U.S. strategy in the Middle East, seeing it as overly militaristic, simplistic, and ineffective. But the great paradox is that Europe, despite these complaints and its long-standing associations with the region, has outsourced its Middle East strategy to Washington. For years, Europe avoided developing the capability to influence developments in the region. European states cut back their militaries, assuming that the Americans would take care of any threats. But Europe has been hugely vulnerable to the effects of the Syrian conflict, while the United States is far less directly exposed. Syrians—whether refugees or fighters—cannot easily travel the approximately six thousand miles, including across the Atlantic Ocean, to reach the United States. As the situation in the Middle East deteriorated, President Obama decided that the instability in Syria and Iraq did not directly threaten U.S. interests in a way that merits the costs of a greater intervention, which he thought would likely not succeed in any case. The infamous red line episode of September 2013 when Obama called off air strikes against Syrian regime targets was greeted with dismay in Paris. The consequent worsening of the situation, however, actually reinforced Obama's calculus.

The Syrian civil war does directly threaten vital EU interests, as we have seen with the massive refugee flows in the autumn of 2015 and the ISIS attacks on Paris and Brussels. Europe found itself in the position of having to rely on the United States at precisely the point when many Americans questioned whether stabilizing the Middle East is possible or worth the cost. The inconvenient truth may well be that U.S. interests are simply not at stake in the region to the degree that Europe's are. Europe was left hoping it could persuade the United States to act in a way compatible with European interests, but there was little sign that it even knows what it wants Washington to do.

Obama also worried that greater U.S. involvement could increase tensions with Moscow and create a U.S.-Russia confrontation. In fact, the United States concentrated on the Russia angle in its diplomacy on Syria and marginalized Europe. The U.S. focus on ISIS meant that some in the United States believed the Russian offensive was compatible with U.S. interests, even though it made the refugee problem worse.

Frustration with the United States over the refugee crisis was just one element of a growing transatlantic divide. When the Obama administration announced its pivot to Asia, many Europeans felt that it was a pivot away from Europe. The administration, particularly senior officials working on Asia, went to great lengths to explain that it was a pivot with Europeans and not away from Europe. But while it is true that the architects of the pivot did not intend it to be a shift away from the transatlantic alliance, it is also true that President Obama reduced America's engagement with Europe over the course of his two terms.

The prism through which President Obama looked at Europe was shaped by the principle that everyone ought to tend their own garden.[42] According to this principle, Europeans are wealthy and well-equipped with the means to deal with their own challenges, if they show leadership and political will. Europe's travails are its own fault and responsibility, and it must find its own way out. The United States can help, but it will take a back seat: Europe must lead. If the situation in Europe threatened core U.S. interests, Obama would make his views known—as his Treasury Department did over the question of Greek exit from the Eurozone, which could have destabilized the global economy, and as he did on Brexit—but otherwise, Obama felt that the United States should leave the European Union to Europe.

This was a significant shift. Previous American presidents have directly engaged Europeans on European integration. George H. W. Bush sat down with Helmut Kohl and François Mitterrand to agree on German reunification. Bill Clinton worked closely with John Major, Tony Blair, and Gerhard Schroeder on NATO expansion and the future of the Balkans. Even George W. Bush built close ties to several European leaders, particularly Tony Blair, and he drove the expansion of NATO to include the Baltics. Prior to the end of the Cold War, American presidents always saw European integration as a core U.S. interest. Indeed, the United States was a pivotal player in the creation of the European Economic Community in 1956. Washington did not do Europe's work for it; it was not a question of all or nothing. Rather, successive administrations believed that the United States had to make a steady investment in European integration to protect its interests over the long term.

The absence of the United States from the process of European integration has created a vacuum that Europe's leaders have been unable to fill. The European Union has only one leader of any real stature—Angela Merkel. Merkel played a vital role in responding to Russia's aggression in Ukraine, but she also made several mistakes. As we saw earlier, the German government's choices worsened the euro crisis and exacerbated the divisions within the European Union. She also reinforced Obama's desire to remain aloof from the European Union, which deepened America's disengagement.

European frustrations with Obama seemed to pale into insignificance in comparison with what would come next. Donald Trump was elected to the presidency after calling NATO's original mission obsolete, questioning the mutual defense clause Article 5, criticizing Merkel directly for her handling of the refugee crisis, and embracing Nigel Farage, the UK nationalist who spearheaded the effort to extract Britain from the European Union. Trump's presidency is likely to put great strain on the transatlantic alliance and will exacerbate all of the crises that Europe was already facing.

A PERFECT STORM IN EUROPE

This series of stunning events means that security competition has returned to Europe. The European Union finds itself weakened by several crises, both internally and externally driven, and faces a revisionist Russia and a growing terrorist threat. Meanwhile, the United States has reduced its engagement with its allies and appears to hold the view that they should handle their problems largely on their own. It is easy to point out that European nations could deal with these challenges by increasing their cooperation, deepening integration, and spending more on defense. Europe could build a real economic union—with common taxes, debt, and spending plans—and establish EU control of its borders with an equitable distribution of refugees throughout its member nations. It could take a common position toward Russia and speak with one voice on critical foreign-policy questions. In effect, European countries could create a United States of Europe. But this will not happen because the politics are too toxic. Calling for such a union is only marginally less fanciful than calling for world government. As these crises continue, the domestic politics become even less hospitable to a great leap forward in integration, even if it could help. Trust is gone. Voters are turning to those politicians who promise to defend the national interest. Even if nationalists do not make it into government, they are powerful enough to stop major treaty change in its tracks. At best, left to its own devices, Europe is doomed to a prolonged period of drift and introspection.

As it struggles to cope with its problems, the European Union will face a motivated and able rival. Putin has shown himself capable of strategic surprise. As he told the Valdai Forum in 2015, "The streets of Leningrad taught me one thing, if a fight is inevitable you should punch first."[43] He annexed Crimea, invaded the Donbass, and intervened in Syria—each time surprising and wrong-footing Western leaders. His intelligence forces were more active still, interfering most notably in American and European domestic politics, but they left few fingerprints. As Putin's position becomes less secure, he is likely to take great risks to advance Russia's position and weaken its rivals. These could occur in any of a number of places—the Baltics, the Balkans, Cyprus, Lebanon, or Libya, to mention but a few. Putin sees the European Union as a threat to his vital interests and he would like to weaken it and the transatlantic alliance as much as possible. He certainly wants to work with individual European leaders, but on his own terms and preferably bilaterally. If Russia's economic predicament worsens, he will grow more confrontational and more willing to embark on risky maneuvers.

The penny has certainly dropped in Europe that it is in trouble and needs help. In January 2016 the *Guardian*, a left-of-center newspaper that is frequently critical of the United States, ran an opinion piece—by the former executive editor of *Le Monde*, no less—headlined "Europe is in crisis. Once more, America will have to step in to save us."[44] The debate had come full circle. Ten months later, on November 8, 2016, America would give its answer—you're on your own.

As we will see in Chapters 6 and 7, the United States has a fundamental choice to make about the role that it will play in Europe over the next decade. On the one hand are strategies of restraint. The United States can argue that it has enough problems of its own. European nations are wealthy and capable and should take care of their own neighborhood. On the other hand is a choice that I call "responsible competition"—a deepening of U.S. engagement in order to strengthen the European order and push back against Russia.

Responsible competition includes providing active support for European integration, playing an intermediary role to produce a Brexit agreement that results in a strong and independent United Kingdom and a successful EU, bolstering democracy in Central and Eastern Europe, strengthening deterrence of Russian aggression, countering Russian efforts to interfere in Western politics, and deepening economic cooperation with the EU through a reformed and much more expansive Transatlantic Trade and Investment Partnership. Success in Europe has been at the heart of America's success internationally since World War II. For a while, that success seemed to have its own momentum, but now the United States must play an active, supportive role to keep it moving.

3 CHINA'S EAST ASIA CHALLENGE

American strategists may have been surprised by the deteriorating situation in Europe, but they have long expected problems in East Asia. They have tended to see Europe as America's past, the Middle East as its present, and East Asia as its future, both in terms of threats and opportunities. The more optimistic point to the incredible economic dynamism of the region as a whole and the necessity of a holistic approach that will deepen U.S. engagement there economically, culturally, and militarily. The more pessimistic worry about how China's spectacular ascent seems to neatly fit preexisting narratives, dating back to ancient Greece, about the dangers inherent in the rise and fall of great powers. There seems to be an endless supply of books, articles, and reports on whether war with China is inevitable or avoidable.

China is very different from Russia. It is a rising power and deeply integrated in the global economy, which ties its fate to that of the United States. Beijing has historical grievances but they are not as recent as Moscow's. China has a strong military but does not rely on hard power alone—it has emerged as the most important economic power for other Asian nations, which gives it special leverage in discussions on the future of the region. The United States has never before faced a competitor as complicated and multi-faceted as China. To understand the challenge China poses, we must start with understanding a key contradiction in its behavior—should it be judged by its foreign policy regionally or globally?

REVISIONIST OR NOT? DECIPHERING A CONTRADICTION

On April 8, 2012, a Philippine surveillance plane spotted eight Chinese fishing vessels near Scarborough Reef, an area in the South China Sea that is claimed by the Philippines, China, and Taiwan. The Philippines used a decommissioned U.S. Coast Guard cutter ship it had received from the United States to inspect the vessels and found them to be illegally carrying endangered sea life. The crew were arrested and detained. China reacted furiously and sent vessels of its own. The Chinese navy worked closely with Chinese fishermen to trap the Philippine vessels inside the reef. China also retaliated in other ways—it prevented Philippine banana imports from reaching their markets in China and it issued a travel ban that reduced the number of Chinese tourists to the Philippines.[1]

The United States intervened as an intermediary to negotiate a mutual withdrawal and de-escalation of tensions. The talks were led on the U.S. side by U.S. Assistant Secretary of State Kurt Campbell, a veteran Asia expert, and on the Chinese side by Fu Ying, a hardliner who was the second-ever woman to hold the position of China's vice foreign minister. In an article on the Scarborough Reef crisis, Ely Ratner, who served in the State Department's Bureau of East Asia and Pacific Affairs at the time, wrote, "After weeks of discussions, demarches and negotiations,

US officials in mid-June brokered what they thought was a deal for a mutual withdrawal. Exhausted, outnumbered and lacking viable alternatives, Manila withdrew its remaining ships under the face-saving auspices of an oncoming typhoon. China, on the other hand, failed to comply with the agreed-upon deadline and retained its maritime vessels at the shoal, where they remain today on near-constant patrol."[2]

A senior U.S. official involved in the talks would later say privately that being unable to stop China from reneging on its commitment was the single greatest regret of his tenure.[3] In his account of the crisis, Ratner noted that China relied on nonmilitary vessels as the "leading edge" of its coercion. Beijing also understood the importance of calibrating its assertiveness—it pressed its "advantage right up to—but still below—the line of militarization, which would have increased the likelihood of response by the US Navy."[4]

In the years that followed, China pressed its advantage throughout the South China Sea and then began to reclaim land by building islands where there were none. China's primary instrument was its civilian power, which includes the world's largest coast guard fleet.[5] In 2014 and 2015, China reclaimed over 2,900 acres of land, which is over seventeen times that reclaimed by all other claimants combined. This was no accident. As researchers Andrew Erickson and Kevin Bond have shown, China used to lag far behind other nations in its "dredging" capability, but it carefully built it up in the 2000s to over three times its 2000 size and has now "created a fleet capable of literally altering geography, creating 'islands' in the span of eighteen months where before there were only reefs and shoals."[6]

Over the past two years, China has sabotaged a Vietnamese fishing boat around the Paracel Islands, patrolled around the disputed James Reef, used its coast guard to fire a water cannon at two Philippine fishery ships around Scarborough Reef, launched an oil rig near the Paracel Islands before removing it six weeks later, and expanded its land-reclamation efforts to the extent of preparing to install military installations on them, including a three-thousand-meter airstrip on Fiery Cross Reef and a runway on Subi Reef.

Throughout this time, China's neighbors have sought to engage Beijing diplomatically to agree to a Code of Conduct or another means of ensuring that territorial disputes do not spiral out of control. China displayed no interest in reaching a binding agreement and instead concentrated on pressing its advantage to gain control of the South China Sea, which Beijing sees as Chinese. The 2013 edition of the Chinese People's Liberation Army's (PLA) influential publication *The Science of Military Strategy* asserted that "around 1.5 million square km of [China's] jurisdictional waters are under the actual control of other nations, and over 50 islands and reefs have been occupied by other states."[7]

Beijing also reacted angrily to U.S. efforts to reassure its allies and discourage China's unilateral actions. Fu Ying, who had gone on to chair the Foreign Affairs Committee of China's National People's Congress, wrote an op-ed in the *Financial Times* titled "The US World Order Is a Suit That No Longer Fits." Fu accused the United States of wanting "to fuel a geopolitical contest by elbowing its way into regional disputes." To "meddle in the problems China has with its neighbors," Fu wrote, "risks elevating territorial disputes into strategic rivalry."[8]

Few analysts, even those who take a benign view of China's rise, would disagree with the claim that China has become much more assertive and revisionist in its actions in the South China Sea. Most would also acknowledge that China is more confident and pushy throughout East Asia. But many point to countervailing evidence outside of East Asia. Over the past five years China has been much more cooperative and responsible about addressing global challenges, including economic crises, climate change, nuclear proliferation, and counterterrorism. China has been a constructive member of the G20—indeed America's greatest critic on economic policy has been its ally Germany, not China. China has abided by the rulings of the World Trade Organization (WTO). And when Beijing set up its own institution—the Asian Infrastructure Investment Bank (AIIB)—it built on the rules of the World Bank.

China was cooperative with Western countries in the Paris climate talks, in stark contrast to its combative behavior at the Copenhagen climate change summit in 2009. And as Beijing faces the threat of violent extremism to its west, it has grown closer to Washington on counterterrorism, with many Westerners believing that increased Chinese engagement in Central Asia and the Middle East would be consistent with U.S. and European interests. China was also a responsible member of the P5+1 talks on stopping Iran from acquiring a nuclear weapon. More generally, unlike Vladimir Putin, China has not articulated a harsh critique of American global power, and it has demonstrated little desire to overturn the U.S.-led global order.

A great deal has been written on China's rise and what it means for U.S. foreign policy. Much of this analysis involves calculated guesswork about China's intentions and what countries do when they rise rapidly. But the key to unlocking China's effect on the global order has received remarkably little attention. There is contradictory evidence on China's intentions. It is very assertive in the South China Sea, somewhat assertive in the rest of East Asia, and generally cooperative on global issues. How should we think about this contradiction? The answer lies in another question: What are we really worried about as China rises? Are we worried about regional disputes, the integrity of the global order, or something in between? Is greater Chinese influence on the international system always bad for the United States, or is it only bad when directed or expressed in a certain way?

Many scholars believe that China will truly threaten the global order only if and when it becomes assertive on global issues. The regional challenge can be managed, or so the argument goes. Princeton University professor G. John Ikenberry is optimistic about China's rise not only because China needs an open global economy for its own economic growth, but also because the global order "is easy to join but hard to overturn."[9] Ikenberry points out that China does not have an alternative vision for how to structure the global economy, tackle climate change, or deal with nuclear proliferation. It does not want to abolish the United Nations, the IMF, or the World Bank. It may want reform so it has a greater voice but this is consistent with strengthening the order.

Globally, U.S. hegemony has been very good news for the Chinese Communist Party, certainly economically, but also geopolitically. The U.S.-led international order created an environment in which China could grow rapidly. This was not an accident; in fact, it was an intended consequence of U.S. strategy. As another Princeton professor, Thomas Christensen, has put it: "With a few rare exceptions, such as restrictions on arms sales and military relevant technologies, US China policy in the past few decades has been nearly the opposite of our containment policy toward the Soviets throughout the Cold War and toward China itself in the 1950s and 1990s."[10] The United States has actively promoted and facilitated Chinese growth, partly because of a belief that prosperity would shape China's choices in a positive way.

Christensen, who served in the State Department in the George W. Bush administration, argues that the challenge with China is less that Beijing will overturn the order and more that it will not play its part in upholding it. He calls this global governance issue "the biggest challenge of all."[11] Brookings Institution scholar Jeffrey Bader, who served as senior director for Asia in the Obama administration, poses the question another way: "Do China's unacceptable actions in the South China Sea portend how China will behave more broadly in the world if and when it acquires the military capacity to do so?"[12] Bader's answer is no. China lacks the capacity to project power and has no allies other than Pakistan and North Korea. For Bader, it is only if and when China uses military force to achieve its objectives that the West will need to worry that it is seeking to destabilize the regional order in East Asia. These experts believe that the regional challenges—including the maritime tensions and China's assertiveness—are important but can be, and are being, adequately dealt with under current policy approaches.

We have been conditioned to think about China as part of a long-running historical drama about the rise and fall of great powers. The story always goes like this: a country is on top of the heap, with the world at its fingertips, until one day it is challenged by the new power on the block, which then has its moment in the sun. This notion is very prevalent in international relations theory and also in popular culture—in 2006 Chinese television broadcast a twelve-part documentary on the rise and fall of the great powers.[13] The question we continually ask ourselves is, Is this happening now? Is China about to replace the United States as the global superpower? In this context, China's acceptance of global institutions offers reassurance. However, this rise-and-fall view is based on a fundamental misunderstanding of what the global order is and how it may come apart. As described in Chapter 1, the global order depends on healthy regional orders. How China behaves toward its neighbors and on the matter of territorial borders is much more indicative of its disposition toward the order than is its behavior in the IMF, the WTO, or the World Bank, as important as that is.

The geopolitical risk is that a Chinese attempt to overturn the regional order will destabilize East Asia, which consists of some of the most economically advanced, militarily capable, and populous countries in the world. East Asia is also a region where nationalist sentiment and historical grievances run deep. China's neighbors worry that Beijing is looking to reconstitute its old tributary system whereby it exercises great influence over the foreign and domestic policies of many of its neighbors. Were the United States to be pushed out of East Asia, security competition would immediately intensify and the risk of war would increase significantly. A conflict in this part of the world would be a calamity on a par with the major European wars of the first half of the twentieth century. Such a regional challenge would also have catastrophic consequences for the global economy and change how China behaves globally, because it will be more motivated to develop a foreign policy that helps it advance its regional interests. It may not seek to overturn the global order but it might, for instance, choose to drive a wedge between the United States and Europe on East Asian security, build economic institutions that are independent of the United States, or make the world safe for authoritarian capitalism.

It is important to realize, however, that just because a Chinese challenge in East Asia would pose a severe geopolitical problem for the United States, this does not mean that Chinese activism in other regions is equally problematic. China is located in a particularly complex geographical position. It shares a land border with eleven states but is contiguous with twenty when one counts maritime territory. According to China specialists Andrew Nathan of Columbia University and Andrew Scobell of the RAND Corporation, China is part of six separate regional subsystems, which consist of forty-five countries in total.[14] China has had difficult relations with many of these nations in the past. And today it faces many challenges. Take China's western neighborhood as an example. In contrast to the east, in the west China faces threats from Uighur militants in Xinjiang, fueled by instability in Pakistan and Afghanistan, and even Syria and Iraq. In a book on the China-Pakistan relationship, German Marshall Fund senior fellow Andrew Small wrote that "looking west from China, the obvious images that come to mind are fragile states, rising forces of Islamic militancy, major narcotics flows, and the world's fastest growing nuclear arsenals."[15] In other words, these are the same challenges that the United States and its allies are invested in confronting in South and Central Asia and in the Middle East. The risk of a major interstate war is much lower. Some people warn about China-India tensions but their escalation is unlikely because India actually benefits from leaving the door open to China's steadying hand in Pakistan.

Yet China is remarkably passive, particularly when compared with other East Asian nations. As Small put it, "Shifts in the economic and military balance of power in the Asia Pacific have so far moved inexorably in China's favor. It is Beijing's impatience, its assertiveness, that is the greatest risk to China's rising power. In China's western neighborhood by contrast, it has been Beijing's caution and its unwillingness to try to steer developments in a direction consonant with Chinese interest that pose the greater problem."[16] Small concludes: "Unlike Beijing's carefully calibrated escalations in East Asia, the threats emerging in its west have caught it looking seriously unprepared."[17]

These observations highlight that the problem is not rising Chinese influence per se as much as the effects of China's strategy and behavior in particular regions. The effects of this influence are very dangerous in East Asia but much less so to China's west. This also applies to other parts of the world. As a rising power, China is increasing its ties to Africa, Latin America, and Europe. This may pose specific problems for the United States but it is not a major challenge to the global order. The challenge China poses to the U.S.-led liberal order is in East Asia. So what exactly is China up to?

UNDERSTANDING CHINA'S EAST ASIA STRATEGY

It used to be said that China's strategic intentions were a mystery, not a secret. A mystery is something that is unknown, even to Chinese leaders. A secret you can steal, but a mystery will only unfold over time, if at all. The mystery versus secret analogy was supposed to show that China's intentions could change as its power rose (or fell). Some of this remains plausible of course, but China's strategic goals, and its strategy, have come into sharper focus over the past five years.

It is clear now that China is not satisfied with the status quo but is also aware that a major strategic offensive would be massively counterproductive—it would provide the cohesive glue for a coordinated response by the United States and its allies, which China does not have the capabilities to match. Chinese leaders must design a strategy that stands a reasonable chance of success. And they appear to have found one. Based on its behavior over the past five years and scholarly assessments of the Chinese debate on strategy, China's regional strategy can be stated as achieving power parity with the United States in East Asia and the Western Pacific. This is the minimum objective. Ideally, Beijing would like to enjoy an advantage over the United States in East Asia and the Western Pacific.[18] There are two elements of this strategy: (1) build a Chinese sphere of influence up to the second island chain by means short of the use of force, and (2) persuade the United States to accept power parity with China.

What is not widely appreciated about Chinese strategy is that to succeed it requires the absence of conflict with the United States and Japan.[19] China is looking to revise the regional order by means short of war—not only out of preference but also out of necessity. It cannot afford an escalation to war at this time. In the event of conflict, China's new islands would become strategic liabilities and would be destroyed. The Chinese regime would be endangered, and the region would be mobilized against it. But if peace prevails, and if China can accrue enough marginal gains without consequence, that would amount to a fundamental change in the region.[20] At some future point—maybe in ten or fifteen years—the rest of the region and the United States would either have to accept China's newly acquired influence and role or initiate a conflict to roll it back. China knows that the United States would be extremely unlikely to use force in such circumstances. In fact, China repeatedly raises the question of whether the United States really wants to risk a conflict—one that would destroy the U.S.-China relationship—over territorial issues in which the United States has no claim.

This is a very sophisticated strategy that maximizes China's advantages, puts the United States in a difficult position, and manipulates the legitimate concerns that Americans have about a conflict with a major power. It has an attainable goal: not to kick the United States out of East Asia, but to put China in a position whereby the two countries share the region between them. Based on its track record so far, is has a good prospect of success. If China succeeds, it would transform East Asia. China would be in a position to control the sea and airspace within its sphere of influence; it could dictate key economic, political, and foreign-policy decisions to its neighbors; it would most likely roll over its neighbors' territorial claims and weaken U.S. alliances; and it would have a platform for future assertiveness. The two elements of this strategy, then, merit a closer look.

Creating a Sphere of Influence in East Asia

China recognizes that the United States will not leave the Asia Pacific anytime soon but it is determined to change the fact that U.S. forces are the preeminent power in all of East Asia, including right up to Chinese shores. Chinese strategists find U.S. surveillance missions intolerable. They resent their neighbors using American preeminence as a license to advance territorial claims in waters they regard as Chinese. And they feel that Beijing's regional influence and standing have been artificially constrained by the U.S.-led regional order. The first step toward righting these wrongs, in Beijing's view, is to build a sphere of influence in East Asia—a sphere where it is China that calls the shots, not the United States. The contours of this sphere are widely known. China wants to gain control of the maritime space up to the first island chain, and it wants to prevent the U.S. Navy from controlling the seas between the first and second island chains. This means controlling the South China Sea, being the dominant force in the East China Sea, being the most influential external power compared to many of its neighbors, and having a clear strategic advantage over Japan. Admiral Harry Harris, the commander of U.S. forces in the Pacific, described China's goal as being to dominate East Asia out to the second island chain, which he labeled "hegemony" in East Asia.[21]

China enjoys great advantages over its neighbors, especially in Southeast Asia, because it is so much larger than all of them. This affords China the opportunity to extend its influence without resorting to the use of military force. For example, China has a far larger civilian fleet than other nations. According to U.S. experts Andrew Erickson and Conor Kennedy, the already-large fleet of the China Coast Guard (CCG) greatly outnumbers the fleets of Japan, Vietnam, Indonesia, Malaysia, and the Philippines combined, and was projected to grow by 25 percent from 2012 to 2015 as newer and larger ships replaced smaller, older ones.[22] China has trained its fishermen to sail deliberately into disputed waters as part of a "fishing militia." An adviser to the government of the port town of Hainan Island where this training takes place said, "The maritime militia is expanding because of the country's need for it, and because of the desire of the fishermen to engage in national service, protecting our country's interests."[23]

Avoiding the overt use of military force has been, and is still, the key feature of Chinese revisionism. China, for instance, has not forcibly removed other country's forces from disputed islands. Since 1999 Philippine marines have been on the *BRP Sierra Madre*, a dilapidated ship that the Philippine navy ran aground on a contested shoal in the Spratly Archipelago merely to stake a claim.[24] China could easily kick them off but it does not, preferring simply to make life difficult for them by obstructing the resupply lines. China has also eschewed the use of force against Taiwan and against Japan in the East China Sea.

Even though it avoids military force, China is using its raw power to create a new reality in the South China Sea. It spurns efforts at arbitration, rejects the notion that disputes must be settled multilaterally, and is using the vast resources and capabilities at its disposal to act unilaterally and create new realities in the region. As a matter of principle, this is not fundamentally different than what the other claimants have done in the past. If Vietnam or the Philippines had the capability to change the status quo in its favor, it's a fair bet that they would do so. But they do not. Of all the claimants, only China has the power to act truly unilaterally and upset the equilibrium.

China is choosing to use its power to beat the other claimants, albeit in a gradual and subtle way. As Patrick Cronin of the Center for a New American Security put it, "China is enhancing its strategic position through its incremental salami slicing tactics, which accrete to major changes to the status quo while warding off escalation."[25] This is a crucial difference between Chinese and Russian strategy. Russia violated international norms in Crimea. China is using a precedent set by others but it is doing so on such a scale that it has a massive strategic effect. In effect, it is taking a small opening and driving a truck (or in this case, a navy) through it.

Over the past five years, China has used a variety of tactics to shift the maritime balance in its favor. China has used its coast guard fleet and fishing vessels to bully and push other countries off contested territory.[26] Whenever the region reacted, China would make some modest concessions—such as engaging in discussions on a code of conduct—until the next time. Then Beijing shifted tack to construct islands in disputed waters. China was not the first to engage in land reclamation—Vietnam, the Philippines, Malaysia, and Taiwan have done so in the past. But as the then U.S. secretary of defense Ash Carter explained, "One country has gone much further and much faster than any other. And that's China. China has reclaimed over 2,000 acres, more than all other claimants combined . . . and more than in the entire history of the region. And China did so in only the last 18 months. It is unclear how much farther China will go."[27]

Indeed, some estimates put Chinese reclamation at over 2,900 acres in 2014 and the first half of 2015 alone. For comparison, Vietnam reclaimed 80 acres over many decades, Malaysia reclaimed 70, the Philippines 40, and Taiwan just 8. Thus China reclaimed seventeen times more land in twenty months than all other claimants had over forty years.[28] And it has not stopped yet. China has since begun to build military features on these islands.

So why does China's maritime assertiveness matter? After all, as we have seen, many claimants, not just China, have acted unilaterally. China just has more capability. Should it be treated differently for being larger than the others? The short answer is yes. China's size means that it alone has the capacity to remake the geopolitical map of Southeast Asia. Control would give it great influence over its smaller neighbors. There are other factors too. China's actions—forcing its neighbors off reefs and building islands—increase the risk of a military clash that could poison geopolitics in the region with dangerous long-term consequences. If China takes control of the South China Sea, it also stands to benefit from vast resources—the United Nations estimates that 10 percent of global fisheries are located in the South China Sea while the U.S. Energy Information Administration says that the region contains approximately 11 billion barrels of oil and 190 trillion cubic feet of natural gas reserves.[29]

Some people say that U.S. concerns are overblown because it would never be in China's interest to cut off access to crucial sea lanes—after all, China relies on international trade (30 percent of which transits the South China Sea), so a cutoff would come at an enormous cost to China.[30] But this misses the point. From China's perspective, the contest for the Asia Pacific is about a gradual struggle for preeminence; it is not the first step in a plan to shut down maritime commerce. Joint custody of the sea lanes would give China great influence over its neighbors, just as it enhances U.S. prestige now (even though it is unthinkable that the United States would use that role for geopolitical leverage outside of a full-blown conflict). China's maritime assertiveness is a crucial component of its strategy to build a sphere of influence in Southeast Asia and to increase its influence in the region.

China has also become much more assertive and aggressive around the Senkaku/Diaoyu Islands since those islands were purchased by the Japanese government and nationalized in 2012. There have been 144 Chinese intrusions into Japanese territorial waters since September 2012.[31] In 2015, Japanese aircraft scrambled 571 times to intercept Chinese aircraft.[32] In November 2013, China unilaterally declared an Air Defense Identification Zone in the East China Sea. Chinese aircraft became increasingly adventurous and passed through Japanese airspace in the Bashi Channel in March 2015 and the Miyako Strait in May 2015 for the first time.[33] The Japanese believe that China is looking to establish dominance over the East China Sea, which would have dire implications for Japan's security. As one senior Japanese official put it, "China's history of being invaded has left it with a psychological need for a buffer zone. In this, China is similar to Russia. But, it has adopted this buffer zone mentality for its maritime space, not just its land borders. China is determined to create a great wall in the sea."[34]

Compelling the United States to Accept Power Parity

The centerpiece of this component of China's strategy is its concept of a new model of major power relations. This concept was first rolled out in 2012 but is closely associated with President Xi Jinping. The basic notion is attractive: nations are not destined to repeat the mistakes of great powers in bygone eras, especially when they have so many shared interests and are interdependent with each other. The Obama administration initially welcomed this concept but then grew more wary of it. It is a curious proposition because it proposes a new trajectory for a relationship whose characteristics are not new at all. U.S.-China relations tick many of the boxes of previous tragic episodes of a rising power meeting an established power: the United States and China have very different political regimes and distrust one another; China feels aggrieved that it has been taken advantage of over the past two centuries and has been denied its rightful role in its region and maybe the world; East Asia is home to several competing nationalisms and most of China's neighbors are distrustful of its rise. The only truly successful example of a rising power taking over the mantle from an established power was Britain and the United States in the 1940s, which was the result of a truly unique situation: both were democracies, they faced a common threat, and Britain recognized that it was a spent force.

In truth, though, this does not matter because China never intended the concept to mean that some special dynamic or features in the relationship would produce a good outcome.[35] What Xi means by it is that the leaders of the two countries can avoid conflict or a cold war by making different choices than the leaders did in previous situations. The problem is that both Washington and Beijing differ on what those decisions are. In Washington, it means that as China rises its leaders will accept the legitimacy of the international order—including at the regional level—and so forsake the strategic goals held by past rising powers. In Beijing, by contrast, it means that as China rises, the United States will accommodate it by respecting its "core interests."

China's core interests have multiplied over the past decade.[36] The phrase was first used in 2003 to highlight Chinese concerns about Taiwan seeking independence. In 2006, Tibet and Xinjiang were added to the list of China's core interests. And in July 2009, at the U.S.-China Strategic and Economic Dialogue, State Councilor Dai Bingguo listed three, much more expansive, core interests: to "uphold our basic systems, our national security; and secondly, the sovereignty and territorial integrity; and thirdly, economic and social sustained development."[37] Various other statements leave no doubt that the first of these refers to the continuation in power of the Chinese Communist Party. The second remains vague but is widely understood to encompass the nine-dash line in the South China Sea in addition to Taiwan, Tibet, and Xinjiang.[38] In 2015, these three interests were codified in a sweeping National Security Law.[39]

As they are understood, of these three core interests, the United States accepts only the third—economic development. Chinese strategists recognize this and have highlighted it. In a 2012 article on how China understood the new model of great power relations, Cui Tiankai and his co-author Pang Hanzhao wrote: "China has never done anything to undermine the US core interests and major concerns, yet what the United States has done in matters concerning China's core and important interests and major concerns is unsatisfactory."[40]

There is absolutely nothing new about a rising power calling on an established power to accommodate its core interests. Virtually all rising powers in modern history have made the same argument. If the United States and China differ over core interests, why bother with the concept of a new model of great power relations? The reason is that Beijing sees it as a useful diplomatic tool to gradually socialize the region and the United States to its ambition. Perhaps its most pernicious aspect is its assumption that no other country in Asia is a great power, so those countries should be subservient to China and the United States. The concept also assumes a linear project of Chinese power relative to the United States. The message is unambiguous: China's rise is inevitable, so accept these core interests and overcome the centuries of history that suggest rivalry between emerging and established powers is inevitable. Right now, the United States will not accept this deal. But if China can undermine the alliance system, create new realities in the region, and gain leverage over the United States, Beijing hopes that a future American president will accept it as a necessary evil to reduce tensions and maintain a constructive relationship with China.[41]

The flip side to China's new model is the risk of war if the United States rejects it. China may require the absence of war to build its sphere of influence in East Asia, but China also wants to maintain the illusion that the two countries are close to an inadvertent conflict. Such an illusion induces an abundance of caution among American policymakers. For instance, in 2011, the Chinese vice foreign minister Cui Tiankai warned that Southeast Asian nations "are actually playing with fire" in the South China Sea, "and I hope the fire will not be drawn to the United States."[42] Cui would go on to serve as ambassador to the United States. It was in that capacity that he authored an article urging Americans to focus on areas of global cooperation with China instead of the more competitive aspects of the relationship.[43]

Beijing is also trying to sow seeds of doubt in the region about America's staying power. It is using its military capability to deny access to maritime regions—what is known in security circles as anti-access and area denial (A2/AD)—as a way of undermining the credibility of U.S. security guarantees well before the United States formally accepts the Chinese sphere of influence. Beijing also hopes that its economic leverage—it serves as a market for the rest of the region and a source of growth—will sugarcoat the pill of revisionism and help socialize its neighbors to its new role as co-manager of the East Asian order.

Without the United States, the balance of power fundamentally shifts and China is in the ascendant. One way of illustrating this is to look at diplomatic ties between the United States and China and what happens when China's neighbors deal with China on their own. Asian nations struggle to have a frank dialogue with Beijing. China resists multilateral discussions on thorny issues because it does not want to be put in a position where it is outnumbered. Beijing also knows that the cards are stacked in its favor in one-on-one discussions given that it is much bigger than all of its neighbors except India. But even in one-on-one talks, China's neighbors find that Beijing is not very forthcoming. Meetings with Xi Jinping are allowed to focus only on soft issues, and criticism of China's behavior, especially in the South China Sea, is not allowed. One senior Japanese diplomat pointed out to China that Presidents Obama and Xi felt free to criticize each other and exchange views frankly and was told by the Chinese side, "Japan is not the United States. Only the United States is the United States."[44] The meaning was clear. China would deal with the United States on different terms because it was a superpower (and because of this status China had no choice in the matter), but smaller countries should not have such pretensions. They must respect Beijing's superior power and preferences, much as foreign peoples did in the tributary system of the Middle Kingdom.

If China can reach an accommodation with the United States whereby Washington recognizes power parity in Asia, including a Chinese sphere of influence in the western part of the western Pacific, Beijing can turn to the rest of Asia and say something to the effect of "We have come to an arrangement with the United States to co-manage the region. You must stop resisting and recognize the new reality." At that point, most countries in the region would have little option but to acquiesce. Japan would likely try to balance against China, especially in the East China Sea, but the other countries in the region would not have enough power or leverage to do so on their own. They would be compelled to bandwagon with Beijing and accept Chinese preeminence in East Asia. The struggle to preserve the U.S.-led regional order would be lost.

A BALANCING ACT

If China's audacious bid to share East Asia with the United States fails, it will be because of a counter-reaction. The United States and most of China's neighbors are increasingly anxious about China's behavior and they are balancing against it. The United States is looking to capitalize on this anxiety by deepening its engagement with East Asian nations to strengthen security and economic cooperation among like-minded nations. Japan's nationalist prime minister, Shinzō Abe, is using the opportunity to introduce domestic reforms that will enable Japan to do more to balance against China, both on its own and with other nations. And the region as a whole is working with the United States and one another—through arms sales, training exercises, joint patrols, and diplomatic cooperation—to balance against China.

Washington and Tokyo hope that this balancing will be enough to deny China its strategic objective, but it may not be enough. Before we look at why it might fail, let's first look at what the balancing effort entails.

A U.S. Pivot

After the initial attempt at convergence with China in 2009, the Obama administration's strategy shifted dramatically as it began to implement its most famous strategic innovation: the pivot, or rebalance, to Asia. Announced by President Obama to the Australian Parliament in 2011, the pivot has been presented as increasing America's investment in the world's most dynamic and vibrant region.[45] But in fact the United States began to increase its engagement in the region from the mid-2000s on.[46] That is, even though officials go to great lengths to say that China is not the target of the pivot, there is no doubt that the primary driver of current U.S. policy is a desire to counter-balance China's challenge to the regional order.

When one looks at the various components of the pivot, it becomes clear that they are primarily in the military realm.[47] The United States is deepening security cooperation with its allies and what it calls its partners—countries, like Vietnam, that are not formal allies but share America's concern over China's rise. In practice, this means that the U.S. Navy has been invited back to places like Subic Bay in the Philippines and Cam Ranh Bay in Vietnam, both of which it had been excluded from for many decades. The Philippines and Vietnam understand very clearly why the change has taken place: to bolster the deterrent to China in the South China Sea.

Another component of the rebalance is sustaining the capability to project power into the area to support U.S. allies. Again, this sounds relatively innocuous, as if the U.S. Navy were struggling to cope with a severe weather pattern rather than inhibited navigation. But, of course, it is nothing of the sort. The Chinese military has been pouring resources into means of blunting America's ability to project power into the region. In the jargon of the navy, they have been investing in A2/AD capabilities, like anti-ship missiles. One purpose of the U.S. pivot, then, is to come up with clever ways of circumventing or defeating these measures.

Even the nonmilitary parts of the pivot are about balancing against China. Increasing U.S. diplomatic engagement in East Asian institutions serves the general purpose of strengthening the regional order but it is also about using multilateral forums to put pressure on China not to act unilaterally to change the status quo. The since-abandoned Trans-Pacific Partnership (TPP) was about promoting economic growth and it was open to China in principle, but there is no getting around the fact that the Obama administration's primary selling point was that "if the United States does not set the rules, China will."[48]

As it pivoted, Washington sought to deepen its dialogue with Beijing along a parallel track, through forums like the Strategic and Economic Dialogue. Balancing is not containment. It does not seek to stop China from rising. It only aims to push back against specific Chinese policies that challenge the regional order. The purpose of the engagement track is to clearly communicate this to China and to keep open avenues of cooperation on vitally important shared interests—like climate change, the global economy, and nonproliferation—even as the regional competition heats up.

The purpose of the U.S. pivot to Asia was very clear. It is to take advantage of regional concerns about Chinese foreign policy to balance against China so it is unable to overturn the U.S.-led regional order. More than any other metric, U.S. engagement in Asia, whether called a pivot or not, will rise or fall on whether it achieves that goal, regardless of how it may be sugarcoated in the public presentation.

Japan

Shinzō Abe served as Japan's prime minister for twelve months in 2006–2007 and returned to power in December 2012 after a particularly volatile period in Japanese politics in which five prime ministers served in five years. Abe's formative experience was as a six-year-old when he sat on the lap of his grandfather, Nobusuke Kishi, who was then prime minister of Japan. Kishi had previously served in Tojo's cabinet in World War II and had been arrested by U.S. forces as a suspected war criminal. On the day that the young Shinzō was with his grandfather, he could hear tens of thousands of people protesting loudly outside Kishi's office against his effort to revise and ratify the U.S.-Japan security treaty.[49] Kishi would succeed in his goal, but only by using strong-arm tactics that led to his resignation and loss of power. It was an experience that Abe would never forget.

When Abe returned to power in 2012, relations with China had already turned sour. In fact, it was the souring of relations of China that propelled Abe back into office. His party, the Liberal Democratic Party (LDP), wanted a strong national security leader to challenge the incumbent Democratic Party of Japan (DPJ) and restore Japan's position vis-à-vis China. Abe's view is that China is seeking a sphere of influence in East Asia, in order to weaken the U.S. alliance system and create a regional order in which other countries are subservient to China. He set out on a mission to transform Japan's strategy and its capabilities, so it could effectively balance China and prevent it from achieving its goal.[50]

Abe's grand strategy has three components. First, he seeks to preserve the balance of power in Asia whereby there is an effective counterweight to China. Japan's military shares the assessment offered here that to succeed, China's strategy requires the absence of war. As one senior Japanese naval officer put it, "The Chinese are expansionist and revisionist but they are also pragmatic and a believer in the balance of power. Unless they believe they have achieved superiority over U.S. forces they will not wage war to expand."[51] The linchpin of this counterweight is the U.S.-led alliance system, but it also includes closer bilateral ties with China's neighbors. Japan has deepened its cooperation with Australia, India, and the Philippines in a myriad of ways—with joint military exercises, closer diplomatic ties, and by relaxing its restrictions on arms sales. Abe has led an effort to normalize Japanese security policy by revising the post–War World II restrictions on what Japan can do in the world. In early 2016 he secured passage of controversial security legislation that allows Japanese armed forces to intervene overseas if strict criteria are met. He is hoping to revise Article 9 of the constitution, which caps Japanese military spending at 1 percent of GDP and forbids the country from having an army. The Japanese public is uneasy about the security reforms, but it is unlikely that they will be reversed if introduced.[52]

Second, Abe wants to promote economic integration within the region, both with China and with other nations in the Asia Pacific. The Trans-Pacific Partnership, a mega trade deal between twelve Pacific countries including the United States but not including China, was at the heart of this vision. Third, Abe seeks to make democracy and the rule of law a central part of his strategy. This approach has helped to consolidate and unify America's allies in the area. As one senior naval official put it, "This is not a dispute over rocks. It is a war over international norms."[53]

European countries should be concerned about the South China Sea because of what it says about Ukraine and Crimea. It also provides an ideological underpinning and positive message for the competition with China. As China cracks down on dissent and opposition, most of China's neighbors are committed to a very different model—liberal democracy. As one senior Japanese official explained, "We tell the Chinese time is on our side, not yours. We will never go communist but some day you will become a democracy."[54]

Abe's strategic shift has not been without difficulties. The greatest has been the revival of Japanese nationalism that has renewed controversies over World War II and thus alienated South Korea while hardening attitudes in China. American friends of Japan have put considerable pressure on Japanese officials to moderate their tone and to reach out to Japan's neighbors, especially South Korea but also China. These efforts have enjoyed some success. In 2015 Abe met with Xi Jinping for the first time, and in early 2016, Japan and South Korea reached an agreement over the "comfort women" issue.

The Regional Web

Some of China's smallest neighbors—Thailand, Cambodia, and Laos—already have demonstrated an inclination to accept Chinese leadership, or accepted it outright, but the rest are determined to resist. By most metrics, these are large countries. Vietnam has 90 million people, the Philippines has over 100 million people, and Japan has more than 150 million people. By contrast, Germany has 70 million, Britain has 58 million, and France has 50 million. China is so large that all other nations seem small by comparison, however, and none are fully capable of standing up to China on their own. Consequently, they are deepening their security cooperation with the United States and are increasingly working with each other to build networks of cooperation that make it more difficult for China to overturn the regional security order. They are moving beyond the old hub-and-spoke model whereby East Asian states worked bilaterally with the United States but not with each other to create instead what researchers from the Center for a New American Security have dubbed an "Asia Power Web."[55]

This web of cooperation cuts across defense, economics, and diplomacy. In the defense realm it means much greater cooperation on intelligence, surveillance, and reconnaissance (ISR), undersea warfare, and amphibious operations, as well as the development of joint capabilities. Countries like Japan, Australia, and India are at the forefront of this effort but it also includes Vietnam, which opened its key naval base, Cam Ranh Bay, to its partners, Singapore and South Korea. On the diplomatic front, Asian nations have developed the so-called ASEAN plus process, which provides numerous forums for cooperation among defense ministers, foreign ministers, and heads of government. Asian countries are also cooperating with each other to promote norms and the rule of law, particularly in the maritime domain, as a way of pressuring China. In addition, we see much closer bilateral ties between Australia and Japan, Australia and India, and India and Japan. The December 2015 agreement between Japan and South Korea raised the prospect that those two countries may be able to put the painful legacy of World War II behind them and work more closely together on shared interests in Northeast Asia. And finally, Asian nations are looking to diversify their economic ties so they will be less dependent on China. The Trans-Pacific Partnership was supposed to be a key component of this broader economic web.

THE COMPETITION FOR EAST ASIA

Some people believe that the very fact that China's strategy has triggered counter-balancing by the United States and the region means that Beijing will fail in its bid to overturn the regional order. As Edward Luttwak succinctly put it, "China's rising power necessarily evokes increasing resistance, so that it may well become weaker at the level of grand strategy because of its own rising military strength—a paradoxical outcome rather common in the realm of strategy."[56] But the situation is not so clear-cut. Balancing has some problems and Beijing has some moves of its own.

The first problem with balancing is that it does not offer a way of deterring China from revisionist actions or of rolling them back once they occur. China has decided it is willing to pay the costs being imposed on it so far, and it is not clear that upping the ante will cause Beijing to have a change of heart. Just as China stops short of using force to establish its sphere of influence, the balancing coalition will never initiate the use of force against China to prevent it from building an island or placing an oil rig in disputed waters. In fact, if one state did take military action against China, the coalition would quickly fall apart.

The second problem is that the regional coalition is not as strong as it appears. Only the United States and Japan are capable of continuing to balance against China regardless of circumstances. Other nations are heavily dependent on China for economic growth and do not want to have to choose between Beijing and Washington. They may have a hardline position regarding their own red lines, but they may run for cover if someone else's red line is threatened. Moreover, smaller Asian nations may balk at being asked to do too much in regional security cooperation, which means that the United States must strike the right balance in what it asks others to do.

The third problem with balancing is that the United States is torn over how much to push back against China over regional differences given that it needs Beijing's help on global issues. Few Americans understand why regional territorial disputes—particularly those in which the United States has no formal position—should be so central to the relationship. When crises occur, as they surely will, China may be able to manipulate public opinion in the United States to cast doubt on Washington's commitment to regional stability.

The fourth problem is that there are real doubts about whether U.S. internationalism will endure. The election of Donald Trump and the failure of TPP have contributed to a sense of uncertainty about America's long-term intentions.

The struggle between China's revisionism and regional counter-balancing is not the only thing going on in East Asia. There are common challenges of economic growth, infrastructural development, climate change, terrorism, disaster relief, development, and, of course, the North Korean nuclear threat. How China and the United States help the region in addressing these problems will also play a crucial role in shaping the competition for the region's future.

Consider a few examples. U.S. opposition to the Asian Infrastructure Investment Bank and the failure to ratify TPP undermined America's claim to have the best economic interests of East Asia at heart. If China is able to take advantage of this hesitancy by the United States and show itself to be a responsible leader of a financial institution, it could increase its relative influence. By contrast, the persistence of the North Korean nuclear threat is a major liability for Beijing. China's long-term goal is to neutralize South Korea and pry it away from the U.S. alliance, but this is impossible as long as Seoul faces an existential threat from the North. In addition, the prospect for a new Taiwan crisis increased with the election in 2016 of Tsai Ing-wen of the pro-independence Democratic Progressive Party. Early signals from Tsai are that she is keen to avoid precipitating a crisis, but if Beijing overplays its hand and tries to undermine her government on principle, its strategy could backfire.

Meanwhile, Russia is beginning to play an active role in East Asia. Putin has sought to deepen relations with China with mixed results. But he has not stopped there. Japan is keen to reopen a diplomatic dialogue with Moscow to settle its territorial dispute over the Kuril Islands and to finally agree to a post–World War II peace treaty. Abe is determined to prevent Russia from moving strategically closer to China because it has no other options and he sees this diplomacy as a means of achieving that. Putin seems receptive, yet he has also been willing to make mischief when it serves his interests—he moved closer to North Korean leader Kim Jong-un in response to South Korea's support for a UN resolution condemning Russia's annexation of Crimea. Japan's outreach to Russia has also been complicated by its desire to maintain a united front with the United States and the West on the annexation of Crimea.

WHAT IF CHINA'S RISE STOPS?

What if China's rise has stopped? Several leading experts on China are warning that it is headed for severe trouble domestically. Minxin Pei, a professor at Claremont McKenna College, argues that the Chinese system is riven with corruption and social tensions and is remarkably fragile as a result.[57] David Shambaugh, a professor at George Washington University, has predicted the collapse of the "badly broken" Chinese Communist Party regime.[58] Others, like Ruchir Sharma of Morgan Stanley, warn of severe economic turmoil in the years to come as China comes to terms with rising debt and major economic mistakes.[59] But this does not mean a less assertive China in East Asia. In fact, the opposite could occur.

The emerging strategic competition with China in East Asia is not purely a function of China's rise. Yes, its rise has given China the confidence and capability to challenge the status quo. But countries in decline or in crisis can be even more dangerous than powers that are rising.[60] A rising power believes that tomorrow will be better than today and it can wait. A rising authoritarian power derives legitimacy from economic growth and does not have to stoke the fires of nationalism. By contrast, a country in crisis or decline, especially after rising for many years, has a very different set of incentives. It can worry that its window of opportunity for geopolitical gains is closing so it is better to act sooner than later. It may need to mobilize the country behind a nationalist message to garner legitimacy for one-party rule. And the instability at home could easily spill over into instability in its behavior overseas. It is for this reason that predictions of a coming crisis or decline in China could make matters much worse than they would otherwise be.

Whichever path China takes, the future of East Asia is no longer settled. It is contested. There are multiple actors but the contest is between two very different visions of regional order: the continuation of the U.S.-led liberal order, or a Chinese spheres-of-influence system. As we have seen, China will seek to deter the United States from pushing back against it by raising the specter of an inadvertent conflict along the lines of 1914. Yet the great-power peace in East Asia is quite durable. Neither China nor the United States has any intention of waging a war against each other, as long as they respect each other's true red lines. For China, these are Taiwan, territorial integrity, and regime stability. On other matters, there may be crises and moments of drama, but this competition will play out in peace-time, so the United States can and should take the time and effort to respond to China's actions in the South China Sea with meas-ures of its own to deny Beijing its strategic objective. This means moving beyond the tit-for-tat imposition of costs on Beijing toward a strategy that will prevent China from controlling the South China Sea: a strategy including arms sales to its neighbors, increased military cooperation between Asian nations, and even competitive island-building if necessary. More broadly, further integration of the U.S.-led order, especially in the economic realm, is crucial.

It is important that competition between the United States and China is limited and controlled given the degree of shared interests between the two nations. Transnational challenges like climate change and nuclear proliferation are especially impor-tant, and the key to maintaining high levels of cooperation on these and other issues is to insist that such cooperation not be linked to geopolitical actions. Likewise, the United States should welcome Chinese initiatives on institution building, even if U.S. diplomats disagree with the specifics. The United States should make it clear that it does not oppose rising Chinese influence on principle, but it does have serious concerns about attempts to build a sphere of influence in East Asia, given the region's stra-tegic importance to global order. If China were looking west-ward, a more accommodating position could be taken. Thus far, however, China has shown that it would like to avoid becoming embroiled in the troubles of the Middle East, the region to which we now turn.

4 GEOPOLITICS AND CONTAGION IN THE MIDDLE EAST

The Middle East is an exception in the U.S.-led liberal order. It has, for many decades, been one of the three most strategically important regions to the United States along with Europe and East Asia. Yet unlike those regional orders that the United States encouraged in Europe and East Asia, there was virtually nothing liberal about the U.S.-led regional order in the Middle East. The United States propped up or assented to authoritarian leaders in Arab states and completely failed to democratize and modernize these allies. Nevertheless, the order did promote peace and stability—Egypt and Jordan made peace with Israel, and the U.S.-led coalition that liberated Kuwait in 1991 was applauded as an unprecedented success.

American leaders have long recognized the risks of authoritarianism and excused the illiberalism as a temporary necessity. They also understood that this illiberal regional order could not last forever. And it did not. As my Brookings colleague Tamara Wittes astutely noted, "The United States was a status quo power defending a regional order that worked to its advantage. That order collapsed and now there is no status quo to defend. Every actor in the region is a revisionist power."[1]

To look at the Middle East today is to see a region unraveling in real time. Iraq, Libya, Syria, and Yemen are wracked by civil war and strife. The formal borders of Iraq and Syria have disintegrated. The Islamic State (ISIS) rose rapidly and poses a global terrorist threat. Millions of refugees have destabilized the European Union. The Kurds are increasingly eager to form their own state. Turkey, once hailed as a potential model of Middle Eastern or Muslim democracy, is trending toward dictatorship. And all the while, the conditions that Arabs protested against in 2010 and 2011 remain in place and are, if anything, more pronounced than before.

A full account of the unraveling of regional order in the Middle East is outside the scope of this book. Such an analysis would have to deal in depth with the weakness of the state in Arab countries, the split within Sunni Islam that led to the rise of ISIS, and Shia-Sunni sectarianism, among other factors. Instead my focus is on the role that the Middle East plays, and is likely to play, in great-power competition and how important it is for the global order. After over a decade of war and revolution, the United States is genuinely torn about its approach. Some are in favor of reducing America's role in the region because there are severe limits on what can be achieved at an acceptable cost. Others wish to increase U.S. engagement to prevent the situation both from getting worse and from destabilizing key U.S. allies and interests, including in Europe. America's strategic rethinking occurs in parallel with, and is a contributing factor to, an intensification of a sectarian-fueled cold war between Iran and Saudi Arabia and fought over the vacuums created by the Arab Awakening. Meanwhile Russia has intervened in Syria and signaled its intention to influence the course of events in the Middle East while China takes a back seat, preferring to concentrate on economic ties. All of this occurs against a backdrop of a continuing ISIS terror threat.

The disorder in the Middle East is likely to continue to command the attention of the United States, European nations, and to some extent Russia, for at least the next decade, and probably more. There is no clean exit to be had. But despite hopeful signs in civil society throughout the region, the Middle East is not some prize to be won in a game between the great powers. It is a crisis to be managed with the goal being to limit its deleterious effects on vital national interests and global order more generally.

AMERICA'S REAPPRAISAL OF THE MIDDLE EAST

Obama can claim some credit for foreseeing the upheaval that would rock the Arab world in late 2010 and early 2011. In a *New Yorker* article, Ryan Lizza published extracts from a five-page memorandum that President Obama sent to his senior national-security and foreign-policy officials in March 2010, nine months before the Arab Awakening. Titled *Political Reform in the Middle East and North Africa,* Obama wrote that "progress toward political reform and openness in the Middle East and North Africa lags behind other regions and has, in some cases, stalled," but there was "evidence of growing citizen discontent with the region's regimes." Obama believed that America's allies would "opt for repression rather than reform to manage domestic dissent" but that this would be counter-productive and "our regional and international credibility will be undermined if we are seen or perceived to be backing repressive regimes and ignoring the rights and aspirations of citizens." He noted that "the advent of political succession in a number of countries offers a potential opening for political reform in the region" and according to Lizza, "he asked his staff to produce 'tailored' 'country by country' strategies for political reform." He worried that if the United States managed coming transitions "poorly," it "could have negative implications for US interests, including for our standing among Arab publics."[2]

The preparation, however, was in vain. When the Arab Awakening finally occurred, the Obama administration tried to limit its involvement and let matters take their own course. As Shadi Hamid of the Brookings Institution describes it,

> From the very start, there was a temptation to discount the importance of foreign powers in the Arab Spring. It became commonplace to hear some variation of the following: that the uprisings were a truly indigenous movement and that Arabs themselves did not want other countries to "interfere" in it— meddling that would, the thinking went, go against the very spirit of the revolutions. President Barack Obama and other US officials repeatedly insisted that this was "not about America." In reality, it was partly about America, not just because of the past US role in backing Arab dictatorships, but because of the critical role it would continue to play in the region.[3]

The Obama administration would intervene diplomatically to persuade Hosni Mubarak to step down and it supported democracy in Egypt, including by recognizing and working with the Muslim Brotherhood government that was elected to power in 2012. Initially, it looked like Obama may have been able to midwife in democracy in Egypt and elsewhere in the region. Within a few short years, however, it had become clear that "the Arab Spring" had failed. The Arab Awakening was, as the journalist and author Robert Worth has put it, "not so much a beginning as an end."[4] It was, he wrote, "the final disintegration of something that had been rotting for decades: the Arab republican states, which finally collapsed of their own weight."[5]

The spread of conflict in the region convinced Americans, including the president, that the Arab world was not on the brink of a new era of democracy and progress.

In President Obama's 2016 interview with the *Atlantic*'s Jeffrey Goldberg, the contrast with his 2010 memo on political reform was dramatic. Goldberg quotes Obama:

> "Right now, I don't think that anybody can be feeling good about the situation in the Middle East," he said. "You have countries that are failing to provide prosperity and opportunity for their people. You've got a violent, extremist ideology, or ideologies, that are turbocharged through social media. You've got countries that have very few civic traditions, so that as autocratic regimes start fraying, the only organizing principles are sectarian. Contrast that with Southeast Asia, which still has huge problems—enormous poverty, corruption—but is filled with striving, ambitious, energetic people who are every single day scratching and clawing to build businesses and get education and find jobs and build infrastructure. The contrast is pretty stark."[6]

The president had determined that U.S. engagement in the Middle East had little chance of success. Obama felt helpless in preventing the region from becoming a mess, but he hoped to keep it from being America's mess: consequently he tried to reduce the U.S. role in the Middle East.

Obama worried that he would be pressed to intervene militarily to deal with the aftermath of the Arab Awakening. He was a skeptic of U.S. military engagement in the Middle East prior to the Arab Spring and aware of the pressures on American presidents to intervene and deepen military engagement in ongoing conflicts. Shortly after taking office, Obama sent more troops to Afghanistan only to have his military commanders immediately request tens of thousands more. Obama and some of his key foreign-policy aides believed that the U.S. national security establishment—including much of the apparatus of government—was pushing the administration to intervene militarily in the Middle East, while the administration felt the United States was overinvested in the region and must limit its role.

Obama also steadily reduced U.S. engagement in Iraq, as Emma Sky described in her memoir *The Unraveling*. Sky, formerly the political adviser to General Ray Odierno, who commanded U.S. forces in Iraq, shows how the Obama administration disengaged diplomatically from Iraq upon taking office. Its most catastrophic decision came after the 2010 Iraqi elections. The Iraqiya Party, led by Ayad Allawi, had emerged as the largest party, while the incumbent Nouri al-Maliki came in close second. Allawi was born a Shiite but had a cross-confessional mindset and stood a good chance of unifying the various factions in Iraq. Maliki was deeply sectarian and the chosen candidate of Iran. U.S. commanders in Iraq wanted the Obama administration to make the diplomatic investment to help Allawi form a government. Instead, the Obama administration wanted to reduce its engagement and was loath to make the investment of time and political capital necessary to help Allawi. Vice President Biden, who once advocated for the partition of Iraq, went to Iraq shortly after the elections and backed Maliki, much to the dismay of Saudi Arabia and other Sunnis who had backed the nominally Shiite Iraqiya over sectarian Sunni alternatives.

Maliki could secure the premiership only by winning the support of the Iranian-backed Sadrists, who during the occupation had been among America's fiercest enemies. Iran's price for this support? No U.S. troops in Iraq and a more sectarian government.[7] Sky concluded that "Biden was a nice man but he simply had the wrong instincts on Iraq. If only Obama had paid attention to Iraq. He more than anyone, would understand the complexities of identity and how people can change. But his only interest in Iraq was ending the war."[8] According to Allawi, he "needed American support," but the United States "wanted to leave, and they handed the country to the Iranians. Iraq is a failed state now, an Iranian colony."[9] In the years that followed, Maliki reneged on understandings with Sunni leaders in northern Iraq, doubled down on sectarianism, pushed U.S. troops out, and used violence against Sunni protestors.[10] All of this created fertile ground for ISIS to reemerge and then expand in Iraq starting in 2013.

The instability that followed the Arab Awakening raised the prospect that Obama would be dragged back into Middle Eastern wars despite his best efforts. He was determined to avoid that fate. He opposed intervention in the Libyan civil war until February 2011, when Qaddafi promised to destroy Benghazi and kill off its inhabitants. Having spoken out forcefully against genocide and mass killing, Obama and his team quickly changed their position and played a limited role in the campaign to lift the siege and topple Qaddafi. One adviser famously described the strategy as "lead from behind."[11]

It was after Libya that the United States sought a conceptual framework to describe and rationalize its decision to strictly limit its engagement in the Middle East. Leading from behind in Libya and avoiding engagement in Syria would be part of a broader regional strategy of retrenchment. In an article in *Foreign Affairs,* Marc Lynch of George Washington University called it "rightsizing." "Rightsizing the United States' footprint in the region," Lynch wrote, "meant not only reducing its material presence but also exercising restraint diplomatically, stepping back and challenging allies to take greater responsibility for their own security. Obama has adhered consistently to this strategy, prioritizing it ruthlessly along the way and firmly resisting efforts to force it off track."[12]

This "rightsizing" entailed a significant reduction in America's role in shaping the future of the Middle East. Dennis Ross, who served as Obama's senior director for the Middle East on the National Security Council, wrote that "Obama believes in the use of force only when our security and homeland might be directly threatened," and that this mindset "frames US interests and the use of force to support them in very narrow terms."[13] Some of Obama's closest aides confirmed this point of view. As Obama's deputy national security adviser Benjamin Rhodes described it to *Politico Magazine*: "The default view in Washington is that if there's a challenge in the Middle East, the US has to solve it. Our basic point has been, no, sorry, we learned the opposite lesson from Iraq. It's not that more US military engagement will stabilize the Middle East. It's that we can't do this." Obama, Rhodes said, was "trying to cabin our engagement so it doesn't lead to an overextension" and so the United States could focus on potential opportunities like climate change and Latin America.[14]

Obama's strategic approach culminated in his policy toward Syria. As the Syrian war escalated, Obama ruled out intervening to topple Bashar al-Assad and arming the rebel forces, only to do so later incrementally and without commitment. He drew a red line over the use of chemical weapons and promised to bomb Assad when it used these weapons, mainly as a way of avoiding intervening to quell lower-level violence. When Assad called his bluff, Obama was left with an awful dilemma—make good on his threat and intervene despite his best instincts, or back down. Obama committed to action but had a change of heart while planes were fueling on the runway. When Putin offered an olive branch a couple of days later, the United States was able to strike a deal that led to the removal of much of Assad's chemical weapons arsenal.

In his address to the UN General Assembly weeks after the Syrian red line crisis, Obama made a distinction between core U.S. interests in the Middle East and broader issues of regional security. He identified four core interests—preventing aggression against U.S. allies and partners, ensuring the free flow of energy, dismantling terrorist networks that threaten Americans, and preventing the proliferation of weapons of mass destruction.[15] "We're not in a Cold War. There is no great game," he said. America had no agenda for Syria beyond what was best for its people. He accepted that America had other interests—such as a peaceful, prosperous, and democratic Middle East—but was convinced that these could not be achieved by America alone. These interests could be advanced only with the cooperation and commitment of the international community. If other nations were serious about addressing these issues in a constructive way, the United States would help, but otherwise, it would strictly limit its role.

The logic of this retrenchment was somewhat paradoxical. Obama and many American observers believed that the turmoil in the Middle East was so bad that it was close to hopeless. The United States could do little to arrest the descent into chaos.[16] Obama would often ask advocates of greater engagement where their strategy would lead ten or eleven steps down the road. Could they guarantee that it would ultimately succeed and that they would not be back asking for ground troops? They could never convince him. For Obama, the region was in the midst of a tumultuous upheaval over which America had little control. In his 2016 State of the Union address, Obama declared, "The Middle East is going through a transformation that will play out for a generation, rooted in conflicts that date back millennia."[17]

Philip Gordon, who served as Obama's top White House aide for Middle East Affairs, wrote shortly after leaving the administration, "We cannot master the historical forces that probably mean the region will be plagued by instability for years or even decades to come. But we can and should manage this instability as best we can and protect our core interests, which include defending our allies, preventing regional war, keeping sea lanes open, avoiding nuclear proliferation and preventing a terrorist safe haven from which the United States or its allies could be attacked."[18] In the battle against terrorism, the United States would rely on drones, air strikes, and intelligence operations rather than ground troops. Despite difficult relations with the Netanyahu government, the Obama administration also substantially increased military assistance to Israel.

Bad as the situation was, it was not bad enough to threaten vital interests. Even safeguarding the free flow of energy, a longstanding vital interest, no longer requires the same level of intense U.S. engagement in the Middle East as it has since World War II: the surge in natural gas supplies due to domestic hydrofracking has considerably reduced America's dependence on Middle East oil. Further dampening the need for U.S. engagement in the Middle East is the apparent weakening of the link between instability and price spikes. The last three years have been among the most turbulent the region has experienced since World War II, but the price of oil reached near record lows and stayed there for a protracted period.

The Iran nuclear deal is an excellent example of the logic, opportunities, and limits of a narrowly focused Obama Middle East policy. With a laser-like focus, the president succeeded in rallying an international coalition to intensify sanctions on Iran and negotiate an agreement that prevented Iran from acquiring a nuclear weapons capability. A consequence of the deal was that it promised to strengthen Iran's conventional capability by reviving its economy and allowing it to normalize its relations with many states. There is little wrong with that—after all, Iran is entitled to economic prosperity just as much as its neighbors— but this had a strategic consequence, coming as it did in 2015 as regional rivalry in the vacuums created by the Arab Awakening reached new heights. The prospect of a newly empowered Iran alarmed Saudi Arabia and its allies and led to an escalation of the Middle Eastern cold war. Obama argued that this cold war would have been worse if Iran had developed nuclear weapons, which was clearly correct, but he did little to address Saudi fears. He told Jeffrey Goldberg that Saudi Arabia and Iran must learn to share the region. He made it clear that the Middle East was unfixable and he would prefer to be someplace else. And he repeatedly claimed that the rivalry was tribal and sectarian and thus imperious to outside influence. Not everyone agreed. General James Mattis, then head of U.S. Central Command, repeatedly raised his concern that the administration did not have a strategy for dealing with the more general challenge that Iran posed, an assertion for which he was pushed out of his position.[19]

From Obama's perspective, it was simply not worth the cost in terms of lives and resources to engage in the Middle East with a view to propping up authoritarian leaders with whom the United States has little in common. The Gulf states read the "abandonment of Mubarak" as a sign that the United States would not care about internally driven and transnational regime change in their countries. If they wished to fight or compete with each other, they would have to do it themselves. But the Arab Awakening had dramatically increased the rivalry between Iran and Sunni Arab states. The United States was limiting its role precisely when geopolitical risks were growing.

A STRUGGLE FOR REGIONAL CONTROL

Relations between Saudi Arabia and Iran were fraught prior to the Arab Awakening, but contrary to popular perception, the rivalry was much more limited than it is now. One indicator of this can be found in 2009 study by the RAND Corporation on Saudi-Iranian relations since the fall of Saddam Hussein.[20] The report, coauthored by six regional experts, concluded that Saudi Arabia's policy toward Iran was complex and multifaceted. It included elements not only of containment and rollback, but also of engagement and accommodation. The Saudis did see themselves as locked in a zero-sum competition with Iran for the future of Iraq, but they did not see the overall relationship through that prism. The authors concluded that the United States could not count on Saudi Arabia being the backbone of an alliance to contain Iran because Riyadh had adopted a more nuanced approach than the United States.

The Arab Awakening removed the complexity and cooperation from the Saudi-Iranian relationship. Arab states were weak and vulnerable to collapse. Ongoing or latent revolutions created a vacuum inside states of great strategic importance. Sectarianism filled this void and Tehran and Riyadh quickly followed to keep the regional balance of power from tipping in the other's favor. The result was a massive intensification of regional rivalry and the outbreak of a new cold war with the two countries competing to control the weak and collapsed states in the region. Both sides are driven by fear that the other will gain the upper hand.

As Professor Gregory Gause of Texas A&M University put it, the objective of this cold war for Saudi Arabia and Iran, and other countries, "is not to defeat their regional rivals militarily on the battlefield. It is to promote the fortunes of their own clients in these weak state domestic struggles and thus build up regional influence."[21] The key to success, he wrote, "is for a regional power to be able to support these non-state clients and allies effectively in their domestic political battles in the weak states of the Arab world."[22] It is an unconventional struggle. It involves proxy wars, covert operations, and coercive diplomacy. And all participants in the region view it as integral to their very survival.

The two primary protagonists in the Middle Eastern cold war are Saudi Arabia and Iran, but they are not alone. As Gause noted, the non-state clients are the true actors shaping the future. And there are other states. Qatar is a prime example. It is a Sunni state like Saudi Arabia, but it was on the opposite side of the Egyptian revolution to Riyadh. Qatar was a strong financial backer of the Muslim Brotherhood within Mohamed Morsi's government in Egypt. It has an intense rivalry with the United Arab Emirates and the two states found themselves at logger-heads in Libya with each backing rival parties and militias, all of which served only to prolong and worsen the conflict. Qatar has also been active in Syria, backing various Islamist forces. As we shall see later, Turkey and Russia also intervened in the Syrian civil war on opposite sides. Nevertheless, the two most important players are Saudi Arabia and Iran.

The Iran–Saudi Arabia rivalry is deeply rooted in religion but it was not caused by it. In an essay titled "The Sunni-Shia Divide: Where Religion Masks Geo-Strategy," Olivier Roy, a French scholar of political Islam, shows how no monarch used the divide as an instrument of foreign policy from the fall of the Safavid dynasty in Persia in 1736 until the Iranian revolution of 1979. After the Iranian revolution, however, the ayatollahs used Shiism as a means of justifying their regional ambitions. This reignited a sectarian divide that had been largely hidden. According to Roy, "The growing antagonism between Shias and Sunnis had nothing to do with a 'millennial' hatred, but with a strategic realignment . . . The geostrategic struggle for hegemony in the Middle East enlarged and even re-created the religious divide between Shias and Sunnis, as did the wave of re-Islamization, because the latter focused precisely on 'who owns Islam?' "[23]

Roy acknowledges though that religion does not need to be the root cause of the conflict for it to have a profound impact on it. He writes, "The religious divide is not the cause of the conflict between a coalition led by Saudi Arabia and the pro-Iran axis; nevertheless, the exacerbation of religious mobilization makes it harder to find domestic political settlements (in Yemen for instance) and to find a diplomatic solution to the crisis."

Gause has warned that the "sectarian framing profoundly misunderstands the nature of the regional crisis." Sectarianism is a part of the crisis but "it is not imposed on the region by Riyadh and Tehran." They "take advantage of sectarianism but they do not cause it."[24] Indeed, Iran and Saudi Arabia have both reached beyond the religious divide when it has served their interests to do so.[25]

For decades, the Saudi grand strategy has been to keep the United States engaged in the region as a hegemonic power and the provider of order. The Saudis perceived a significant American retrenchment in the region during the Obama administration— as evidenced by America's shunning of al-Iraqiya in Iraq in 2010, its support for the ousting of Mubarak, the way it backed down over the chemical weapons red line in Syria, and its pursuit of the Iran nuclear deal—and this has shaken Saudi strategic assumptions to their foundation. In particular, the Saudis worry that Iran will emerge stronger from the nuclear deal and that it will use its resources to wage and win the cold war in the region. Even worse from the Saudi perspective, the Americans seem to have responded to this prospect with nonchalance.

As the rift between Washington and Riyadh grew, Saudi Arabia has adjusted its strategy under new leadership. King Abdullah died in early 2015 and was replaced by King Salman, who shocked the world by changing the line of succession. He made his nephew Mohammed bin Nayef crown prince and his young son, Mohammed bin Salman, deputy crown prince. Mohammed bin Nayef, the most pro-American of the Saudi royals, has led Saudi Arabia's counter-terrorism efforts for two decades. By contrast, Mohammed bin Salman, who is around thirty-one years old (his exact age depends on whom you ask), has emerged as a very influential and hawkish voice, surpassing the crown prince by many accounts. He is an advocate of domestic reform and a hawkish foreign policy. He is also a critic of American retrenchment and once told the *Economist*, "The United States must realize that they are the number one in the world and they have to act like it."[26]

The shift in power in Saudi Arabia has caused its foreign policy to harden significantly. Having lost confidence in the United States, the Saudis decided to take matters into their own hands and balanced against Iran directly. They led a counter-revolution in the region, which included intervening in Bahrain and providing financial assistance to al-Sisi after he took power in Egypt. In March 2015, Saudi Arabia led a coalition and intervened in the civil war in Yemen against the Iranian-backed Houthis.

Saudi Arabia has also escalated tensions through their actions at home. In early 2016, Saudi Arabia executed a Shiite cleric named Sheikh Nimr-al-Nimir. Al-Nimir was no ordinary cleric. He was a vocal opponent of the Saudi regime who had worked to get more rights for Saudi Shia, who comprise 10 to 15 percent of the Saudi population and who reside in the oil-rich eastern part of the country. Iranian hardliners were outraged by his execution. To the embarrassment of the Rouhani administration, which sought to project an image of regional moderation, the Saudi embassy in Tehran was besieged and ultimately overrun by a hardline mob. In response, Saudi Arabia cut off diplomatic ties with Iran and banned commerce and travel between the two countries. Bahrain and Sudan followed suit, while Kuwait and the United Arab Emirates downgraded their diplomatic relations with Iran.[27]

Other Arab powers have different attitudes toward Iran. The United Arab Emirates is as concerned as Saudi Arabia about Iranian power and influence. UAE leaders feel abandoned by the United States and want Washington to restore trust with its Sunni allies by doing much more to contain Iran. Al-Sisi's Egypt, on the other hand, is less concerned about Iranian hegemonic desires and instead sees Islamic extremism, whether in its Sunni or Shiite form, as an existential threat. Egypt would like to see the United States try to ease tensions between Saudi Arabia and Iran, while providing assistance to Cairo without attaching conditions of political reform.

Iran's strategy also became more assertive and expansionist after the Arab Awakening, although its initial reaction to the revolutions was one of ambivalence. The Iranians first had to come to terms with their own recent history. Much like the protests in Moscow in 2012, Iranian leaders saw the 2009 Green Movement as part of a Western "soft war" against Iran. Iran's leading security institution, the Iranian Revolutionary Guard Corps (IRGC), studied the concept of soft war to understand the threat and how to respond. An IRGC report, *Overcoming Sedition*, compared the 2009 revolution to color revolutions in Georgia, Ukraine, and Kyrgyzstan, and placed the blame squarely on the United States.[28] Thereafter Arab regimes began to fall. On the one hand, Iranian leaders were thrilled to see their enemies, like the Saudis and Hosni Mubarak, in retreat and opportunities opening up for increasing Iran's influence throughout the Arab world. On the other hand, the Awakening was too close for comfort—in form and time—to the Green Movement. It also threatened Iran's close ally in Syria.[29]

Nevertheless, the Revolutionary Guard spearheaded an effort to take advantage of the vacuum. In May 2011 Qassem Soleimani, the head of the elite Quds Force of the IRGC, said in a speech that "today, Iran's defeat or victory will not be determined in Mehran and Khorramshahr, but rather our borders have spread. We must witness victories in Egypt, Iraq, Lebanon and Syria."[30] Iran was aggrieved by Saudi counter-revolution efforts and had responded by launching a covert campaign against Saudi Arabia. Most bizarrely, this included a failed plot to enlist a Mexican drug gang to kill the Saudi ambassador to the United States in 2011 by detonating a bomb at Café Milano, a Washington, DC, restaurant popular with diplomats.[31] The very public failure of the Washington plot, and the fact that Iran's involvement was discovered, spooked the Iranian government and led it to narrow its focus to a more regional emphasis on the Middle Eastern cold war.

The epicenter of this cold war is the Syrian civil war, which as of the spring of 2016 has claimed the lives of over 400,000 people.[32] For Iran, Syria was the linchpin of its influence in the Levant. The alliance with Assad went back to the darkest days of Iran's war with Iraq. For Iran, influence in Syria provided leverage over Israel and the United States and gave it the ability to project power through Hezbollah. Mehdi Taeb, a former commander of the Basij, an auxiliary force of the IRGC, put it bluntly when he explained that "Syria is the 35th province and a strategic province for Iran . . . If the enemy attacks and aims to capture both Syria and Khuzestan [the province attacked in the Iran-Iraq War], our priority would be Syria. Because if we hold on to Syria, we would be able to retake Khuzestan; yet if Syria were lost, we would not be able to keep even Tehran."[33]

Iran supplied vast quantities of arms to Assad and sent military advisers who assisted in setting up new militias, similar to the Iranian Basij, which fought in parallel to the regular Syrian army.[34] For Saudi Arabia, Syria is especially important because Iran has been able to capitalize on changes elsewhere in the region, especially in Iraq. Saudi Arabia knows how important Syria is to Iran and therein lies its importance to the Saudis. If Riyadh cannot deal a blow to Iran in Syria, and Tehran emerges victorious, the Saudis believe that the balance of power in the region could be permanently shifted in favor of Iran. It is not that Riyadh covets influence in Syria for its own sake—it is that the Saudis fear that an Iranian victory there would be a tipping point for the entire region.

This highlights a particularly tragic characteristic of the Syrian civil war, which is that it is also a proxy war between outside powers. Civil wars are most bloody and protracted when outside powers are involved.[35] Powerful external sponsors are strong enough to prevent their side from losing but are rarely willing to intervene on a scale that cannot be countered by another. They are usually content to avoid losing, even at a great humanitarian cost. Proxy wars were common during the Cold War but they largely disappeared after the fall of the Soviet Union. Now they are back.[36] In addition to Iran and Saudi Arabia, Russia, the United States, France, and Turkey are all militarily engaged in Syria in what has become a proxy geopolitical contest for the region as a whole.

Proxy warfare comes with the risk of inadvertent escalation. A striking example of this came in November 2015 when a Turkish F-16 shot down a Russian military aircraft that had violated its air defenses for fifteen seconds. As tensions between Russia and Turkey escalated Western powers looked on with concern that a NATO member state would be drawn into a direct conflict with Russia. The deep divisions created by this conflict are underscored by the fact that prior to the Russian intervention in Syrian civil war, Putin and Erdoğan had been relatively close. Turkey was the only NATO member that did not impose sanctions on Russia after the invasion of Crimea, and Erdoğan sought to deepen ties with Russia when the West was trying to isolate it. Putin visited Turkey in November 2014 and had turned to it as an energy partner. But tensions rose over Syria. Turkey vociferously opposed Assad, while Russia just as vociferously backed him. Erdoğan grew increasingly agitated by Russia's intervention and Putin was infuriated by the shooting down of his plane. Putin retaliated by increasing the pressure on Erdoğan from multiple directions. One European expert on Russia, Ivan Krastev, described Putin's policy toward Erdoğan as regime change.[37] Russian state media accused Erdoğan's son of profiting from oil deals with ISIS. Putin invited the leader of Turkey's Kurdish

People's Democratic Party to Moscow. Russia suspended its visa waiver program for Turkish citizens, cut tourism to Turkey, and imposed new restrictions on Turkish business. Erdoğan attempted to deescalate tensions but Putin responded by escalating. It was only in August of 2016, after a failed coup in Turkey that Erdoğan blamed on the United States, that he and Putin mended fences. The spat revealed just how dangerous civil wars in the Middle East can be. Each side in each conflict has outside backers and the risk of escalation is ever-present. It also demonstrated how tactical, flexible, and temporary partnerships and rivalries can be in the new Middle East.

The Syrian civil war is a calamitous conflict that has ravaged Syria and destabilized much of the region as well as Europe. Its unintended consequences have rocked the entire world. One of the most worrisome of these unintended consequences has been the rise of the Islamic State (ISIS). ISIS is a horrific symptom and catalyst of disorder in the Middle East but it is not the underlying cause. ISIS, which first arose during the turmoil of the U.S. invasion of Iraq and Iraq's civil war, found a second breath in the vacuum created by the Arab Awakening. It benefited in several ways from the emerging regional rivalry. First, Bashar al-Assad empowered jihadism in Syria by targeting the mainstream opposition and allowing the rise of Islamist extremism to force the choice to become one between his regime and rule by the latter, rather than between his regime and a moderate alternative. In this, Assad was helped by Iran and later by Russia.

Second, Soleimani and the Quds force made a catastrophic mistake in Iraq. When Soleimani helped Maliki retain power in 2010, he insisted on a more sectarian government and the removal of U.S. forces from Iraq. The result was brutal repression of Sunnis in northern Iraq—including mass killings of Sunnis in

Buhriz, Fallujah, and Ramadi in the spring of 2014—and a vacuum that ISIS could fill. The ISIS takeover of much of northern Iraq in 2013–2014 was initially a calamity for Iran and weakened Soleimani's position for a while.[38]

Third, the United States deserves some of the blame because its diplomatic disengagement from Iraq in 2010, which was driven by the American desire to extract itself from the situation, led Washington to miss an opportunity to encourage a more inclusive Iraqi government and to allow for a continuing U.S. presence that would have gathered intelligence, maintained networks with Sunnis, and been alert to the risk posed by ISIS.

The fourth, and most important, way that the regional rivalry has bolstered ISIS is as a distraction. The decisive defeat of ISIS is not the number-one priority of any state in the region. Assad wants to preserve power and sees the mainstream rebels as the greater danger. Iran sees ISIS as a foe but is more concerned about protecting Assad. Saudi Arabia sees Syria through the prism of its struggle with Iran. Limiting Iran's influence is its top goal. ISIS comes in third among Turkey's perceived threats in Syria, after the Kurds and Assad. Even the Russians, who intervened in Syria in 2015, saw other Syrian rebel groups as a greater threat to its interests than ISIS, as evidenced by the targets of their September air campaign.[39] If ISIS had taken over large swathes of Syria and Iraq in the mid-2000s, it is inconceivable that the region and outside powers would not have cooperated to prioritize its defeat. The uncomfortable reality is that in the present context of advanced fragmentation and rivalry, the major powers have competing priorities.

The United States initially saw ISIS as a local actor. In early 2014, President Obama told David Remnick of the *New Yorker* that we should be careful not to exaggerate the threat posed by

Islamist terrorist organizations in Iraq. "The analogy we use around here sometimes, "Obama said, "and I think is accurate, is if a jayvee team puts on Lakers uniforms that doesn't make them Kobe Bryant."[40] ISIS's rise, and its progression from an organization focused on local fights in Iraq and Syria to one with global ambitions, were game changers. Repeated attacks in Western countries, and even more horrific attacks throughout the greater Middle East, captured the world's attention, deepened tensions between the West and Islam, and sparked a major rethinking of U.S. strategy. President Obama would find himself dragged back in to Iraq with more than four thousand U.S. ground troops, including special operations forces in Syria. Military disengagement was not an option if a terrorist organization with global reach and hostile intent could find a safe haven.

LOOKING AHEAD: LIKELY APPROACHES BY THE GREAT POWERS

The deterioration of the Middle East after the Arab Awakening and the attempted retrenchment of the United States showed that the problems of the region would have major implications for global order. The Middle East is destined to play a role in strategic competition, not as a new great game or prize but as a crisis to be managed. The major powers, and leaders in those countries, will differ on how this should be accomplished.

The United States

Because the United States is deeply divided on how to approach the Middle East, its role is uncertain. As we saw earlier one school of thought, led by President Obama, posits that the Middle East is just not that important to the United States as long as a narrow set of interests—the defense of Israel, counter-terrorism, the supply of oil—are protected.[41] Advocates of this position will argue for military engagement if they feel like they have no other option, but they will do so grudgingly and with strict limits, much as Obama has done to counter the ISIS threat. The irony is that despite his best efforts to retrench, Obama found himself drawn back in to the Middle East to wage war against Islamic State in Iraq and Syria.

The second school of thought is that ignoring the Middle East was a major strategic mistake and it is imperative to reengage in the region, even if it is only to achieve the least-bad outcome attainable. Historically when a region has been allowed to descend into war and anarchy, the effects are very rarely contained. Already the conflict in the Middle East has spread to four countries. It has pulled in outside powers. The refugee crisis is threatening the stability of the European Union, which has long been a vital U.S. interest. And although terrorist organizations like ISIS still find it difficult to carry out attacks in the United States, they are attacking Western targets with greater intensity, especially in Europe. If the situation deteriorates further, it could become a hub for nuclear proliferation. It is true that there are few good options, but the United States must reengage with its allies, as imperfect as they are, to restore a sense of regional equilibrium and stop the unraveling. If the Middle East is in the early stages of a Thirty Years' War, then surely it makes sense to do everything possible to reverse this troublesome trajectory.

The debate between these two positions also must be viewed in the context of a global strategy. If the United States invests heavily in restoring an equilibrium in the Middle East, will that detract from priorities elsewhere? During his second term, Obama very clearly was convinced that it would. But others believed that a deteriorating Middle East would be catastrophic for vital U.S. interests, especially those in Europe but also those in East Asia. The American strategic debate on the Middle East is no longer just, or even mainly, about the Middle East. It is now about the strategic importance of the region for U.S. global interests, including the future of the liberal order.

It is unclear which of these two views the Trump administration will take. Trump has signaled that he views the Middle East as of greater strategic importance than Europe or East Asia, but he also has less desire to uphold regional orders. However, the debate between these two views will continue for many years. Even if the United States retrenches, there will be powerful voices favoring renewed engagement. Thus, the United States is very unlikely to be capable of disengaging from a chaotic Middle East.

Russia and the Middle East

As Vladimir Putin sees it, the United States has willfully ignored Russia's interests and wreaked havoc in the Middle East. It has toppled or weakened the legitimate governments of Iraq, Syria, Libya, Egypt, and others in pursuit of a utopian dream. In the process, it worsened the terrorist threat from the region. In September 2015, Putin gave an address to the UN General Assembly that was scathing in its criticism of U.S. policy in the Middle East. He said: "Aggressive foreign interference has resulted in a brazen destruction of national institutions and the lifestyle itself. Instead of the triumph of democracy and progress, we got violence, poverty and social disaster. Nobody cares a bit about human rights, including the right to life. I cannot help asking those who have caused the situation, do you realize now what you've done?"[42]

Putin increased Russia's engagement in the Middle East for two reasons. The first was to deal Russia in on diplomacy in the region so that its interests would not be ignored. The intervention in Syria meant that the United States had to take Russia's interests into account. Russia believes that Assad is the best bulwark against Islamic extremism in Syria and it wants a pro-Russian regime in Damascus. Putin wants to uphold friendly regimes and raise the cost to the West of deposing regimes not to the West's liking, or even prevent this from happening altogether. He sees economic opportunities for Russia, especially through coordination with energy producers in order to keep the price of oil high and for investment and trade. The second reason is that the Middle East offers Putin an opportunity to reestablish Russia as a great power outside of Europe. According to Dmitri Trenin, "Moscow seeks to present itself to countries in the region as a pragmatic, non-ideological, reliable, savvy, no-nonsense player with a capacity to weigh in on regional matters by both diplomatic and military means. As a major outside power, Russia offers itself as a credible partner to those seeking to diversify their foreign policy."[43]

Iran does not trust Russia, but there is common ground between the two countries on trade, on the Syrian civil war where they are de facto allies, and on rivalry with the United States. But Russia is also aware of the risk of being seen to side with Iran in its struggle with Saudi Arabia and Sunni states—a risk that is heightened as a result of Russia's intervention in the Syrian civil war. Putin has no interest in alienating Saudi Arabia and other Arab states, so he will attempt to maintain some neutrality in regional geopolitics.

China and the Middle East

As the United States relies less on the Middle East for its energy supplies, China has become more reliant on it, with 52 percent of China's oil imports now coming from the Gulf.[44] It is not surprising, then, that China has been increasing its engagement in the region. In January 2016, President Xi was the first foreign leader to visit Tehran after the nuclear deal. He also stopped in Riyadh and Cairo. Around the same time, China released a strategy paper on its approach to the Arab world, which emphasizes energy cooperation, investment, and infrastructural development.[45] It has also dabbled in diplomacy in regional crises. Foreign Minister Wang Yi invited representatives of the Syrian government and opposition to Beijing for meetings.[46] Previously, China had hosted Israeli and Palestinian officials and reportedly tried to ease tensions between Saudi Arabia and Iran. Over the longer term, China's One Belt, One Road initiative is intended to increase economic engagement with the Middle East, among other regions. So does this mean that China is about to become a player in the great game for Middle Eastern energy resources? No, it does not.

Even as China pays more attention to the Middle East, it is also abundantly clear that China is very reluctant to play a substantial role in trying to stabilize the region. High-profile diplomatic meetings are one thing, but taking responsibility for the region, with all of the tradeoffs involved, is quite another. China has tried to stay impartial and friendly with all countries in the region—which would quickly become an impossible task if it really tried to stabilize or shape that part of the world. Chinese policymakers are wary of becoming embroiled in the Middle East and they are reluctant to undermine the role the United States chooses to play.[47] They are aware that they lack expertise on the Middle East and that any big play entails a high likelihood of failure. They will play a constructive role if asked—as in the Iran nuclear talks—but otherwise they prefer to concentrate their geopolitical efforts on East Asia and leave the problems of the

Middle East to others. In any event, Chinese and U.S. interests in the Middle East are well aligned. Both want stable governance, no safe haven for terrorists, and the steady flow of oil. Democracy promotion used to be a point of contention, but the post–Arab Awakening trajectory makes this less of an American objective, at least in the short run.

The greatest risk the Middle East poses to the United States is not that it will fall into Russia or China's orbit. China does not even seek to play a major geopolitical role in the region, and it is content for the United States to take the lead. Russia has and will challenge U.S. interests there, but it is nowhere near capable of replacing the United States in its role. The real risk is that the regional security competition—driven by Iran and Saudi Arabia with interventions by outside powers, including Russia—will deteriorate to the point that it endangers key U.S. interests in the Middle East and in Europe. It may even drag the United States into a general regional war. It is not just a matter of the United States staying out. Leaving Sunni states to fend for themselves may lead them to become more hawkish and risk acceptant vis-à-vis Iran. And as much as the United States may try to stay aloof, there is always a chance, as in Europe in 1917 and 1941, that things will get so bad that it gets dragged in anyway.

Chaos in the Middle East also threatens the global order even if it stops short of a general war. Migration flows from Syria will continue to undermine the European Union, and if other states were to collapse this problem could get much worse. Conflict zones in the Middle East provide a base for terrorist organizations like Islamic State and Al-Qaeda, putting much of the world at risk. Although the Iran nuclear deal provides some respite, the nuclear proliferation risk has not vanished and could easily return, thus undermining the global non-proliferation regime. And the Middle East is still important for oil supplies, even though prices are relatively low at the moment.

Apart from the risks posed by the region, we should also remember that there are signs of hope. There is a constituency for liberalization—in civil society and even in some Arab governments. The Middle East is not destined for conflict because of ancient hatreds or tribalism. These green shoots have been hard to see in recent years, but they are there. A period of stability may provide them with the time and space to grow.

The United States should seek to play an active role in stabilizing the Middle East, not just to protect narrowly defined U.S. interests, but also because the broad goal of a stable Middle East is itself a key U.S. interest. There is no doubt that doing so will be extremely difficult. Getting the geopolitics right will not be sufficient, but it will be a necessary component of a successful strategy. The United States must restore the balance of power in the region by working with Sunni states to balance against Iran and to stabilize the region against Sunni extremism. Once that balance has been restored, and if Iran's behavior improves, Washington could engage Tehran from a position of strength with a view toward cooperation beyond the nuclear file, including on Syria.

5 INTERDEPENDENT COMPETITION

The return and intensification of geopolitical competition is happening in an era of unprecedented interdependence. For almost a quarter century, the major powers have made economic, financial, and technological integration an end in itself. Now they are waking up to the fact that interdependence means they may have leverage over, and be vulnerable to, their geopolitical rivals. Some of these consequences are inherent to integration: authoritarian states like China and Russia, for example, are being exposed to information flows through the Internet that may prove inconvenient or even threaten the stability of their regimes. Part of this shift is also due to the broader array of active measures that globalization has made possible. Interdependence provides means of coercion—such as sanctions and cyberwarfare—that are far more attractive than the use of military force because they entail a lower risk of escalation, cause fewer casualties, and are less controversial. Such new threats will encourage rivals to carve out spheres of independence for themselves to hedge against the downside risks of being reliant on others. Countries will try to wall themselves off from their rivals, even if only in a limited way. Globalization will continue, but not as we've known it.

Using interdependence for strategic advantage is not new. The past century is replete with examples of great powers using any advantage they might have in the international economy as a weapon in war or in a struggle for supremacy. Britain sought to use German reliance on its financial system as a weapon against it in World War I, only to be persuaded otherwise by the United States.[1] After World War I, France and Britain sought to suppress German power through punishing reparations, only to see their strategy backfire when the Nazis came to power. The Nazis used Germany's economic weight to bully and co-opt its neighbors in Central Europe in the 1930s. In 1940–1941, the United States sought to choke the Japanese economy to punish it for its aggression in Asia, only for the Japanese leadership to decide that it should attack Pearl Harbor. In 1956, President Eisenhower threatened a selloff of the British pound to force Great Britain to remove its forces from Egypt during the Suez Crisis. During the Cold War, the United States created the Coordinating Committee for Multilateral Export Controls (CoCom), which was designed to organize the Western world in withholding crucial technologies from the Soviet Union. Since the Cold War, the United States has employed sanctions against many states and private actors, including Russia, Iraq, Iran, North Korea, Cuba, and Serbia, as well as al-Qaeda and other terrorist networks.

The historical record is very clear: it is impossible to separate the economic from the geopolitical. Dependency on rivals will be ruthlessly exploited in a time of crisis. But doesn't international relations teach us that interdependence should decrease tensions between states? Why would it become a tool of warfare?[2]

The key to understanding the strategic effects of interdependence on a bilateral relationship is to see that it is not a monolithic force. Some types of interdependence will encourage cooperation and decrease tensions. Others will have the opposite effect, increasing tensions and friction. How can we tell the difference between the two? The positive type of interdependence is one where the benefits are shared and it is difficult for either side to turn it into leverage that can be used to inflict disproportionate damage on the other. The negative type of interdependence is one where one side gains disproportionate leverage over the other and has the ability to use this leverage as an economic weapon at a time of crisis. In addition, if one side has an asymmetric vulnerability that the other side tries to exploit, it might retaliate in another area where it holds an asymmetric superiority. This increases the risk of miscalculation and of a crisis that can spiral out of control.

The economist Albert O. Hirschman described this dynamic in 1945 in a seminal book called *National Power and the Structure of Foreign Trade*.[3] Hirschman was born in Germany to Jewish parents who subsequently converted to Presbyterianism. As a young man, he became active in the struggle against the Nazis and fascism, fighting with the Republicans in the Spanish civil war. During World War II, he was active in anti-fascist efforts in France and in 1941 he fled to the United States.[4] As a scholar at UC Berkeley, Hirschman sought to explain how Nazi Germany was able to use international trade as part of its strategy of aggressive revisionism in Europe. It was an unprecedented study that cut across academic fields (and, as a consequence, was overlooked for decades). Hirschman showed how in the years before World War II aggressive countries, like Nazi Germany and Fascist Italy, traded internationally with a "bully commercial strategy" rather than abiding by a fair, rules-based system.

Hirschman found that countries are vulnerable if they are too dependent on a single country that is not equally dependent on them. Hirschman focused on trading relations between a large country and a small country under certain conditions, but his insight can be applied to other types of interdependence between countries of approximately equal size. If China is heavily dependent on the United States for energy or the United States is heavily dependent on China for finance, each will be especially vulnerable to unilateral actions by the other.

During the Cold War, the United States and the Soviet Union had very little to do with each other economically. Trade was miniscule; there was no investment between the two; each had its own economic bloc. After the Cold War, countries across the globe integrated with each other to unprecedented degrees. World trade grew from 38 percent of world GDP in 1991 to 59 percent in 2013, a sixfold increase in absolute dollars.[5] Global Foreign Direct Investment (FDI) stocks were worth $23 trillion in 2012 compared with $1.7 trillion in 1992, a fourteenfold increase.[6] Financial systems have also become tightly integrated. Little or no thought was given to the risks of interdependence because great-power rivalry was presumed to be a thing of the past. Now, as geopolitical rivalry returns, the world remains interdependent. Thus we are entering a world characterized by "interdependent competition." Countries are competing with each other but they are also closely linked; consequently, they are gradually exploring how to use these linkages to their own advantage. As Mark Leonard of the European Council on Foreign Relations put it, the major powers of the early twenty-first century are engaged in "connectivity wars."[7] Russia brandishes energy as a weapon. China uses its enormous size as an export market to influence its neighbors. But thus far, one country has stood out from all others in its use of interdependencies for its own advantage—the United States.

THE ROLE OF AMERICAN FINANCIAL POWER

In terms of GDP and financially, the world may be becoming more economically multipolar.[8] But the United States has a major advantage when it comes to controlling the commanding heights of the global economy and the capability to convert that influence into geopolitical power.

America's greatest asset may be the role of the dollar as the world's reserve currency. Possessing the world's reserve currency bestows "an exorbitant privilege" that allows a great power to operate under far looser fiscal and monetary constraints than all other countries.[9] It is widely believed that the United States can run huge deficits to finance high levels of defense spending because its debt is denominated in its own currency. The owner of the reserve currency is also able to make momentous decisions that affect all countries on the basis of its own narrow interests.[10] The United States and its key allies, particularly the United Kingdom, provide the financial centers of gravity for the global economy. There is not a global bank or financial institution that can survive and prosper if it defies U.S. or European law. As a report by the Eurasia Group put it, "Access to the US marketplace and US banks, and Washington's ability and willingness to use them, are becoming more important as instruments of foreign and security policy."[11] The dependency of other countries and financial institutions on the United States means that Washington can use targeted sanctions to cut off others from capital markets and the financial system. The Eurasia Group called this the weaponization of finance.

The United States has worked closely with the European Union to consolidate its control over the international financial system and to convert that influence into geopolitical power. Over the past two decades, it has refined and deployed economic weapons against Iran, North Korea, terrorist networks, and now Russia. The United States has, in other words, become very adept at the use of financial warfare, which former senior U.S. Treasury official Juan Zarate describes as "the use of financial tools, pressure, and market forces to leverage the banking sector, private sector interests, and foreign partners in order to isolate rogue actors from the international financial and commercial systems and eliminate their funding sources."[12] These states and rogue groups have recognized this power as strategically valuable. Jack Lew, Treasury secretary in the Obama administration, said that economic sanctions are "a new battlefield for the United States, one that enables us to go after those who would wish us harm without putting our troops in harm's way."[13]

Thus far, the U.S. and European use of financial weapons has been carefully calibrated. In the conclusion to his book endorsing their use, Zarate argued that it was very important not to expand the use of sanctions to include diplomatic goals instead of focusing on rogue state conduct. He writes, "Illegal or suspect conduct must remain the primary driver for attention and isolation. Though financial suasion may appear to be a tantalizing and powerful tool to achieve political or diplomatic motives, its efficacy will be drastically diminished if diplomatic goals take precedence over conduct based drivers."[14]

As Walter Russell Mead put it, "the more powerful the sanctions weapon becomes, and the more we try to use it, the greater the incentive we create for other people to challenge it."[15] U.S. policymakers are cognizant of the risk and have been extremely cautious about using the core infrastructure of the international financial order—such as the SWIFT payments system for the world's banks—for strategic ends. But they have not hesitated to use modest financial sanctions to retaliate against U.S. rivals.

THE CASE OF CRIMEA

As we saw in Chapter 2, Russia's annexation of Crimea—the first unilateral territorial expansion in Europe since 1945—and its subsequent support for separatists in eastern Ukraine were widely viewed in the United States and European Union as revisionist acts and significant challenges to the post–World War II international order. But it was also clear from the outset that the United States (to Europe's relief) chose to take a military response off the table. NATO would not undertake any action, including lethal assistance to the Ukrainian military or boots on the ground, that could lead to armed conflict between the West and Russia. But there had to be a response. And sanctions appeared to fit the bill.

Sanctions on Russia

Sanctions were a very appealing option. They were already at the top of policymakers' minds because the United States had threatened sanctions and imposed visa bans on the Yanukovych government for the crackdown on the Euromaidan protests. Russia was the world's eighth largest economy in 2013, just before the annexation of Crimea, but it is heavily reliant on energy exports and is not a major player in international finance.[16] Overall, Russia is much more dependent on Western markets than vice versa. Thus sanctions offered the prospect of imposing costs on Russia while limiting the costs incurred by the United States and Europe. The United States was able to implement the first of several rounds of sanctions unilaterally and press Europe to do more, which it did in a progressive way as Russian aggression continued.[17] A tipping point was reached with the downing of Malaysia Airlines flight MH17 by Russian-backed forces on July 17, 2014, killing 298 people: after this attack, the European Union introduced a new round of sanctions targeting the Russian financial system and Russian companies.

The U.S. and EU sanctions included asset freezes and travel bans against individuals close to Putin as well as sanctions against sectors in the defense and energy industries believed to be engaged in aggression against Ukraine. Several Russian banks—including Gazprombank, Vnesheconombank, and Rosselkhozbank—were prevented from raising debt or equity with a maturity longer than ninety days.[18] U.S. energy companies were restricted from cooperating with their Russian counterparts. Licensing systems were used to prevent trade in dual-use technologies as well as in energy exploration equipment.[19] EU sanctions were more consequential and controversial domestically than U.S. sanctions, since the European Union is Russia's largest trading partner and Russia is the European Union's third largest after the United States and China.[20] The United States engages in far less trade with Russia.[21]

At a meeting in late July 2014 to toughen sanctions, the European Union warned Moscow in an official statement that "destabilizing Ukraine, or any other eastern European neighboring state, will bring heavy costs to its economy."[22] The same day, President Obama declared: "The sanctions that we've already imposed have made a weak Russian economy even weaker. Foreign investors already are increasingly staying away. Even before our actions today, nearly $100 billion in capital was expected to flee Russia. Russia's energy, financial, and defense sectors are feeling the pain. Projections for Russian economic growth are down to near zero." The new sanctions will "ratchet up the pressure on Russia, including the cronies and companies that are supporting Russia's illegal actions in Ukraine."[23]

Although the sanctions were limited in scope, their effect was compounded by the fall in the price of oil. Together, these events had a devastating effect on the ruble, which collapsed in value, falling from 34 rubles to the dollar on July 1, 2014, to 69 to one on January 30, 2015.[24] Russian GDP contracted by 4.6 percent from July of 2014 to July of 2015—its greatest drop since 2009.[25] Capital flight for the first half of 2014 was estimated at $75 billion.[26] Russian companies were advised not to list on the London Stock Exchange.[27] Inflation rose to 11.4 percent in 2014 and was at a 15.8 percent annual rate by August 2015.[28] Living standards plummeted for the first time since the 1990s—international air travel fell by 20 percent, car sales fell by 36 percent, and shops stopped stocking many Western food products.[29]

As bad as this was, Russians experienced much worse in the not too distant past. They adjusted, as they have done many times before. The United States and the European Union stopped short of imposing sanctions that would truly hurt the Russian economy; instead they held such sanctions in reserve as a means of deterring further aggression.

The Russian Response

Putin has long been suspicious of Russian integration into the global economy. He believed that Russia was too reliant on international sources of finance in the 1990s, which in his view made it a captive of the West and the politically motivated conditionality imposed by the IMF and the World Bank. He also saw a Russia ravaged by resource crises, including a food shortage in St. Petersburg while he was a city official there. He concluded that Russia would only succeed and maintain its sovereignty if it was more self-reliant. In their biography of Putin, Fiona Hill and Clifford Gaddy show how the idea of strategic reserve is central to his philosophy of governing. In the 1990s Putin learned, Hill and Gaddy wrote, that "Russia's ultimate guarantee of survival—and of the country's wealth and development—is its natural resources. They should therefore be kept in strategic reserve." This was also an important theme of Putin's dissertation for a graduate degree in economics, which he received in the mid-1990s. In this dissertation, according to Hill and Gaddy, he argued that "Russia must not allow itself to be dependent on any foreign country or countries for the infrastructure crucial to ensuring the export and import of key commodities and goods."[30]

Putin implemented this philosophy as president. When he became president for the first time in 2000, Russia's foreign-currency reserves were only $8.5 billion while its external debt was $133 billion. Eight years later, Russia's debt was down to $37 billion while its foreign currency reserves had skyrocketed to $600 billion. A fourteenfold increase in the price of oil, from $10 per barrel in 1998 to $140 per barrel in 2008, helped Putin, but he also displayed skill and resolve in ensuring that the bene-fits went to the state and not just the oil companies. At the height of the financial crisis in October 2008, Putin told a group of foreign investors that while they were unprepared for the turbu-lence, "we did not allow ourselves to be caught by surprise. When we formulated our long-term economic and financial policy, we took into account potential risks and threats . . . We were sometimes even criticized for being too conservative. Well, I think that conservatism proved justified."[31]

After the annexation of Crimea, Putin turned once again to self-reliance—but this time using China as an interim bridge. Reports surfaced in the Russian media, originating from the

Russian government, that Russian aerospace and military-industrial companies were planning to purchase electronic components worth several billion dollars from China until they could adjust their manufacturing industry to produce these parts at home. Andrei Ionin, chief analyst at GLONASS Union, an association of Russian firms working on navigation systems to rival GPS, said that "establishing large-scale cooperation with Chinese manufacturers could become the first step toward forming a technology alliance involving BRICS member states."[32] In July 2014, Putin warned that the "very notion of state sovereignty is being washed out. Undesirable regimes, countries that conduct an independent policy or that simply stand in the way of somebody's interests get destabilized." He promised "additional steps to decrease the dependence of the national economy and financial system on negative external factors," including "political risks."[33] Putin has tried to follow through on this promise. His goal is to provide a safety net for Russia, and potentially other countries disenchanted with Western economic dominance, as a way of reducing the West's ability to expel its rivals from the global economy and as part of a comprehensive response to Western sanctions.

Pure self-reliance in an age of globalization will come at a cost, which Russia is already experiencing. But Russia was willing to pay this cost and has succeeded in its objective of thwarting the West's strategy to bring Ukraine into the orbit of the European Union. Few nations will voluntarily follow in Russia's footsteps, but the experience of all the players in the Ukraine drama has taught other nations and companies that involvement in the global economy can be turned against them in a time of crisis. Governments may not be able to be wholly self-reliant, but they can take steps to reduce their exposure, particularly in areas of strategic importance such as finance, information networks, and military power. In other words, Putin's diagnosis of the problem—integration means that you are strategically exposed—will resonate even if the radicalism of his response, full self-reliance regardless of the cost, is rejected.

WHY CHINA IS ALSO WORRIED

The failure of the U.S. model of globalization and the return of economic warfare in Europe will have far-reaching implications for the U.S.-China relationship. Prior to 2008, China bought into the idea that interdependence would be a stabilizing force in world politics, even though there were large imbalances and reasons for concern. In many ways, this belief has continued. But the crisis also proved to many Chinese that the U.S. economy and the U.S. financial model were a force for instability rather than sustainable prosperity. As Cornell University professor Jonathan Kirshner has argued, the crisis created the space for a "new heterogeneity of thinking about money and finance," whereas before there was only one approach to which all serious people and economies adhered. "The loss of faith in the American model," Kirshner wrote, "has transformed China's international economic strategy" because it began to seek ways to hedge against the volatility inherent in the U.S. system.[34]

The perceived failure of the U.S. model of globalization is not the only element of the interdependent order that worries China. The Chinese Communist Party is concerned that the open flow of information may undermine its regime. What makes this concern particularly dangerous is that the flow of information is intrinsic to interdependence and not the result of a deliberate decision made in Washington. For instance, in 2012 the *New York Times* conducted a major investigation of public records in China and exposed the seemingly illicit wealth held by the families of

Chinese government officials.[35] Beijing put severe pressure on the *New York Times* and other media outlets, to the point that *Bloomberg* promised to curb stories critical of the regime so as to continue operating in China.[36] Beijing has also spared little effort to limit the freedom of the Internet. In addition, the Chinese government, concerned that travel abroad by Chinese scholars and experts could result in the spread of Western ideas, has cracked down on nongovernmental organizations and imposed restrictions on scholarly travel.

While the inherent nature of an open and interdependent order is a concern, Western sanctions on Russia have also raised the possibility that such measures could be used against China in retaliation for aggression abroad or for human rights abuses at home. This may seem far-fetched but it is hardly less likely than the prospect of a full-scale war between the United States and China, which is, after all, a contingency both countries plan for. There is also recent history. The United States imposed sanctions on China after the Tiananmen Square massacre in 1989. If the United States could hit Russia with sanctions after its annexation of Crimea, it seems at least conceivable that smart sanctions would be on the table if the Chinese government put down a revolution or felt compelled to make a move against Taiwan. U.S. officials have done little to assuage these fears. During the Ukraine crisis, U.S. Assistant Secretary of State for East Asia Daniel Russel explicitly drew a link between the U.S. response to Russia's annexation of Crimea and how the United States would react to aggression by China. Russel said the retaliatory sanctions on Russia should have a "chilling effect on anyone in China who might contemplate the Crimea annexation as a model," especially given the extent of China's economic interdependence with the United States and its Asian neighbors.[37]

These two concerns—a loss of faith in the U.S. model and fear of sanctions—are mutually reinforcing and they point in one direction. China wants more influence in the global order, particularly in the economic, financial, and information realms, to ensure that the global order can never be turned against it. It is not that China wants to replace the U.S.-led economic order for all countries; it just does not want to be fully dependent on it. China is in a position quite different from that of Russia. It is the world's second largest economy. It is not heavily dependent on energy as a source of income. In fact, it is an energy consumer, not an energy provider. China's economy is much more diversified than Russia's. China occupies a crucial position in global supply and manufacturing chains. It is the dominant trading partner for much of East Asia, especially Southeast Asia. It is inextricably bound up with the U.S. economy, especially with the U.S. financial system. It is the European Union's second largest trading partner and has massively increased its investment in Europe since the financial crisis.[38]

China is also in a stronger position in terms of developing its own tools of interdependent warfare. Russia had few economic means of retaliating in kind against the West. Western economic warfare had a limited economic cost for Europe and the United States, and it was one they were willing and able to pay as the price of ratcheting up pressure on Moscow. China, conversely, has means and the cost would be immense. To put it bluntly, over the next decade, and if it puts its mind to it, China poses as much of a potential economic threat to the United States as the United States does to China. One could be forgiven for thinking that the relative equality of the United States and China means that economic warfare will be taken off the table. It will not be. Both countries are preparing military options to use against each other in the event of a major crisis, such as over Taiwan or Japan. Given that war would be more costly than sanctions, it follows that as long as traditional conflict is thinkable, so too is economic coercion. In fact, in the event of a major crisis, policymakers are likely to turn first to the economic tools because they are perceived as less likely to escalate than military force. The incredibly dense linkages between the American and Chinese economies will be subjected to deep study by military planners as they seek to identify vulnerabilities to exploit and defend against.

BLUNTING THE AMERICAN ADVANTAGE

So globalization is here to stay, but China, with Russia's support, has a strategic incentive to reduce the risks of interdependence with the West. Moscow and Beijing are going about this task in a number of ways.

Changing the Incentive Structure inside the West

Interdependence is by its very nature mutually beneficial to the two countries involved. If Russia trades with Germany, both economies will benefit, although perhaps to varying degrees. If it were not mutually beneficial, trade would quickly come to an end. Mutual benefit means that both sides will pay a price if sanctions are introduced. Analysts tend to look at the way in which the threat of sanctions can increase pressure on a country like Russia to cease acts of aggression, but the flip side of the coin is that interdependence constrains the West's response to such acts. Thus it came as no surprise that the European Union, which has substantial economic ties to Russia, was much more skeptical of economic sanctions than was the United States. As Stuart Gottlieb and Eric Lorber wrote: "Greater interdependence might, in fact, reduce the likelihood of conflict between nations or groups of nations. After all, it increases the cost of conflict for all of them. However, as the EU-Russian case shows, the logic can also work in reverse. It is incredibly difficult to punish economic partners for international aggression. The rational fear of economic backlash creates high tolerance for international wrongdoing."[39]

Some Western companies are paying a significant price. ExxonMobil found oil in the Russian Arctic but could not develop the field because its partner was Rosneft, the major energy company subject to sanctions.[40] Shares in Adidas dropped by 15 percent after it was forced to close stores in Russia. Joe Kaeser, chief executive of Siemens, warned that broader geopolitical tensions posed "serious risks" for Europe's economy. The Erste Group, Eastern Europe's third largest lender, warned that the economic fallout in the region could include banking failures. The U.S. credit card companies Visa and MasterCard have also been affected, not just in Russia but also more widely, due to market concerns about hedging against the future risk of sanctions elsewhere. Royal Bank of Scotland, Citigroup, and Bank of America all reduced their investments in Russia prior to the toughening of EU sanctions in July 2014.[41] And then there is France, which canceled its sale of a second Mistral naval vessel to Russia.

This economic dynamic quickly melds into the political world. The writer Anne Applebaum has noted: "As they began to do business in Europe in the 1990s, the Russians learned very quickly about the importance of politically connected companies. As a result, they have begun to acquire shares in more of them."[42] This includes Rosneft's purchase of 13 percent of Pirelli, the Italian tire giant, and Rosatom's expansion of Hungary's only

nuclear power plant. Several of Europe's most politically important companies have deep ties to Russia, including E.ON Ruhrgas
(a German gas company), Eni (the Italian state gas company),
and Royal Dutch Shell. Or take Nord Stream, a Baltic Sea pipe-
line controlled by Russian giant Gazprom, which has former
German chancellor Gerhard Schroeder as its chairman. When
Schroeder celebrated his seventieth birthday in 2014, at the
height of the Crimea crisis, Putin was one of the attendees at a
bash put on by Gazprom. In Germany, analysts speak of the
Russia *verstehers* (understanders) who sympathize with the
Kremlin's position, often because they are economically engaged
with it.

These costs have not prevented Europe from adopting sanctions on Russia, but they do demonstrate the difficult headwinds
that any such strategy faces. Interdependence does not just
constrain aggressor states; it also constrains the response to their
aggression. It suggests as well that new fault lines have been
created within democracies, weaknesses that they will have to
work around as they cope with the rise of revisionist states.

Diversifying the Economic Infrastructure

China is seeking to build a parallel infrastructure in the global
economy to reduce its dependence on Western-dominated institutions. The goal is not to replace the existing order but diversifi-
cation. Toward that end, China has created a series of regional
economic institutions designed to inaugurate a Sino-centric
Asian economic order. The Asian Infrastructure Investment Bank
came into being in 2015 over the objections of the United
States and Japan but with the support and membership of many
U.S. allies, including the United Kingdom, France, Germany,
South Korea, and Australia. China also rolled out the New Silk

Road, which seeks to link East and Central Asia through two initiatives.[43] The Silk Road Economic Belt promotes overland investment in Central Asia by means of a network of railways, energy pipelines, investment, and the greater use of the renminbi.[44] The Maritime Silk Road seeks to expand maritime trade through investment in ports in the Indian Ocean and the Persian Gulf.

China is also undertaking other initiatives, often with the other BRICS. In 2015, the BRICS launched the New Development Bank (NDB), also known as the BRICS Bank. Based in Shanghai, with five members that have an equal voting share and $100 billion in capital, the NDB will compete in the same space as the World Bank.[45] China and Russia are also exploring a way of depriving the United States of its "nuclear economic weapon." Andrey Kostin, chief executive of VTB, Russia's second largest bank, told the 2015 Davos meeting: "We have already created a domestic alternative to the SWIFT system . . . and we need to create alternatives internationally."[46] Russia has been pressing the rest of the BRICS to help it create an international alternative but thus far the talks have been only informal.[47]

China is also looking to reduce its reliance on the dollar and to increase use of the renminbi. Di Dongsheng, an associate professor at the Renmin University of China, has written about a debate in Beijing about the internationalization of the renminbi. One constituency worries that internationalization will increase volatility in the Chinese economy, while another believes that it will help advance economic and social reforms. There is also a third group. As Di describes it, "Foreign policy experts with close ties to the People's Liberation Army also hope to accelerate the pace of renminbi internationalization" because they "tend to believe in the great currency–great power nexus, which would require more assertive diplomacy and power-projection capabilities."[48]

Di argues that the debate has shifted decisively toward those favoring internationalization. Internationalization is part of a more general rebalancing of China's economy under which it will import more, thus giving it potential leverage over some of its trading partners. Internationalization will also increase Beijing's incentive to abandon its principle of noninterference in the sovereign affairs of other countries because it will seek to protect its interests overseas.

The dollar will remain the world's premier reserve currency. But a successful Chinese effort to increase the role of the renminbi in East Asia will have two major strategic consequences. The first is that China, and perhaps others, will be able to protect itself from a U.S. strategy of using the dollar for strategic purposes. If the world has two currencies in widespread use, the impact of any Western sanctions will be lessened. The second is that China will be able to use the renminbi for its own strategic ends in its own neighborhood if the renminbi becomes the dominant currency in East Asia. That is, the renminbi does not need to replace the dollar worldwide to have a strategic impact.

CHINA AND RUSSIA LOOK TO THE OFFENSIVE

China and Russia are developing their own tools of economic statecraft and warfare. They would like to have the means of deterring U.S. financial and economic power—either to dissuade Washington from using sanctions or to retaliate if it does.

In 2008, at the height of the financial crisis and less than two months after Russia's invasion of Georgia, which put relations between Moscow and Washington into deep freeze, Russian officials approached the Chinese government and proposed a coordinated dumping of Fannie Mae and Freddie Mac bonds in an effort to force another massive bailout and badly damage the U.S. economy. Chinese officials declined the offer and promptly informed U.S. Treasury Secretary Hank Paulson, who subsequently told the tale in his memoir. Russia's attempt to destabilize the U.S. economy shows the risks of requiring the cooperation of a state that may have a geopolitical interest in your failure even if they would also suffer from the economic shock.[49] Thankfully, Russia's economic weight was very limited in 2008, but imagine how difficult and complicated it would be to tackle a new Asian financial crisis if China and Japan were at each other's throats in the East China Sea.

At the end of June 2015, foreign investors held $6.175 trillion in U.S. debt.[50] Of that, China holds approximately 20.5 percent, the largest of any foreign holder. (Japan is the second largest, with approximately 19.3 percent.)[51] While U.S. officials maintain that China's holdings exercise no influence over U.S. policy, some Chinese officials and analysts have hinted that they would consider such a strategy if China's sovereignty was threatened.[52] Most analysts believe that China cannot use its holdings of debt as a weapon because China's economic interests would be badly damaged if it began to dump U.S. debt.[53] This is true most, but not all, of the time.

If the United States and China were on the brink of conflict over Taiwan or disputed islands in the East or South China Sea, China may calculate that unloading U.S. debt would hurt the U.S. economy more than the Chinese economy, either in absolute terms or in the relative pain that each country could endure during the crisis (if the Chinese felt more strongly about Taiwan than did the American people, for example, this balance would be in their favor). Even if China did not execute this strategy, giving the impression that it would be willing to do so could be effective, especially if Chinese policymakers were simply trying to deter the United States from taking an action (such as entering a conflict on the side of an ally) rather than compelling it to do something.

The risks of China's vast holdings of U.S. debt should not be exaggerated, but neither should they be dismissed. China is refining its ability to use sanctions and the tools of economic coercion against countries that are smaller, and thus easier to intimidate, than the United States. China has imposed sanctions on bananas and tourism in a dispute with the Philippines over the Scarborough Shoal, on rare-earth metals in a dispute with Japan over the arrest of a Chinese fisherman in 2010, and on salmon exports from Norway after the awarding of the Nobel Peace Prize to Chinese dissident Liu Xiaobo. It has also encouraged informal boycotts of Japan in response to Japan's purchase of the Diaoyu/Senkaku Islands in September 2012.[54] This is part of a strategy to use China's economic importance, especially in the region, to raise the costs of opposing Beijing.

LEVELING THE PLAYING FIELD WITH CYBERWARFARE

Interdependence reaches well beyond economics and finance, of course, and the playing field begins to level out for China and Russia in these other arenas, especially technology and cyber security. Yes, the United States enjoys considerable structural advantages in cyberwarfare. The National Security Agency is immensely capable. The world's largest technology companies are American. And the United States has been at the cutting edge of developing offensive cyber weapons. Most notably, in 2012, word leaked of a U.S. covert operation called "Olympic Games" that was designed to sabotage the Iranian nuclear program by planting a virus known as Stuxnet, one of the most advanced and sophisticated viruses ever developed.

Yet the United States is also incredibly vulnerable given the technological nature of the U.S. economy and the country's reliance on information networks in all fields, including in the military. This vulnerability is one that China and Russia have been all too willing to exploit to gain a strategic edge over the United States in the emerging geopolitical competition. China has been repeatedly identified by U.S. agencies and the U.S. Congress as the number one cyber threat to the United States.[55] China's cyberwarfare operations are the responsibility of the PLA's General Staff Department's Third Department, which has over 130,000 people attached to it.[56] The Chinese military believes that the U.S. military's reliance on information networks offers China an opportunity to occupy "the new strategic high ground."[57]

By their very nature, cyberwar operations are shrouded in secrecy. It is widely believed that China has engaged in massive state-sponsored espionage of Western corporations to steal vast quantities of highly valuable intellectual property. The U.S. government has complained repeatedly about this, pointing out that it crosses the boundary of what is commonly regarded as acceptable espionage. But perhaps even more notable is what China has being doing that is regarded as legitimate by the United States. In 2015, it was revealed that China is building a vast database of Americans, particularly those in sensitive government positions, by hacking government departments, health-care companies, and other organizations. Perhaps the most high-profile hack was of the U.S. Office of Personnel Management (OPM), which compromised the records of over 21 million people. OPM holds personnel files on millions of American government workers, including in the Pentagon, State Department, and White House. The files include the security clearance form filled out by all government employees, which contains details on every foreign national the employee knows, old addresses, financial information, and personal weaknesses. The files for background investigations into each employee, which could involve romantic entanglements and other potentially embarrassing and compromising information, were also reportedly compromised.

As Director of National Intelligence James Clapper put it, the OPM breach was "a gold mine for a foreign intelligence service."[58] One U.S. government official told the *Washington Post*, "This is part of their strategic goal—to increase their intelligence collection via big-data theft and big-data aggregation. It's part of a strategic plan."[59] This is not an illegitimate or shocking action. It is what countries do in a strategic competition. Current and former senior U.S. intelligence officers said as much. Clapper said, "You have to kind of salute the Chinese for what they did . . . If we had the opportunity to do that, I don't think we'd hesitate for a minute."[60] Michael Hayden, a former head of the National Security Agency and the Central Intelligence Agency, struck a similar note. OPM, he said, was a "legitimate foreign intelligence target. To grab the equivalent in the Chinese system, I would not have thought twice. I would not have asked permission . . . This is not 'shame on China.' This is 'shame on us' for not protecting that kind of information."[61]

What made the OPM hack special was that China used interdependence—in this case information networks—to turn an American strength into a strategic liability. It was a victory that would have been inconceivable before the age of the Internet. We are likely to see similarly ambitious operations, on all sides, in the years to come.

Russia's cyberwarfare operations are even more secret than China's. Russian hackers are regarded as among the best in the world and the Russian government is suspected of being closely involved in major cyber attacks on U.S. interests. One of the most spectacular occurred in 2016 when Russia was named by U.S. intelligence as the likely source of cyber attacks on the Democratic National Committee (DNC). These attacks accessed thousands of internal documents, which ended up in the possession of WikiLeaks, which in turn released them to maximize political pain on Democratic nominee Hillary Clinton. There were other leaks of the personal emails of leading political figures—including Colin Powell and John Podesta—in the fall of 2016, while Russia was also believed to be behind fake news, whereby false stories were planted in social media. The interference was widely perceived as Putin's revenge on Clinton and the Obama administration for what he saw as U.S. meddling in the Russian elections in 2012 and in Ukraine in 2013 and 2014. Putin may also have seen Donald Trump as more aligned with Russian interests in Europe and the Middle East.

Russia's gambit was successful—Clinton's candidacy was hurt by the drip-drip effects of the leaks, Trump was elected, and the credibility of American democracy was damaged by its vulnerability to outside pressures.

As the United States and Russia compete with each other, one can expect active measures to distort and influence the domestic politics of each. Putin has responded to the threat he perceives from the West by cracking down on nongovernmental organizations, targeting opposition figures, and consolidating his power. But the United States is an open system and much more vulnerable to external interference. It has never had to deal with this type of threat before—one where a rival power could interfere with its domestic democratic process on such a large scale. Dirty tricks surely happened in the past, but their dangers have become magnified in the era of big data and cyberwarfare. This raises difficult questions about how to respond and deter Russia from such actions in the future.

THE FUTURE OF GLOBALIZATION

Fears of cyberwar and the weaponization of interdependence are taking a toll on investment.[62] The United States is concerned that China is using market openness to preemptively penetrate U.S. companies and technologies in ways that Beijing could strategically exploit at a time of crisis. In a 2013 interview, former director of the CIA and the NSA Michael Hayden explained, "If you've got a foreign company supply[ing] you with essential communications infrastructure and/or helping build your network, the detailed knowledge that company obtains can be a powerful intelligence tool for foreign security services to leverage off to map out and target your telecommunications network for espionage and other malicious purposes."[63]

Later in the interview, Hayden singled out Chinese technology giant Huawei, saying that it represents an "unambiguous national security threat" to the United States and Australia. In 2012, a House Intelligence Committee Report into the activities of Huawei and ZTE, another Chinese telecommunications company, recommended that both be viewed with suspicion and be banned from mergers, acquisitions, and takeovers in the United States or from supplying vital components to the U.S. telecommunications infrastructure.[64]

Huawei and ZTE are meeting with stiff resistance in the United States, but they have had a more mixed experience elsewhere. Taiwan, Germany, India, and Australia blocked Huawei and/or ZTE from major contracts.[65] But Huawei enjoyed the support of former UK prime minister David Cameron in making a £1.3 billion investment in the United Kingdom (despite considerable concerns from Parliament), and the European Union as a whole continues to do business with it.[66]

Concerns have spread from the technology sector to other infrastructure areas. Cameron backed Chinese investment in an £18 billion project to build a nuclear power plant at Hinkley Point despite security concerns, such as that China could threaten to turn off the plant if it was engaged in a dispute with the United Kingdom. After Cameron's resignation, the new British prime minister, Theresa May, paused the project and subjected it to further review due to those same concerns, before finally approving it.[67] In Australia, the Turnbull government blocked a deal that would have seen Chinese investors take a majority stake in the country's largest electricity company, Ausgrid, again citing national security concerns.[68]

Unconditional interdependence would allow Chinese companies and investors to fully avail themselves of all the opportunities that globalization offers—but there is widespread recognition that technology infrastructure is a special case where "Trojan horse" concerns are real. Further integration is unlikely to ease tensions; it will only exacerbate them.

As tensions rise between the world's major powers, they will use whatever leverage they have to advance their strategic goals. The use of force is too high-risk, except as a last resort, and reassuring allies or pre-positioning forces is insufficient as a coercive tool. Consequently, countries will prepare for limited economic warfare, more in the financial arena than in trade, and they will make widespread use of cyberwarfare. They will also seek out other means of using a rival's reliance on and participation in the global system to their own advantage. This development will have enormous repercussions. Globalization will continue but not as we have known it. Countries will delink from each other where they perceive a strategic vulnerability. They will maximize their leverage where they can. They will develop means of retaliation. And they will continue to test each other.

6 DEVISING A STRATEGY

Crafting a strategy and a foreign policy is harder for America than for other great powers because the United States has defined its interest as a healthy world order, not just as security for the homeland, surrounding waters, and the geographical locations that impinge on both. This expansive definition dates back to the 1940s, when American strategists built a liberal international order in Western Europe and Northeast Asia. They chose this path because isolationism had proven to be a catastrophe and they did not want to simply replace Imperial Britain as a master of real-politik—because that too had failed and it offended the sensibilities of the American people. If the United States could not avoid the world by isolating itself, it would have to transform it. The United States would have to stand for something and against something— and on a global scale. And what it stood for would have to provide real benefits for the United States and the world. One key top-secret American national security document of the day summed up the strategic goal as to "foster a world environment in which the American system can survive and flourish," which, in turn, necessitates "our positive participation in the world community."[1]

U.S. strategists elected to create an international order whose institutions, policies, and values were liberal in character. Liberal in this context draws from the classical definition—distinct from its partisan meaning—which describes a system that safeguards rights and prevents tyrannical rule. The liberal international order had three components.[2] On the security side, it entailed forward deployment of U.S. forces and creating alliances with the dual purpose of containing the Soviet Union and ending security competition between the major powers in the Western bloc. On the economic side, it consisted of an open global economy and the creation of cooperative international financial institutions, such as the International Monetary Fund and the World Bank. The third component was that in exchange for the cooperation and support of other countries, the United States would restrain itself: America would work within the framework of the order it created, and provide its friends and allies, even those that were relatively small and weak, with real influence. This order was tremendously successful. It did not just outlast the Soviet Union; it created an engine of prosperity and innovation that powered the Western bloc forward while political cooperation between the allies surged to new and historically unprecedented heights.

But such a broad American definition of interests and order also had extreme effects on U.S. foreign policy. During the Cold War, the United States had to convince the Soviet Union that it would respond to a conventional attack on Germany with nuclear weapons even though such a war would result in the incineration of American cities. It was a disproportionate and grotesque response by any measure, but it was deemed rational and necessary to maintain a liberal order that was otherwise vulnerable to a Soviet invasion of Europe.

Indeed, from the very beginning of the American led-liberal order, U.S. strategists had to convince other nations that they would react to aggression in a manner that greatly exceeded the direct threat to the American homeland. It was the Catholic theologian Reinhold Niebuhr who first put the central point clearly when he wrote about what he called "America's Tragic Dilemma," saying: "Though confident of its virtue, it must hold atomic bombs ready for use so as to prevent a possible world conflagration. It may actually make the conflict more inevitable with this threat; and yet, it cannot abandon the threat."[3] Every American president has tried to manage this dilemma and to ensure that the U.S. strategy is proportionate to the interests involved. But the Niebuhrian dilemma was a problem that could never be resolved. It could only be managed.

From the beginning of the postwar period, the United States also confronted a second, less terrifying but equally controversial, dilemma—whether to bear a vastly disproportionate share of the cost of proactively building the liberal order. While World War II was still raging, the Franklin D. Roosevelt administration carefully developed plans to build a liberal postwar order, but by 1946 these ideas—including an interest-bearing loan to Great Britain—encountered fierce resistance in Congress and appeared doomed. Many Americans wanted the United States to come home and mind its own business, to look out for its own narrow economic interests instead of rebuilding ruined nations, and to be unbound by international rules and norms. The rapid emergence of a Soviet threat provided the Truman administration with the opportunity to mobilize support for internationalism under an anti-communist banner. As Dean Acheson put it, Truman portrayed the threat as "clearer than truth" in order to secure passage of his program.[4] Without anti-communism, it is possible that Truman's Marshall Plan and alliance with Western Europe would have been defeated in much the same way that President Wilson's Treaty of Versailles was rejected by Congress.

The communist threat sustained an outsized American strategy throughout the Cold War. After the Soviet Union collapsed, American leaders continued to make the moral case for upholding the order, and because no power sought to balance against the United States, the costs of upholding the order appeared to be manageable. It was easier to maintain the status quo than embark on a risky change. Today, we have reached a point where the costs of upholding the order have escalated considerably, although they are still far below those at the height of the Cold War. The post–Cold War expansion of the liberal order to a truly global scale widened the horizon of U.S. responsibility. Pushing back against Russia in Ukraine or China in the South China Sea seems to run the risk of war with a major power. Stabilizing the Middle East seems to require yet another ground war in an Arab country—something people are loath to do after the 2003 invasion of Iraq. Even the cost of alliances has become more controversial when viewed against the backdrop of the Great Recession. A grandiose foreign policy seems like an indulgence to many.

These two dilemmas—deterring threats against nonvital interests and paying the costs for building a liberal order—have reemerged, but many people are tempted to argue that they are actually not dilemmas at all. Some say it is easy to deter aggression in faraway places without incurring great risk or that one can have a liberal order without paying a disproportionate share of the costs. But the essence of these dilemmas is that not all good things go together. There are important tradeoffs and no way of avoiding them. Further, understanding these tradeoffs is the essence of strategic thinking. The real debate in American strategy is between two schools of thought with very different ideas on how to manage the dilemmas—one favoring restraint and retrenchment, and the other, increased engagement and competitiveness. These dilemmas emerge in two strategic problems facing the United States.

THE PROBLEM OF REVISIONISM

Under the current international order, there is a distinction in international relations between status quo and revisionist states.[5] Status quo states are generally satisfied with their position in the international system. They may have ambitions, or even desires for substantial changes, but they pursue them through the legitimate processes of the international order. Nor do they use their military power to seize territory or subdue other states. When all states are status quo states, war occurs only when miscalculation or a security dilemma ignites a serious conflict.[6] For instance, if China were a status quo power, it may build up its military not for conquest but for the purpose of protecting its interests. Nevertheless, the United States may still find this threatening, and respond by balancing against China. This could lead to an arms race and spiraling tensions, a situation prone to crisis and war. The answer to a "security dilemma" is transparency, reassurance, and restraint, so it will be clear to all that neither state seeks to threaten the status quo.[7]

Revisionist states, by contrast, use their military power, or the threat of military power, to change the status quo. They seek to acquire more power, either by seizing territory, imposing their preferred form of government on other states, or by unilaterally and fundamentally rewriting the rules of the game.[8] Transparency, reassurance, and restraint are ineffective in dealing with revisionist states. Revisionism is a recurring feature in world politics: consider the Spanish and Austrian Hapsburgs; Russia in the eighteenth, nineteenth, and twentieth centuries; the United States in its hemisphere in the nineteenth century; Prussia in the 1860s; and Germany and Imperial Japan in the twentieth century. Revisionist policies often lead to conflict—usually of a limited nature, but sometimes in the form of a general war—because they invite collisions, either between the status quo and revisionist powers or between multiple revisionists. One of the remarkable features of the past quarter century is the near absence of revisionism. The post–Cold War international order is predicated on the assumption that all the major powers are essentially status quo powers.[9]

Today, though, revisionism is on the upswing. We often think of revisionist powers as countries hell-bent on global domination, like Nazi Germany or the Soviet Union. But revisionism rarely manifests itself with all-out world war; revisionists instead can aim for sizable regional gains that simply disrupt the status quo. Revisionist states traditionally go after the nonvital interests of their great power rivals, because doing so generally doesn't provoke the retaliatory strike that would come from attacking a vital interest. Threatening nonvital interests—for example, by attacking a non-ally—leaves the status quo power torn over how to respond, debating whether it's worth it to commit the blood and treasure.

Of course, the term "nonvital interest" is somewhat misleading. It only holds true when viewed narrowly and in isolation from a wider strategic picture. The way in which a state increases its influence affects the distinction between vital and nonvital interests profoundly. While annexation of territory and unprovoked invasion clearly constitute a breach of the peace and threaten vital U.S. interests, seizing small rocks or strips of territory is a more ambiguous threat. Such acts appear to be of limited strategic importance, until, in the aggregate, they acquire a much greater value. It is, in effect, a salami slicing strategy. At the outset, the fact that no treaty has been breached and the territory in question seems to be of limited importance shapes the psychology and dynamics of the crisis. It is precisely the small strategic value of the territory in dispute that causes the dominant power to refrain from going to war over it at an extraordinary cost that would be vastly disproportionate to the disputed territory's value.

This is the great advantage that a revisionist power has, and one that it can ruthlessly exploit as long as it doesn't overstep its mark. After all, what American president wants to risk nuclear war for the Donbass in eastern Ukraine? To put it another way, how many vital interests is a state willing to jeopardize for a nonvital one? Therefore, if the revisionist power is smart, and it usually is, it will pick territories precisely because they lack significant strategic value to great power rivals, even if they are important to the smaller country upon which the revisionist preys.[10]

This is not a new problem. It is textbook revisionism. Its purpose is to make deterrence extremely hard and to encourage rival great powers to accommodate the revisionist state diplomatically or to limit the response, rendering it ineffective. It was for this reason that the British Empire used accommodation as a pillar of its grand strategy for half a century prior to its catastrophic failure in the late 1930s. Indeed, until 1938, accommodation or appeasement was viewed very positively in Britain because it seemed to offer a way to stave off a major power conflict by making modest concessions from a position of strength.[11]

The revisionist challenge is the most complex problem with which a major power can be confronted. A regular security dilemma between two status quo powers can be addressed with reassurance and transparency, but a revisionist power will not be satisfied with the restraint of others. It needs major concessions so it can accomplish its objectives; at times regimes pursue revisionist policies for their very domestic survival. The return of revisionism has put the Niebuhrian dilemma right back in the center of American strategy. If Russia and China continue to pursue revisionist foreign policies, and if they are adept at choosing their targets, they will put immense pressure on American policymakers, who will be faced with the choice of risking conflict with a nuclear power or accommodating them and setting the stage for similar acts in the future.

BUILDING A LIBERAL ORDER IN A NATIONALIST AGE

America's second strategic problem is how to continue to build and sustain a U.S.-led liberal international order in a more nationalist and geopolitically competitive age. After the Cold War, the U.S.-led Western order went global thanks to globalization, NATO expansion, democracy promotion, and the strengthening of human rights norms. The process was never easy but it was made possible by the forces of convergence. As we saw in Chapter 1, many nations embraced the U.S.-led order; Russia and China acquiesced to it. Today, as those forces of convergence wane, the United States finds itself with global responsibilities in an era heavily influenced by nationalism and populism.

There are multiple dimensions to this problem. One of the most severe is that some of the core goals of the U.S.-led order—including a prosperous global economy through globalization and democracy promotion—no longer appear to offer what they once promised. As we saw in Chapter 5, the international financial crisis of 2008 and 2009, the Great Recession and lack of economic growth, and the political salience of inequality have undermined public and elite support in the United States and overseas for measures to maintain, or increase, the openness of the global economy. It is telling that the actions taken in 2008 and 2009 to save the global economy remain highly unpopular today. Major trade deals have stalled. And populist politicians have become increasingly successful in Western democracies, most notably with Donald Trump's victory in the 2016 U.S. presidential election.

Democracy promotion was also discredited in the eyes of many after the Iraq War. Humanitarian intervention is frequently perceived by other countries as a U.S. tactic to topple an anti-American dictator and replace him with a more amenable alternative. For their part, many Americans believe that their government is utterly incompetent when it comes to fostering positive change abroad. And it is not just American ideas that are in doubt. There is also a general sense—not necessarily true—that international governance has failed, whether it is in the form of the European Union, efforts to curb climate change, or the nonproliferation regime. This sense of failure strengthens those who want to focus exclusively on national solutions.

A second element to this problem is when and how to intervene to stop mass atrocities and uphold basic standards of human rights. Later in this chapter, we will see how in recent years the United States has distinguished between problems that pose a direct threat to U.S. interests and those that do not but are matters for the international community to address. Military action was judged to be justifiable in cases where direct threats to

U.S. interests were involved; other situations very rarely were deemed to require a military response. The difficulty is that it is not always possible to identify clearly what poses a systemic threat to core U.S. interests.

This problem is particularly acute in the Middle East where there is widespread disagreement on the systemic risk that disorder in parts of the region poses to the region as a whole and to vital U.S. interests elsewhere, especially in Europe. Those who believe that disorder can largely be contained are wary of increased U.S. engagement, of potentially throwing good resources after bad, whereas those who worry that the disorder is highly contagious want to increase engagement if only as a means to put a lid on the region's problems.

A third element is how to balance those global issues requiring cooperation with other nations—especially climate change, terrorism, and nuclear proliferation—with geopolitical concerns. Sometimes it may seem as if there is a tradeoff to be made between the two. Perhaps the United States needs to make a concession on a regional issue in exchange for cooperation on a global issue. Or it may have to choose which to invest its time and energy in. The regional issues, as we have seen, are critically important to the global order but transnational challenges are also absolutely vital.

This problem of juggling cooperation around global issues with geopolitical concerns has come up before. In 1943, U.S. Secretary of State Cordell Hull let it be known that his number one priority was the new United Nations. Hull wanted the Soviets to join but worried that they would stay out. The Soviets had no strong opinion one way or the other but they saw an opportunity for leverage. At the Moscow Conference in October and November of 1943, the Soviets played hard to get and criticized the United Nations, only finally to "concede" in exchange for what they wanted on Poland. Hull was none the wiser and assumed he had extracted extremely difficult concessions for what he saw as the secondary issue of territory in Eastern Europe. In reality, the Soviets had played him and "given up" something they never cared much about in the first place.[12]

The trick is to be able to increase cooperation across a wide range of areas—globally and regionally—without leaving one hostage to another. The lesson is as pertinent today as it was in 1943. The building of a liberal order advanced in leaps and bounds after the Cold War, largely because the environment was permissive. Today, it is anything but. The United States has to cope with mounting opposition at home and considerable skepticism overseas. Overcoming this problem is a key challenge for U.S. strategy.

These two strategic problems, and the dilemmas inherent in them, run through today's debate on U.S. foreign policy. Although it is rarely explicitly framed in this way, how one approaches these dilemmas shapes one's response to the problems, and, by extension, to U.S. foreign policy as a whole. But before we look at America's strategic options, we must first ask, What is the United States capable of? Is it a power in decline, with less capacity than before, or can it still uphold a liberal international order if it so chooses?

HOW POWERFUL IS THE UNITED STATES?

Over the past ten years, many people, including Donald Trump, have argued that the United States is in decline, either in absolute or relative terms.[13] If true, this has enormous implications for U.S. strategy. After all, a superpower in an inexorable decline will soon find itself overextended and in retreat on multiple fronts. There are certain things it cannot do. Americans have been terrified by the prospect of decline since the United States became a global power after World War II. The Soviet acquisition of the atomic bomb, *Sputnik,* the mythical missile gap of the 1960 election, the supposed emergence of a multipolar world in the late 1960s and 1970s, the rise of Japan in the mid-1980s, and now the ascension of China have all induced high levels of anxiety in the American people. And just because Americans have been unduly alarmed in the past does not mean that alarm is an inappropriate response this time around. After all, in the end the boy who cried wolf did meet the wolf.[14]

Assessing power is a tricky task. The seventeenth-century British philosopher and statesman Francis Bacon famously warned that nothing is "more subject to error than the forming of a true and right valuation of the power and forces of an empire."[15] Power is usually conceived of in relative terms, which complicates matters further. Analysts tend to rely on metrics like GDP and military spending, although less tangible and often overlooked factors—including strategic competence, military innovation, and the attraction of a country's model to others—are often crucial.

Let's start with relative power. Surely it is stating the obvious to say that the United States is in relative decline given China's rapid economic growth, isn't it? Not necessarily. For one, GDP growth is a very narrow metric. As William Wohlforth and Stephen Brooks explain, "GDP was originally designed to measure mid-twentieth-century manufacturing economies, and so the more knowledge-based and globalized a country's production is, the more its GDP underestimates its economy's true size."[16] China's success is largely explained by the size of its population and the fact that it is starting from a low base so it can take advantage of so-called catch-up growth. But the United States enjoys long-term advantages in key industries, patents, and higher education. In terms of military clout, too, the United States is an unrivaled global power. True, America's military advantage is somewhat blunted by the fact that China, as well as Russia, have the edge in contested areas, like eastern Ukraine and the South China Sea. But what matters is not overall military power but that the United States possesses the ability to deploy effective forces in a crisis. With enough political will, the United States could choose to have the most military might overall in almost any crisis or conflict. Finally, when compared on a global scale of relative power, it is clear that the United States is surpassing most other nations. The GDP gap between the United States and Russia is growing, and the United States has outperformed European countries following the financial crisis.

Contrary to predictions of decline, then, in many respects the United States is actually a power still on the rise. The United States continues to grow economically and demographically year over year. It continues to benefit from an influx of immigrants, particularly those with high levels of education and expertise. One result of large-scale immigration in the United States is that U.S. demographic trends are much healthier than for other Western societies, many of which are aging. The shale gas revolution has reduced U.S. dependence on foreign oil and has given U.S. industries a competitive edge. The United States is at the cutting edge in key sectors, particularly technology. To take just one example offered by Wohlforth and Brooks, "The United States has an enormous advantage as a source of innovative technologies, with $128 billion in receipts in 2013 for the use of its intellectual property compared to $1 billion in receipts for China."[17] The U.S.

military had a tough decade in the 2000s, but out of adversity came major military innovations, particularly in the use of unmanned technologies. The return of revisionism also amplified U.S. soft power as other nations sought to deepen their ties to the United States; even if the U.S. model wasn't necessarily attractive, the ability to balance their regional rivals was.

Yet the United States does have a power problem. Since World War II, U.S. power has always been bound to its alliances, and now some of America's key allies are in decline in relative, or in some cases even in absolute, terms. As we have seen in earlier chapters, Western European nations are stuck in an economic lost decade with no end in sight. Low growth has led to continental lethargy. Britain, France, and Germany slashed their militaries and have only recently begun to arrest this trend. As discussed in Chapter 2, Brexit has deepened Europeans' introspection and sense of crisis. Meanwhile, in Asia, Japan has fallen behind China over the past decade and is still struggling to overcome a prolonged period of stagnation and economic malaise. Shinzō Abe's efforts to kickstart Japan's economy and strengthen its national power offer reason for hope, but there is no doubt that the balance of power between China and Japan has tipped in China's favor.

So the picture is complicated. America's allies are struggling. The United States continues to grow, but the balance of power with China is complex and multifaceted. Russia is in decline economically but has increased its military and diplomatic power. The binary concept of decline is simply not very helpful for describing and assessing the strategic situation. A more fruitful and useful conceptual frame is to ask what advantages and disadvantages the various competitor nations have in the emerging geopolitical competition for the future of the world order.

Looking at advantages and disadvantages allows us to deal with contradictory evidence broadly and in particular circumstances.

The United States has two advantages over its rivals. The first is that it enjoys preeminence over global systems. It has no peer in the international financial system. It is the only country that can project its military power around the world supported by command and control systems that are second to none. America's second advantage is its soft power. With the exception of its strategic rivals (Russia, China, and Iran) and maybe a few emerging powers like Brazil and South Africa, other nations see their interests as best served by a U.S.-led order compared to any other model, be it a spheres-of-influence system dominated by regional hegemons or a global alternative led by China. This gives the United States an enormous advantage because other countries will act as power multipliers for it.

America's rivals, however, also have several advantages when it comes to regional competition: proximity to a likely crisis, superior resolve, and the initiative. Despite having far less power than the United States, Russia, China, and Iran often have the ability and political will to deploy power more quickly and in greater quantities to a crisis in their region than the United States does, because the United States is both far away and constrained by Congress. These countries also have the advantage of being able to take the initiative, which means that they can choose to challenge the U.S.-led regional order with scenarios that maximize their relative advantage. Globally, they are at a distinct disadvantage, but they may be able to benefit if other nations feel that the United States is abusing its influence in the international order: for instance, if the United States is seen as too willing to opt for sanctions or is perceived as using humanitarian intervention for geopolitical purposes.

THE NECESSITY OF STRATEGIC CHOICE

It is easy to get distracted by definitions and critiques of national security and grand strategy. The concept of national security was devised by U.S. strategists after World War II to signify something broader than military policy.[18] As Henry Kissinger explained, "In its widest sense," national security "comprises every action by which a society seeks to assure its survival or to realize its aspirations internationally."[19] This fits neatly into the notion of grand strategy, which MIT professor Barry Posen insightfully defined as a state's theory about how to cause security for itself.[20] The art of American foreign policy is not to devise a strategy for how to defend the homeland or key sea lanes. It is much broader than that. It entails having an overarching vision for advancing the state's long-term national interest and a plan for realizing it even as other countries work to frustrate it. To be useful, a grand strategy also must address the challenges that policymakers confront on a daily basis. It should help guide and shape the decision-making process and not be just a collection of self-help bromides.

To apply these ideas today means that the United States needs a strategy for a more geopolitically competitive world. The post–Cold War strategy is based on assumptions of convergence that are no longer applicable. A new strategy must provide a theory and narrative about what the United States needs from the world to realize its long-term interests. It must have something to say about Europe, the Middle East, and East Asia. And it must offer a solution to the two strategic problems outlined earlier: deterring revisionism and continuing to build the liberal order. It must also be cognizant that other powers are working to ensure that the U.S. strategy will fail. A strategy does not need to be one-size-fits-all, but it must be coherent. For example, one

cannot simultaneously claim that the United States should prioritize East Asia above all else without identifying which region
can be safely neglected and how the United States should cope
with the consequences of that neglect.

As we seek strategic options, it is useful to keep in mind an
analytical distinction made by Stephen Sestanovich, a scholar
at the Council on Foreign Relations. In his book *Maximalist*,
Sestanovich argued that there are two types of American grand
strategies—maximalist approaches and retrenchment. Maximalists
seek a broad array of ambitious countermeasures against threats,
whereas retrenchers look to "shift responsibilities to friends and
allies, to explore accommodation with adversaries, to narrow
commitments and reduce costs."[21] Presidents Truman, Kennedy,
and Reagan were maximalists, while Eisenhower, Nixon, and
Carter were retrenchers. The impulses that Sestanovich identifies
are alive and well today although the context has changed.

The United States faces a choice between retrenchment, or
restraint as it is often called, and a more forward-leaning,
competitive approach designed to strengthen and enhance the
U.S.-led liberal order. Advocates of retrenchment and restraint
believe that the risks of broadly defining vital interests to include
much of the world outweigh the benefits. They also worry that
the United States is becoming overstretched and weakened by
the extent of its obligations. Supporters of a competitive approach
to uphold liberal order worry that reduced U.S. engagement will
lead to the unraveling of the order and a deterioration in
America's strategic environment that will be hard to reverse.
They argue that over the course of seventy years, the risks that
the United States undertook were worth it given the outcome.

In their own unique ways, the Clinton and George W. Bush
administrations pursued a forward-leaning and expansive foreign

policy; but the invasion of Iraq and the financial crisis created an opening for a swing toward restraint, one that the 44th president was willing to take.

The Obama Doctrine of Restraint

Many Americans, feeling a heightened sense of risk and economic pressures at home, want to reduce the U.S. role in upholding the liberal order, even as they simultaneously want the benefits of that order. Consequently they are looking for ways of doing less in the world without causing a significant deterioration in it. The search for this middle path was, in many ways, the core mission of President Obama during his two terms in office. Obama saw it as America's responsibility to uphold the liberal international order. He believed that the United States provided indispensable leadership for solving problems the world shared—problems like climate change, terrorism, and economic volatility. He also believed that the U.S. alliance system was a force for stability in Europe and East Asia. "For all of our warts," he told Jeffrey Goldberg of the *Atlantic,* "the United States has clearly been a force for good in the world. If you compare us to previous superpowers, we act less on the basis of naked self-interest, and have been interested in establishing norms that benefit everyone. If it is possible to do good at a bearable cost, to save lives, we will do it." "I am," he went on, "very much the internationalist."[22]

Obama was also of the view, however, that the United States was prone to overextending itself in pursuit of the goal of upholding the liberal order. He told Goldberg, "There's a playbook in Washington that presidents are supposed to follow. It's a playbook that comes out of the foreign-policy establishment. And the playbook prescribes responses to different events, and these responses tend to be militarized responses. Where America is directly threatened, the playbook works. But the playbook can also be a trap that can lead to bad decisions."[23]

For Obama, the United States is a relatively secure country. The long-term trends domestically are positive and there is plenty of good news in the world. Yes, the Middle East may be in flames, but America can find wonderful opportunities in Southeast Asia and Latin America. Yes, there are threats, but they are not existential and the greatest risk they pose is that they could elicit an overreaction. Obama was clearly frustrated with America's overextension in the post–Cold War period, particularly during the George W. Bush administration. But his real complaint was with U.S. strategy from the late 1940s on, which, as we saw earlier, relied on the notion of a blurring of vital interests and interests in the order as a whole.

Obama also resented that other nations did not carry their weight in upholding the order, acknowledging that "free riders aggravate me."[24] He tried to play hard to get so that others would be compelled to do more. Foreign-policy analyst Nina Hachigian, who would go on to become President Obama's ambassador to ASEAN, and foreign-policy analyst David Shorr, called this the "Responsibility Doctrine."[25] Obama complained about how the United States was the first nation others called in a security crisis, regardless of where that crisis was happening. European governments had slashed their defense budgets but relied on the United States to take care of nearby threats in North Africa. Sunni states wanted the United States to wage war with Iran. Obama's solution to this problem was to set a high threshold for U.S. action in those cases when what he saw as core interests—the security of the United States or its citizens, of surrounding territories, and of U.S. allies—were not directly threatened. For these threats, such as mass atrocities and the security of non-allies, the United States would act only multilaterally, if others did their fair share, and if the costs were relatively low. He explained that "one of the reasons I am so focused on taking action multilaterally where our direct interests are not at stake is that multilateralism regulates hubris."[26] Obama was essentially trying to define U.S. interests as other major powers do by distinguishing between core and peripheral concerns.

The Obama administration did accept that the world was becoming more geopolitically competitive, but it was determined not to be defined by that fact. It would push back against Russia by imposing economic costs on it for its aggression against Ukraine. Obama acknowledged, however, that Ukraine, as a non-NATO country, "is going to be vulnerable to military domination by Russia no matter what we do."[27] Obama was aloof from Europe's struggles and the European Union's existential challenges and saw little reason for the United States to become more involved. In dealing with Russia, Obama tolerated its intervention in Syria and even rewarded Putin by making him the centerpiece of his diplomacy. In East Asia, the Obama administration conducted freedom-of-navigation operations and deepened cooperation with regional partners to counteract Chinese assertiveness in the South China Sea, but it stopped short of trying to deny China its strategic objective. Concerned by rising tensions, the White House even instructed the Pentagon to drop the term "great power competition," which had been a staple of speeches by senior military officers and of the secretary of defense, Ashton Carter.[28] Meanwhile, in the Middle East, as we have already seen, Obama argued that Saudi Arabia and Iran must share power in the region, but he trusted the Saudis and Iranians to reach this conclusion on their own as the United States reduced its involvement in the regional competition.

Obama's strategy of restraint encountered several problems. The first is that the design of the liberal order requires an outsized American role for its maintenance and nobody has come up with a perfect formula for how to provide clarity as to when the United States will act and when it will not. When clarity is provided, as it was in 1950 when Dean Acheson said that South Korea was outside the U.S. defense perimeter, or in 1990 when U.S. Ambassador to Iraq April Glaspie signaled U.S. indifference to Saddam Hussein over the Iraq-Kuwait dispute, conflict has followed. The converse is also true; the blurring of the lines led to several egregious mistakes—the Vietnam War in particular— and it created the mindset that led to the invasion of Iraq in 2003. But this ambiguity also led to many successes—the defense of non-allied South Korea in 1950, the liberation of non-allied Kuwait in 1991, intervention in Bosnia in the mid-1990s, intervention in Kosovo in 1999, and even the collapse of the Soviet Union in 1991, which rested on the disproportionate strategy of Mutually Assured Destruction. One could argue, as Niebuhr did, that the very existence of the liberal world order rested on this irrational threat. The ambiguous expansion of U.S. interests can lead to policy mistakes, but it also performs an indispensable role in reducing conflict by providing a credible deterrent to aggression.

The second problem is that smaller threats can pose a systemic risk to the international order even if they do not immediately endanger core U.S. interests. For example, Obama would be pilloried for downplaying the threat posed by ISIS in 2013, calling the group the "jayvee team," but the episode illustrated the difficulty of correctly diagnosing long-term threats to U.S. interests. Obama was right that ISIS was focused on local sectarian issues, but he underestimated the risk that instability in Iraq and Syria would pose to the region as a whole and beyond to the European Union.

The third problem is that once the president stops making the case for why the United States has a special obligation to act when the stability of the order is threatened, even in faraway lands, the public tends to seek ever-greater levels of retrenchment. For instance, in August 2013, Obama tried to rally the public for strikes on the Assad regime in Syria after it violated his red line on using chemical weapons. But after over a year of hearing that Syria was of marginal importance and there was little the United States could do, they were unwilling to support strikes. With Congress restless, and with his own doubts about striking, Obama reversed course. This was the same problem that President George H. W. Bush had in Kuwait in 1990 and that President Bill Clinton had in the Balkans in the 1990s—only by using the bully pulpit of the presidency could they secure sufficient public support for their foreign policy. If the presidents did not frequently make the case, the public would be difficult to convince when they wanted to act.

As we look past the Obama administration, one obvious path for future presidents is to maintain an approach that is deeply skeptical about the use of military power in pursuit of interests that do not entail a direct threat to Americans, and seeks to shift the burden to others, while preserving the liberal order. Such a strategy will be difficult to sustain, however, because it tries to do two things simultaneously that will likely prove to be mutually incompatible. It tries to reduce the burden on the United States, while maintaining the liberal international order as it is today. Yet the recalibration of U.S. strategy to limit the U.S. response to indirect threats may destabilize the international order over time. As President Obama acknowledged in his interview in the

Atlantic, U.S. allies were unable to adequately cope with the additional responsibilities that he tried to shift onto them in Libya. As a result, postconflict operations in Libya were a failure, the terror threat increased, and U.S. interests in Europe were badly damaged.

Looking forward, eventually the United States will be presented with one tough choice after another by revisionist powers. Washington will rightly want to avoid a great-power war, but in pursuing this aim it will by definition avoid any steps that could increase the risk of one—which will leave very few options for responding to revisionism. In a relatively short period of time, a future president will be compelled to make a choice—to compete with rival powers or to concede a sphere of influence to them. It is for this reason that policymakers inclined toward restraint and retrenchment will be increasingly drawn to alternative strategies. Two such strategies are waiting in the wings.

The Strategy of Offshore Balancing and Neo-Isolationism

Some experts, scholars, and policymakers believe that the Obama administration did not go far enough in scaling back America's commitments overseas. They agree with Obama that other nations free-ride on American security guarantees, but they ask why then did he deepen U.S. alliances and not put real pressure on the allies. They question the forward positioning of U.S. forces and whether it really matters if China controls the South China Sea or if Russia is in charge of Ukraine. This school of thought is rooted in the realist school of foreign policy. Realists tend to define U.S. interests narrowly, and feel skeptical of international institutions and of the liberal order.

The name most commonly given to realist foreign policy is offshore balancing. Offshore balancers believe that the United

States ought largely to withdraw from Northeast Asia, Europe, and the Middle East. America should intervene only if another major power is poised to conquer and dominate one of these regions. As University of Chicago's John Mearsheimer and Harvard University's Stephen Walt have written: "The aim is to remain offshore as long as possible, while recognizing that it is sometimes necessary to come onshore. If that happens, however, the United States should make its allies do as much of the heavy lifting as possible and remove its own forces as soon as it can."[29]

Those who adhere to a realist foreign policy believe that power is sufficiently dispersed in each of these regions so as to make conquest unlikely, if not impossible. The key element to understand about offshore balancing is that it accepts as a necessary byproduct increased security competition between regional powers. For instance, if the United States leaves NATO or dramatically reduces its role, European nations can and should rearm to balance against Russia. They may even fight a limited war against Russia. The United States should intervene only if Russia is poised to overrun the rest of Europe. Similarly, in East Asia, Japan could rearm, including by acquiring nuclear weapons, and work with its neighbors to check China's rise. Only if China were poised to deal a crippling blow to Japan would the United States intervene. Offshore balancers see the 1930s as a model to follow. At that time, the United States let others fight it out, intervened late into World War II, and took most of the spoils.

Other realists call for an even more sweeping retrenchment of U.S. power, something like a twenty-first-century version of isolationism. The most advanced and sophisticated case for this approach appears in the 2014 book *Restraint* by Barry Posen, a professor at MIT and perhaps America's top academic defense expert.[30] *Restraint* explains in detail why and how the United

States should divest itself of its international security commitments and give up the liberal international order. Posen argues that the United States should pull out of NATO and out of alliances in Asia over a ten-year period.

The case for restraint has made it into the wider public debate on foreign policy. For instance, Ian Bremmer, CEO and founder of the Eurasia Group, has proposed a strategy he calls Independent America, whereby the United States would dramatically reduce its international commitments by ceasing to be the security guarantor of last resort for NATO and Japan, and by withdrawing entirely from the Middle East.[31] Neo-isolationism unexpectedly reemerged as a force in American politics during the Republican primary campaign in 2016 with the rise of Donald Trump. Trump questioned America's alliances and its leadership of the international order. He harkened back to the days of a more isolationist and mercantilist United States.[32] Trump even embraced the slogan "America First" used by Charles Lindbergh, a leading isolationist in the 1930s. Trump's foreign-policy message was crude and often strewn with factual errors, but it was unmistakably different—the United States would no longer provide security or economic growth for the rest of the world. It would look out only for itself. As we will see in the Epilogue, if Trump governs as he campaigned, the implications for world order could be severe.

These views could not be further from the U.S. postwar tradition. For over seven decades, the United States has sought to quell and reduce regional security competition in Western Europe and East Asia. Yes, the alliances were intended to contain the Soviet Union. But they were also intended to create a community of nations that did not fear each other. And they were designed so that the United States could restrain its allies and prevent events from spiraling into conflict. Thus the United States provides for much of Japan's security so Japan will not build capabilities that worry South Korea or others. And even after the Soviet threat disappeared, the United States has gone to extraordinary lengths to promote regional integration and cooperation in Asia and Europe—expansion of the European Union and NATO, for instance, has helped to consolidate democracy in Eastern Europe and reduce the potential for rivalries and territorial disputes.

Realists believe that many of these steps, including NATO's expansion, were mistakes. When it is pointed out to them that if the Baltics were not in NATO today, Russia may have invaded, their response is that the United States has no interests there. They recognize that retrenchment may make the world a much more dangerous place. They just believe that these regional conflicts will not affect the United States, asserting that America can protect itself behind its oceans and nuclear deterrent and would have time to intervene if a rival power was poised to dominate Europe, East Asia, or the Middle East.

Full-scale retrenchment will inject unprecedented risk and uncertainty into world politics. It is a revolutionary strategy. The day after the president of the United States adopts a neo-isolationist strategy will be the day that every defense planner and diplomat the world over scrambles to understand how to survive in the post-American world. Alliances will be worthless. The glue that held everything together will no longer stick. The United States would have created the mother of all vacuums. Japan would likely rearm, and may even go nuclear, to defend itself against China. China would see a window of opportunity to establish its dominance over East Asia. In Europe, Russia would likely move on the Baltics to put the final nail in NATO's coffin and would establish full control over Ukraine. Some Western European countries would rearm, but the overwhelming impulse would be to seek a balance of power. It is unlikely that globalization would survive the return to full-throated rivalry, which in turn would result in massive economic costs for the United States.

It is unlikely that any president—even Donald Trump—will voluntarily take the risk associated with neo-isolationism without being under overwhelming pressure to do so. To proactively dissolve America's alliances and retrench from the world would not only be geopolitically dangerous; it would also be politically dangerous because any crisis would be seen as self-inflicted. For these reasons, a president with retrenchment or isolationist tendencies is much more likely to seek a more orderly means of retreat—which brings us to accommodation.

Accommodation: Another Strategy of Restraint

One strategy that may make a comeback as tensions between the major powers rise is strategic accommodation. Strategic accommodation means negotiating with China, Russia, and maybe Iran to grant them a sphere of influence in their region in exchange for respecting a more limited U.S. role in their regions and U.S. leadership on global issues. The logic is that it is better to share power deliberately and through negotiation than by means of a disorderly retreat, as would occur if the United States unilaterally withdrew from its global role. The United States would remain a global power but it would be less hegemonic than it is now.

There is no doubt that this strategy would be highly contentious. For almost a quarter of a century, the United States has said that it opposes a return to a spheres-of-influence order of the kind that existed in the Cold War or prior to World War II. In fact, in 2013, Secretary of State John Kerry even formally repudiated the Monroe Doctrine.[33] Successive presidents have endorsed a Europe "whole and free" and the principle that states should be able to decide their own foreign relations.[34] This policy has had real and positive consequences, especially in Europe—since the collapse of the Soviet Union, NATO has expanded from sixteen countries to twenty-eight and the European Union from eleven to twenty-eight. But it was relatively easy to oppose a return to spheres of influence when no other major power was actively trying to reconstitute it. Now that revisionism has returned, some scholars and experts believe that accommodation offers a way of avoiding a great-power war.

Hugh White, an Australian strategist who is one of the leading advocates of sharing power with China, summed up this approach, writing that when the balancing strategy fails, "I fear that Washington will be left with only two disastrous options: either withdrawal from Asia or war with China. It is to avoid either of these outcomes that I advocate a new order to accommodate with China."[35] For White, the answer is an exchange: the United States would give China much greater influence in its neighborhood, and China would agree to respect vital U.S. interests, such as the U.S.-Japan alliance and the presence of the U.S. Navy in the western Pacific. The United States, in his view, should use its current standing in Asia as leverage to negotiate with China, India, and Japan a Concert of Asia, along the lines of the Concert of Europe. This arrangement would, he argues, mean that the United States "can remain in Asia on a new basis, allowing China a larger role but also maintaining a strong presence of its own."[36]

In a book titled *Meeting China Halfway*, Lyle Goldstein, a professor at the U.S. Naval War College, argues that the United

States must make the first move in offering China concessions that will create a spiral of cooperation that can lead to a sharing of power in East Asia. U.S. concessions would start out small but lead to major compromises, including a downgrading of the U.S.-Japan alliance in exchange for Japanese permanent membership in the UN Security Council and a withdrawal of U.S. forces from South Korea in exchange for North Korean denuclearization.[37]

The same logic has been applied in Europe. Samuel Charap and Jeremy Shapiro, two think-tank scholars who have questioned the strategy of confronting Russia, ask, "Are the principles at stake—the right of every country to make its own foreign-policy choices and freely choose its own alliances—really worth" war with a nuclear power?[38] They argue that Obama's strategy of punishing Russia for its aggression while seeking to cooperate with it on global issues is unsustainable. Putin will not accept a return to a status quo that he sees as threatening his regime. As Charap and Shapiro put it, "Politics in Washington and Moscow, and the interaction between them, will make it impossible to sustain. Obama's middle way will likely devolve into the very new Cold War he is seeking to avoid."[39] In their view, then, the United States must be proactive and reach a power-sharing agreement with Moscow that meets some of its demands. The first element of such a power-sharing agreement with Russia in Europe would be for the West to formally end the expansion of NATO and the European Union. The second element would be to open a dialogue with Russia on creating a new, more inclusive European security architecture that would replace, or at the very least downgrade, the role played by the European Union and NATO as the cornerstones of European security. The third element would be to recognize a special role for Russia in its neighborhood. Ukraine would be Finlandized at best. If Russia managed to wrest control of the government in Kiev, a more formal Russian role in Ukraine, including military bases, may be recognized. There would be an understanding that Russia would have a sphere of influence throughout the former Soviet Union. This influence would be more constrained in the Baltic states, but even there Moscow would be allowed a say over the treatment of ethnic Russians.

Accommodation with a view to sharing power sounds like an attractive strategy. It offers the prospect of a managed retrenchment, cooperation with rivals, a continuing U.S. role overseas in the regions, and a global leadership role. It would create a spheres-of-influence order, which, despite being very different from what we have had for the past twenty-five years, has been implemented before. But perhaps the greatest advantage of sharing power is that it will offer a way out in a time of crisis when rival powers appear on track to fight over a territory of marginal significance. As tensions rise, more people will become drawn to this strategy as an option. It is a coherent answer to a set of strategic problems.

A strategy based on power sharing and a spheres-of-influence order may be destined for popularity, but that does not make it wise or prudent. It is true that we have been here before. Sharing power always emerges as an option when a country is confronted by a revisionist rival. So it is important to look back on history and see how things went. It turns out that the only case in which accommodation ever truly "worked" was Britain's appeasement of the United States in the late nineteenth century. But it worked for a very particular reason. British appeasement of the United States certainly did not satiate the Americans. The United States pocketed the concessions and kicked Britain out of the Western Hemisphere. Instead the story had a happy ending only because the United States acted in a way commensurate with Britain's long-term interests. Specifically, the United States intervened on Britain's behalf in two world wars. American hegemony worked out pretty well for Britain, if not for the British Empire.

For a similar strategy to work for and with Russia or China, one would have to believe that these countries are as well-disposed to protecting long-term American interests as the United States was with Britain. To pose the question is to know the answer. For whatever hope there is of thinking that a democratic Russia or a democratic China would uphold the rules of the international order, there is no reason to think that Russia's dictatorship or China's authoritarian regime would do so. Instead, they would likely build on their gains, albeit gradually, and challenge the regional order in Europe and Asia.

It is one thing to say that the United States ought to sit down with its rivals and agree on spheres of influence. It is entirely another to specify where the lines of demarcation between those spheres should be. There are some places that would neatly fit into one sphere or another, but others would be heavily disputed. Moreover, there is no assurance that as the power balance continues to shift, the revisionist powers will not seek to renegotiate or update the bargain in the future. The prospect of further changes will unnerve even those countries that are outside of the revisionists' initial sphere of influence. So which countries are we willing to betray and designate as part of a sphere that they want nothing to do with?

This brings us to another reason that accommodation won't work: we live in a postcolonial world in which subjugated peoples are no longer passed around to satiate great powers. Britain pursued appeasement because it was an empire and existed in an age of empires. It had possessions it could give away, regardless of what the locals felt, and it felt little compunction about selling out small states in Central and Eastern Europe—since the very existence of these states struck them as odd, more the result of an idealist American president than of clear-headed, balance-of-power thinking. On other occasions, formal concerts had emerged after major wars, when the victorious powers sat down and ratified the status quo or some version of it.

We, by contrast, live in a post-imperial age. The United States leads an order in which it enjoys a privileged position, but it shares the dividends of this privilege with other states in an unprecedented manner. Most countries are satisfied with the status quo and their position in it. They see no compelling reason for major change. In an order dominated by democracies, the United States cannot just sit down with its competitors and rewrite the futures of independent countries and their populations. The very spectacle would be stomach-turning and hugely damaging to the legitimacy of the order. Moreover, the states affected would take matters into their own hands. There is no reason to believe that they would simply accept the revised international order. Some would most likely rearm and even seek nuclear weapons. This may even be true of countries that would remain in the U.S. sphere, since they would worry about being cast out in the future.

Accommodation is a real strategic option for dealing with the return of revisionist powers in world politics. Usually rejected in the abstract, it will become more attractive to presidents when they find themselves stuck in difficult crises with few good options. Accommodation deserves to be taken seriously, but the critique offered here is that its consequences could be calamitous. It may not succeed in turning revisionist powers into cooperative partners, and moreover pursuing accommodation would deal a devastating blow to principles that the United States has upheld since World War II.

Restraint is a powerful impulse within U.S. foreign policy and it is sure to shape one or more strategic options in a more geopolitically competitive world. But restraint tends to be most compelling as an option when it is perceived as a necessity, rather than a choice. In other words, its appeal depends in large part on whether there is a viable alternative to pursue a more competitive and forward-leaning foreign policy.

7 RESPONSIBLE COMPETITION

The United States must decide if it wants to remain a liberal superpower. Being the world's only superpower bestows great benefits. The United States leads and shapes an international order conducive to its long-term interests and values. Nobody else has that privilege. The United States also has a major, and often decisive, say in how to tackle global threats and challenges. But being a superpower also comes with an enormous price tag.[1] The country has found itself engaged in places far from its shores and on issues well removed from a narrow understanding of national interests. Other nations free-ride on American leadership and do less than they can do. Looking at this price tag, many Americans wonder if the country should retire from its role as a superpower.[2]

Retirement may appear tempting after a decade and a half of low-intensity but grueling warfare against terrorist networks and insurgents, but it would be an egregious mistake. The liberal international order has been tremendously successful in safeguarding U.S. interests while bolstering the peace and prosperity of most of the rest of the world. A more anarchic world organized around regional spheres of influence would be much less stable and would encourage revisionist states to test the limits of American resolve. Trade and economic performance would suffer. Democracy would continue its retreat. The United States would quickly find itself embroiled in conflict and from a much weaker position than it now enjoys. The real question is, How can the United States maintain its superpower status and continue to lead a liberal international order?

This is not primarily a national power problem. Some experts have argued that if only the United States could fix its domestic problems, all would be well with its foreign policy.[3] Such a view is flawed in two respects. First, the U.S. domestic economy is dependent on the global context. If the rest of the world stagnates or is troubled, the United States will not be immune. Second, America faces difficult strategic problems that will not become much easier to solve if the resources at the president's disposal increased by 10 percent or even 20 percent. Resources always help, of course, but tackling revisionism or dealing with the Middle East would be extremely thorny problems regardless. The real challenge is the management of risk: How much risk should the United States incur to uphold the liberal international order?

Responsible competition offers the best way of preserving America's status as a liberal superpower and the U.S.-led international order. It provides a framework for competition with rival powers that preserves a liberal international order as the organizing principle of world politics. The word "competition" acknowledges the adversarial and zero-sum nature characterizing relations with rival powers. The word "responsible" acknowledges that this competition can and ought to be circumscribed, since the United States must still cooperate with rivals on areas of common interest. If the United States follows a strategy of responsible competition, it will be well placed to take advantage of its global power and the support of other nations. Responsible competition rests on the assumption that the strategy of convergence ultimately failed and cannot be successfully resuscitated until there is a fundamental change in the domestic governance of China and Russia and in the Middle East as a whole.

For the theoretically minded, responsible competition can be described as a strategy of liberal internationalism for a more geopolitically competitive world. It fits with this school because it defines U.S. interests as being bound up in the preservation of a liberal international order and recognizes that the United States must play a leadership role. Responsible competition, however, diverges from more recent variants of liberal internationalism such as convergence or liberal interventionism because it sees the liberal order as facing an existential geopolitical challenge and it puts this challenge at the heart of U.S. strategy.

A NEW MINDSET

The first and most important step is a change in mindset. The United States is in a competition with Russia and China for the future of the international order. It is also locked into a competition with multiple actors in the Middle East. It is not possible to fashion win-win outcomes. Rival powers will try to weaken the U.S. model of international order and advance their own. To compete successfully, one must accept that this is in fact a competition with rational opponents who will adapt and respond to U.S. strategy.

What does this mean in practice? Take, for example, the impasse between the United States and China over the South China Sea. This is not a misunderstanding that can be easily worked out to the mutual benefit of both countries. Rather, the tensions between the two countries are rooted in strategies that are designed to be in conflict with each other: China wants to control the South China Sea, and the United States wants to prevent this. Similarly, in Europe, the United States cannot deal with Russia simply by being more transparent and by reassuring Moscow about benign U.S. intentions, because Putin is engaged in a competition to weaken the European Union and remake the European security order along lines anathema to U.S. interests.

These interactions stand in stark contrast to noncompetitive relationships. The United States and India have their differences, but they are not engaged in a security competition with each other. India is not seeking to weaken the U.S. position in Asia nor does it have designs that bring it into conflict with vital U.S. interests. True, Washington may on occasion want India to do things that it would prefer not to do, but it certainly does not seek to frustrate Indian strategic goals as defined by its government. This dynamic also applies to relations among democracies in general, even if, as in the case of the United States and India, they are not formally allied.

There is a significant literature on the competitive strategy school of thought that is a useful reference but distinct from the strategy proposed here. The competitive strategy literature stems largely from the work of Andrew Marshall, the legendary head of the Pentagon's Office of Net Assessment who retired in 2014 at the age of ninety-six, and his students. Marshall pioneered the approach of competitive strategies, which, as Stephen Peter Rosen describes, "try to get competitors to play our game, a game that we are likely to win. This is done by getting them to make the kind of mistakes that they are inclined to make, by getting them to do that which is in their nature, despite the fact that they should not do so, given their resources."[4] Competitive strategists tend to favor approaches that provoke a rival and encourage it to allocate resources in an inefficient manner. Such a strategy can be effective in long-term competitions, but it is also risky and difficult to execute.

In contrast, the kind of competition applied in a strategy of responsible competition has two components. The first is to identify your rival's strategic objectives that threaten your vital interests and prevent their realization. For our purposes, this may mean denying China control over the South China Sea or denying Russia a weakened European Union. It does not mean stopping rivals wherever they are active. In fact, such an overreaction would be counterproductive. The world will not stay static and it is not realistic to be a purely status quo power, but the world can evolve in a favorable direction. As Henry Kissinger wrote, "An equilibrium can never be permanent but must be adjusted in constant struggles."[5]

The second is to understand and advance your own strategic objectives, including by anticipating and overcoming resistance to them where necessary. This means defining today's liberal international order and designing policies, both domestic and foreign, that advance its objectives. This is complicated by the fact that the United States is engaged in several competitions simultaneously. Some overlap, but each has its own distinct logic and characteristics. Consider again Russia and China as U.S. competitors. Russia is willing to consider limited war in order to achieve its objectives, seeing its superior willpower as a strategic advantage that could give it escalation dominance in a number of contingencies. By contrast, the Chinese government is determined to avoid war, even a limited one, despite benefiting from the illusion of looming conflict. Applying a single, one-size-fits-all strategy in Europe and East Asia that does not account for these differences will meet setbacks. And this doesn't take into account the Middle East, an entirely different predicament in which the United States finds itself competing with friends and traditional rivals alike.

The United States must also balance its competitive instincts by behaving responsibly and bounding the competitions it is engaged in. The goal cannot be the destruction of the rival's state or a full-on competition to contain that state's influence wherever it pops up. Such unrestrained competition led to numerous strategic errors in the Cold War, such as mistaking Vietnamese nationalism for a global communist revolution. It is even less applicable in today's environment of interdependence and regional competition. The United States and China are closely intertwined and rely on one another to tackle shared problems. And China is not seeking to overthrow the global order. Even Russia, which is more dissatisfied with the global order, has a constructive role to play on nuclear proliferation and other issues. The responsible part of responsible competition means understanding the specific challenge that rival powers pose to the international order and responding accordingly, without overreacting or jeopardizing cooperation in other realms.

Doubling Down on the "Liberal" in Liberal Order

One of the reasons that U.S. leadership is more acceptable to other nations than the alternatives is that Americans tend to define their interests inclusively and idealistically. By insisting that the international order be liberal (by its classical meaning of an open global economy, democratic, and multilateral), the United States is offering something that appeals to a wide swath of people across all continents and nations. Democracy, an open global economy that promises greater prosperity, human rights, and a formal say in multilateral structures all speak to basic standards that people have for how they want to live their lives. Even so, in recent years, the idea that the order must be liberal has been challenged from multiple directions.

Some leaders believe that promoting democracy, freedom of the press, freedom of speech, and the rule of law automatically alienates China and Russia and will undermine hopes of international cooperation in the long run. Skeptics argue that the United States has been hypocritical in its support for these values and it should be humble and let events take their natural course elsewhere without intervening. And then there is the argument of some U.S. strategists that a values-based foreign policy damages America's interest, often resulting in the replacement of pro-American dictators with weak anti-American democracies, which many times are dominated by theocrats. On the economic front, those distrustful of global trade assert that Americans would be better served by a mercantilist approach that uses the country's size to negotiate lopsided deals advantageous to the United States.

We can take these objections one by one, but first, it is important to underscore that if any one of these arguments were accepted, American leadership would morph into a more traditional form of hegemony—fostering an order that primarily serves the interest of the hegemon with little to offer other nations beyond a sense of security and predictability. This may play well among a subset of American voters, but it would bankrupt America's legitimacy in the rest of the world. If the United States takes this path, it would become like every other hegemon or empire.

Turning to the first objection, it is true that the United States does have a choice to make as to whether to prioritize its inclusion of Russia and China in an international order over its promotion of liberal values. While inclusion seems like a good idea, it could ultimately backfire if it means compromising on the liberal nature of the order. Such a compromise would change the fundamental nature of the post–World War II order by gutting it of its legitimacy—its major advantage—and so taking the United States down a slippery slope.

Granted, the United States has a mixed record on democracy promotion. As is well known, the United States backed coups in Iran in 1953, Guatemala in 1954, and Chile in 1973. It also backed Saddam Hussein in the early 1980s and was an ally of Hosni Mubarak for several decades. But there is also another tradition whereby the United States has taken real risks to promote democracy to the vexation of pro-American authoritarian leaders—in Chile (1988), Indonesia (1998), and Egypt (2011), among others. U.S. pressure also helped promote democracy in Eastern Europe in the 1990s and in Burma in recent years. Yes, these examples show two clashing traditions, but the actions in support of democracy do refute the argument that the pro-democracy position is merely one of convenience.

In terms of economics, it is fashionable to slam trade agreements and argue that the global economy promotes inequality and unfair outcomes. There is no doubt that the international economic order is hemorrhaging legitimacy, regionally and globally. But the single greatest reason for this legitimacy deficit is not inequality, the terms of trade, overextension, or a democratic deficit. It is the lack of global growth. Economic stagnation, particularly since the 2008 financial crisis, has sapped support for globalization and internationalist politicians. Some economists believe that this is a long-term trend as technological innovation transforms the economy by decoupling productivity from employment. For instance, in his book *The Great Stagnation*, Tyler

Cowen argues that the West has exhausted those innovations that create mass employment and growth and is now seeking small improvements on the margin.[6]

However, abandoning globalization and returning to an era of mercantilism and protectionism is likely to drive growth even lower. Imposition of trade tariffs and capital controls to discourage companies from "shipping jobs overseas" could ignite a disastrous trade war with China and other large economies. At best, mercantilism offers the most powerful countries a way to take a greater slice of an ever-decreasing pie, which ends up being bad for everyone. There are valid concerns about globalization, but as former Treasury secretary Lawrence Summers has argued, there is scope to use globalization to manage the impact of integration on workers, including by eliminating corporate tax loopholes and promoting labor standards.[7]

America's foreign-policy problem is not that there is too much liberalism. It is that many people are losing faith in liberalism because it is no longer delivering what it promised. It is also under assault as authoritarian forces—inside countries and in external state sponsors like Russia—undermine democratic and open systems and push nationalist, protectionist, and populist alternatives. Those who see the merit of maintaining a liberal order must reimagine and reinvigorate it so that it offers value to billions of people the world over in its new context just as it has in the past. This means being faithful to the core principles and values that the order was founded on. It means promoting economic activity between nations, including trade, to fuel global growth. It means insisting that all nations follow basic rules about international behavior, including not unilaterally changing territorial boundaries. It means supporting democracy and human rights where possible, even if inconvenient. On this last point, there will be times when it is not possible, but we should recognize these episodes as failings and look for opportunities to correct course. As my colleague at the Brookings Institution Tamara Wittes explains, it is "not possible to be consistent but it is possible to be persistent."[8]

The U.S.-led order must be liberal, not because it is a nice approach for our global partners. Such an order must be liberal because that is in the long-term interests of America and its allies. The reason why U.S. strategy has succeeded far longer than anyone anticipated is because successive leaders fashioned a vision of the world that has appeal across boundaries and is viewed by the vast majority of nations as more just, legitimate, and advantageous than the alternatives. It is precisely when the world seems to be headed in the wrong direction and people are worried about their future that the United States ought to recommit to advancing liberal values as part of its foreign policy and international order.

Restoring the Balance of Power by Strengthening Allies

China and Russia, and a number of actors in the Middle East, have calculated that the regional balance of power has shifted in their favor. This calculation is not rooted in overall defense spending or in GDP growth. It is based on a sophisticated assessment of deployable power in particular scenarios, such as the contest for the South China Sea, the struggle for influence in Ukraine, or internal interference in the domestic politics of Arab states. A common thread in all three theaters is that the United States and its allies are not willing or able to counterbalance revisionist actions in a real and meaningful way.

To restore a stable equilibrium, the United States must first restore a favorable balance of power. As an isolated statement this may seem absurd—after all, is the United States not an unrivaled superpower? Yes, but the imbalance of power has emerged in specific and vital theaters. There are actions the United States can take: it can pursue a federated defense in East Asia by encouraging Australia, India, Japan, and others to deepen their cooperation; it can permanently station troops in the Baltics to deter Russia; and it can work with Sunni states to counter Iranian interference in their politics and violent Sunni extremism.

On the face of it, restoring a balance of power may be seen as an escalation. But as Andrew Shearer, a former Australian national security adviser, has argued in the case of East Asia, it "should be seen as stabilizing rather than provocative." Improving allied capabilities, he argues, is "instrumental to ensuring that Beijing has realistic expectations about the extent to which other countries will tolerate changes to the regional order—and thereby positively influence China's behavior and choices."[9] The same can be said in Europe and the Middle East. The United States must deepen its engagement with its allies in these regions to convince revisionist powers that it has its allies' back and will be steadfast in opposition to geopolitical challenges to the regional order.

Viewing Free-Riding in Its Proper Perspective

Alliances are the linchpin of U.S. strategy. The U.S. alliance system has been the secret of America's grand-strategy success more than any other factor. Alliances are a power multiplier, a stabilizing force in the regions, and a source of legitimacy. Some people, including Presidents Obama and Trump, have become frustrated with America's alliances because many of them free-ride on American power, which is to say they rely on the United States to provide their security without "paying for it." Americans ask why the allies should not spend more on defense or take care of their own neighborhood. It's tempting to try to square the circle and say that allies must do more, and the United States less, if the alliances are to remain valid. But while this sounds good in theory, it does not work in practice.

To begin with, the allies do not believe that the arrangement is a one-way street. They point out that they repeatedly side with the United States even when they may have disagreed with it. The Iraq War of 2003 is a case in point. Many countries, including the United Kingdom, Australia, Spain, Saudi Arabia, and others, supported the Bush administration in large part because the United States asked them to. Being faithful to the alliance is what mattered, not just the merits and demerits of the case at hand. One can disagree with the invasion of Iraq, but it is important to remember that the loyalty of allies has been a strategic asset of the United States for decades. Japan, for instance, paid for a large part of the first Gulf War. The allies would argue that this solidarity across time is a form of burden sharing.

Beyond this, it is important to realize that some free-riding is part of the price the United States must pay for the benefits of being a superpower. Free-riding has been a complaint of every American president going back to Eisenhower. It occurs because the United States sees it in its interest to partially provide for the security of others. For instance, the United States does not want Japan to build up its defenses, including acquiring its own nuclear weapons, to the point that it worries its neighbors. It is better to have Japan enmeshed in an alliance with the United States. Moreover, if allies are partly dependent on the United States, it is less likely that they will act in ways that undermine U.S. interests. Consider the case of Saudi Arabia. In recent years, Saudi Arabia has done more to provide for its own security because

Riyadh worries about the U.S. commitment to the alliance. But this newfound strategic independence has made Saudi Arabia more insecure and willing to take risks, which included launching an ill-advised intervention in Yemen. You can have allies that engage in some free-riding or you can have allies that might act in ways that the United States does not like. You cannot have the best of both worlds.

The real issue is how to strengthen the alliances to make them more effective. By all means, presidents should press the country's allies to spend more and do more. Donald Trump's surprising victory in the 2016 presidential election provides an opportunity to make this argument anew. Trump can push other nations to spend more on their defense, which he raised as an issue in the campaign. But he should not threaten to disengage from alliance relationships, nor should he demand direct payment to the United States for security commitments. In this more competitive world, both the United States and the allies will have to do more. The United States will inevitably take on a disproportionate share of the burden, but this has never been without recompense.

PROMOTING RESPONSIBLE COMPETITION IN EUROPE

The United States has long seen the value in a stable Europe and played an active role in the formation of the European Union and its predecessor, the European Economic Community. U.S. security guarantees and quiet diplomacy empowered Europe's leaders to make enlightened choices that were previously unthinkable. This resulted in a more united Europe that served U.S. interests in multiple ways, most importantly by transforming Europe from a source of conflict into a bastion of peace and freedom (first in Western, then in Central and Eastern Europe). In addition, a united Europe provided an effective counterweight to the Soviet Union and offers the United States a partner that has been a constructive force in world affairs.

The United States now faces two problems in Europe—a weakened European Union that is gradually disintegrating, and a revisionist Russia that is using hard power to remake the European security order. The United States cannot be impartial or disinterested about the future of the European Union, and it cannot let aggravations about burden-sharing tempt it to disengage from Europe's security problems. It must also recognize that Putin's strategic objective is to weaken the European Union and NATO in order to remake Europe's security order into a great-power spheres-of-influence system. Putin sees the European Union as an existential threat to his regime and has sought to destroy it through a variety of tactics, including funding far right and far left parties, weaponizing refugee flows from Syria to the European Union as a political tool, backing Brexit, and using force on Europe's periphery. This reality is often lost in discussions about whether to extend or suspend sanctions or to reengage with Russia. Regardless of whether the European Union seeks to renormalize relations with Russia, it will have to live with a thinking opponent perched on its border, one dedicated to its demise. If Putin's regime somehow collapsed and Russia became a failed state, the repercussions could be even greater.

There are two strategic questions to answer in designing a strategy for competing responsibly in Europe. The first is how to reengage with European allies in order to strengthen the European Union, liberal democracy, and internationalism so that Europe is a partner in upholding the liberal international order. It is not obvious what role Washington can play in restoring European growth, tackling populist movements, or bolstering the European Union. The second question is how to balance

Russia responsibly so as to avoid a new cold war or an actual war. While Putin has no intention of starting a war with the United States, he is willing to use force as a tactic to advance his agenda. He believes that Russia may prevail in a limited war thanks to its superior willpower and its nuclear arsenal. This makes the situation particularly perilous.

To strengthen the European Union, the United States must fully reengage with it. Some parts of this reengagement will be fairly straightforward and uncontroversial. U.S. diplomats cannot talk about pivoting away from Europe or leaving Europe. The president should spend time developing strong personal relationships with European leaders based on a shared commitment to building a liberal international order. The United States should reinstate exchanges and deepen engagement with large European countries, especially Germany. During the Cold War, there were many opportunities to build networks of American and European politicians, military officers, academics, businesspeople, and journalists. This interconnectedness helped shape a shared worldview.

Apart from greater diplomatic engagement, there are real changes the United States could make to its Europe policy today if it were to adopt a strategy of responsible competition. First, the United States should not jeopardize European security to make a point about free-riding. President Obama once told the *Atlantic* that "it was precisely in order to prevent the Europeans and the Arab states from holding our coats while we did all the fighting that we, by design, insisted" that they lead the Libya intervention. "It was part of the anti–free rider campaign."[10] The failure of the Libya intervention exacerbated the refugee and migration crisis and the ISIS threat. If a similar crisis occurs in the future, the United States should make a realistic assessment about what

Europe is capable of, and its primary objective should be resolving the crisis in a way that enhances U.S. and European security, not grandstanding about burden-sharing.

Second, the United States should work with the European Union and individual European states to find a diplomatic solution to several of the crises that Europe faces. One example is EU-Turkish diplomacy in early 2016. The European Union sought a deal with Erdoğan to stem the flow of asylum seekers to Europe from Turkey, but Erdoğan was aggressive and obstructionist. An imperfect deal was finally reached. At the time, senior German officials privately noted the absence of any American engagement in the talks with Ankara. Had the United States directly inserted itself into these negotiations and used a mixture of carrots and sticks to encourage a deal that would resolve the crisis, the talks would undoubtedly have borne a more effective, legitimate, and less controversial outcome.

Another example is Brexit and the future of European integration. The United States will never be a central player on these issues, but it does have an important supporting role to play. On Brexit, America's objective must be a successful independent Britain and a successful European Union. Washington can work with London to deepen U.S.-UK relations, it can support deeper integration in the rest of the EU, and it can use quiet diplomacy to lobby both sides to avoid grandstanding or excessively hard lines in the Article 50 negotiations, which will determine the mechanics of Brexit.

Third, and this may be the most sensitive issue between the United States and Europe, the United States must revisit economic policy. The United States believes in a Keynesian fiscal policy and in using monetary policy to encourage growth. Germany is a stringent critic of this position and believes in balanced budgets, even with negative interest rates, and a tight monetary policy. There is no easy way to square this circle, but it is clear that the European approach is contributing to a prolonged period of stagnation that endangers the European Union itself. Most other EU member states share these concerns. The United States must continue to press Germany on economic policy and it should not be shy about intervening diplomatically in a time of political crisis, such as the Greek crisis of 2015.

Fourth, the United States should not accommodate Russia's demand to remake the European security architecture so that it has special great-power privileges and influence over the regional order. Russia may frame this issue as one of inclusion and fairness, but in truth it is a means of undermining the principle that all states are equally sovereign and get to decide their own system of government and manage their own foreign relations with other countries. In practical terms, the Russian model of order would mean the substantial weakening, and maybe even the end, of the European Union and NATO.

We need to be very clear-sighted about what rejecting the Russian proposal means. Russia will not accept a return to normality whereby it accepts and engages with a NATO- and EU-dominated Europe. Russia will push back, threatening the European security order at three different pressure points: nonallied countries, the internal politics of the European Union, and NATO deterrence. Let's take these one by one.

Of all three threats, competition over non-allied countries (non-NATO and non-EU) to build a sphere of influence may be the toughest. As described in detail earlier, Russia has a key strategic advantage in its near abroad—it is more willing to fight for its sphere of influence than is the United States or Western Europe. If the West arms the Ukrainian government, Russia will likely respond with further escalation, up to and including a proxy war with Western powers. Some of the other solutions commonly suggested are also not as strong as they first appear. For example, economic assistance to Ukraine is ineffective when Russia can dial up the security threat to the government, both externally through aggression and internally by activating its intelligence assets.

Rather, the United States should deploy to Ukraine nonlethal assistance—such as radar, unmanned aerial vehicles, and body armor—and promise to provide lethal assistance and new sanctions in the event of further Russian aggression. Sanctions are the West's asymmetrical advantage over Putin. Sanctions must be used sparingly, but they are entirely justified in response to territorial aggression. It is true that they are not always effective in the short term—they did not persuade Putin to pull out of eastern Ukraine or to reverse the annexation of Crimea. But they have had a significant effect on his strategic calculations. The fighting in Donbass was largely contained, even though many analysts believed that Putin would strike out to Mariupol and even farther. It is likely that these decisions were affected by the threat of much more severe financial sanctions. The United States should also work with Ukraine and other countries to harden the target by encouraging political and economic reform, including anti-corruption measures; initiating market reforms; strengthening the rule of law; and fostering cooperation between the intelligence communities. This type of cooperation can also occur during peacetime, when it is more likely to be effective.

Meanwhile, the United States and the European Union ought to learn lessons from the Ukraine crisis and exercise caution to avoid providing Putin with a pretext for dramatically escalating a crisis. For instance, the United States can deepen its cooperation with Georgia and Ukraine but it should not press for NATO Membership Action Plans that would very likely lead to immediate military action by Russia and to which Washington would struggle to respond.

The United States must also think through the implications of Russia's interference in Western elections, not just in Europe but also in the United States. Special steps must be taken to increase intelligence-sharing in order to counter Russian infiltration and covert actions designed to help pro-Russian political parties. If Russia does launch cyber attacks to influence an election in a NATO country, the target state should consider invoking Article 5, NATO's mutual defense clause, which was updated in the 2016 NATO summit in Warsaw to include cyber contingencies. NATO should then consider an appropriate and unified response, possibly including a cyber response or sanctions. The United States should also engage diplomatically and economically in Central and Eastern Europe to help democratic and internationalist politicians stave off the new wave of authoritarianism and nationalism. As a superpower and the provider of security in NATO, the United States has special leverage in Poland, Hungary, Slovakia, and other nations.

Finally, strengthening deterrence in NATO will be the mission most familiar to Americans. The challenge is that Russia may wager that many NATO member states would not go to war to defend the Baltic states from a limited Russian attack or incursions. If true, this would give Putin an opportunity to discredit Article 5, whereby an attack on one is treated as an attack on all. NATO officials are aware of this risk and have already taken steps to bolster deterrence by creating a task force of five thousand soldiers that could deploy at short notice. The key to effective deterrence is to convince Moscow that any attack on the

Baltics would immediately involve U.S. forces. This means a trip-wire force in the Baltics—whether permanent or on continual rotation—as well as clear statements from the U.S. president that he or she regards Article 5 as inviolable.

With a responsible competition strategy, the United States should also make it clear that it is balancing Putin's Russia, not Russia itself. This is a shift from the Cold War, when containment was directed against the Soviet Union, not the Soviet leader. Thus when Stalin died, the United States refused to countenance détente with the new Soviet leadership, even though Winston Churchill, then Britain's prime minister, strongly supported exploring it. Churchill saw Stalin, not the USSR, as the problem and he believed that Eisenhower's refusal was a historic error that would prolong the Cold War. This time, the United States should make clear that it is open to détente with a Russia that remains authoritarian as long as it abandons Putinism.

JUGGLING A RANGE OF INTERESTS AND RISKS IN EAST ASIA

U.S. balancing against China must be focused on East Asia. East Asia is a strategically vital region for U.S. interests, and Chinese attempts to upend the East Asian order are stoking nationalism and security rivalries. If China succeeds in building a spheres-of-influence order there, it would destabilize the regional and global orders. By contrast, the westward expansion of Chinese influence—into Pakistan, Central Asia, and the Middle East—is relatively benign to U.S. interests and the global order so the United States should take a much more relaxed view of it. In addition, a growing Chinese economy is in the interests of the United States and its allies, even if it means greater Chinese economic influence in Europe and East Asia. U.S. leaders must clearly communicate that their problem is not with rising Chinese power per se; it is with where and how this power is directed and toward what end. The truly disturbing aspect of Chinese strategy is that its primary goal is the revision of the regional order in East Asia. A secondary concern is that China might try to advance illiberal goals globally—something it has flirted with, although not to the extent Russia has.

The key to crafting U.S. strategy in East Asia is to understand something very fundamental about the Chinese strategy: it requires the avoidance of war to achieve its goals. It is not about preparing to fight and win a conflict with the United States. It is not about preparing to invade its neighbors. It is about changing the balance of power in peacetime so that one day the region and the United States will realize that China has achieved power parity and a sphere of influence, so that the path of least resistance will be to accept that and accommodate China. If war were to break out, it would shatter this plan. Chinese military installations in the South China Sea, which would otherwise have geopolitical influence, would be wiped out quickly. The Chinese leaders also know that if a war occurred and if China were defeated, the Chinese Communist Party regime would surely come to an end.

Current U.S. strategy toward China is confused. Some believe that China can only displace the United States in East Asia by winning a major war and that the primary goal of U.S. strategy must be to prepare to fight and win such a war, which would help deter China from ever starting it. Others take the opposite view, citing the 1914 scenario of inadvertent conflict, and argue that the United States must exhibit great caution to avoid misunderstandings and accidents that could spiral out of control. According to this view, the United States can impose some costs on China for revisionist actions, but it must also reassure China that it is exercising restraint.

Both approaches—war preparations and reassurance—miss the point. Yes, the United States should maintain its military advantage because if that gap closed significantly Chinese strategists could revisit their opposition to war with America. But focusing exclusively on preparation for the next major war misses the peacetime challenge that China poses. And reassurance plays right into China's hands. While the United States should not be careless or overly provocative in its behavior toward China, working relentlessly toward a code of conduct that China rejects or practicing restraint while China pushes its advantage would give Beijing the time and space for its strategy to succeed.

The United States must prepare to wage a peacetime competition to strengthen the U.S.-led regional order and to prevent China from achieving its vision of a spheres-of-influence order. In reality, great-power peace (properly understood as the absence of war) is relatively stable and durable in East Asia, even though it is in China's interest to pretend it is fragile. Even if there were a collision of vessels or a standoff over an island, China would maintain its strategy of incremental revisionism while avoiding war. The United States has considerable geopolitical space to push back against China in peacetime without triggering a crisis or a conflict. This is one way in which East Asia is distinct from Europe, where Russian strategy condones war as a tactic to achieve its goals.

The objective of America's China strategy ought to be twofold. The first is to deny China a significant sphere of influence in East Asia, particularly in the South and East China Seas. This approach would not entail preventing every act of land reclamation or building military installations. China will have individual successes that the United States can do very little about. What matters is the overall strategic effect and preventing the South China Sea from becoming a Chinese lake. The United States should not and cannot allow the Chinese navy to control access to the South China Sea and to bequeath open seas to other nations with the option to take them away. It is a similar story in the East China Sea, where the United States and Japan cannot allow the Chinese navy to become the dominant force.

Such a strategic objective certainly means expanding and sustaining freedom of navigation operations and rendering meaningless any Air Defense Identification Zone. It also means taking proactive steps by working with U.S. allies to ensure that the South China Sea is a contested space. The July 2016 decision by an international tribunal (the Permanent Court of Arbitration) that China's claims in the South China Sea have no basis in international law provides a diplomatic opportunity to build an international coalition in favor of a multilateral approach to settling disputes. If China continues to push the envelope by building islands in the South China Sea, the United States could, for example, equip the Philippines and Vietnam with dredging equipment so they can do the same. The United States could sell anti-access/area-denial equipment to its allies and partners to raise the risk to Beijing of operating in the South China Sea. The United States could even pressure Taiwan to open the archives and release the original documentation on the nine-dash line (what Taiwan calls the eleven-dash line) and subject it to intense legal scrutiny—a step that China has long opposed. The United States should stop short of drawing red lines and threatening war if China continues to build its sphere of influence, however, because such a threat would be disproportionate, unwise, and not credible.

Preserving the liberal order in East Asia does not mean risking war to prevent every Chinese land reclamation, land strip, or maritime advance. The equilibrium in East Asia will never be fixed or permanent, but it can be maintained amid adjustments and persistent competition. The balance of power and the balance of influence may look modestly different than they do today but what is important is that they continue to favor the liberal order strategy instead of the spheres-of-influence alternative.

The second strategic objective must be to build, strengthen, and expand the U.S.-led liberal order so it is in robust health and provides a better alternative to the Chinese-led spheres-of-influence model. The United States should leverage Chinese assertiveness to deepen and strengthen its alliances and strategic partnerships with China's neighbors. This is the most obvious way of imposing costs on Beijing for revisionist behavior and it serves to bolster the existing order. The United States must also provide an economic vision for the region. It can begin by reviving and reforming the Trans-Pacific Partnership, a mega trade deal with eleven other countries that was negotiated by President Obama but disowned and opposed by President Trump. The TPP could be renegotiated to address thorny issues like the role of state-owned enterprises in investment decisions and currency manipulation.[11] The United States should deepen its relations with India, the world's largest democracy. India's strategic history precludes a formal alliance but there is a great deal that can be done short of that, including greater defense cooperation, assisting India in building its maritime capabilities, and working together on energy and climate change. The United States should also encourage closer strategic ties between Asian nations, including between Japan and Australia, India and Australia, India and Japan, and Japan and South Korea. As scholars from the Center for Strategic and International Studies have argued, Asia needs a federated defense whereby America's allies work closely with one another through "aligned strategies, force postures, operating concepts, [and] training and logistics," all of which would be "delivered through shared defense capabilities, facilities and other infrastructure, and jointly developed and acquired systems."[12]

China does have some red lines that it could not avoid going to war over: three in particular. There is every reason to think that Beijing cannot accept Taiwanese independence and that it would go to war to prevent it from happening. It will also use economic sanctions and other punitive measures on any government, presumably a Democratic Progressive Party (DPP) government, that moves in that direction. The second red line is the collapse of North Korea. There is reason to believe that China would use its army to prevent a unified Korea allied with the United States from reaching the Chinese border, if the house of Kim falls. And the third red line is any threat that could topple the Chinese Communist Party (CCP) regime. With its back to the wall, the Chinese government may choose war over regime collapse. It is hard to know what form this could take. It is unlikely to be simply nationalist disquiet over an island dispute. The United States must take these three red lines seriously. It should continue its balanced Taiwan policy; it should exercise great caution and consult with Beijing in the event that the house of Kim falls; and it should be careful not to take advantage of a Chinese domestic crisis to advance regime change in China.

North Korea poses a particularly difficult problem. Long the outlaw of Asia, North Korea has relied on blackmail, calculated aggression, and its nuclear program as the pillars of its foreign policy. The rise to power of Kim Jong-un has injected even more uncertainty and volatility into the situation. Kim has angered

China with his behavior, including by killing his uncle, Jang Sung-taek, who was one of the leading interlocutors with Beijing. He has also accelerated North Korea's efforts to develop an intercontinental ballistic missile capable of hitting the continental United States with a nuclear weapon. Kim seems to believe that this would be a game-changer that would deter the United States from defending South Korea and would allow him a freer hand to engage in acts of aggression in the region.

China is stuck in a bind on North Korea. It has little sympathy for Kim but it does not want to see the country's collapse, which could cause millions of refugees to pour into China and lead to a unified Korea allied with the United States. North Korea's increasingly erratic behavior and its pursuit of an ICBM capability, however, change the equation. The United States cannot tolerate the threat of nuclear attack from North Korea and will be tempted to act preemptively. To avert this, Washington and Beijing must deepen their cooperation on North Korea before Pyongyang acquires such a capability and consider new ways of putting additional pressure on the regime and of imposing credible red lines regarding threats to the United States.

MIDDLE EAST: THE CASE FOR INCREASED U.S. ENGAGEMENT

The U.S.-led regional order in the Middle East was never very liberal to begin with, but what was there lies in ruins. The question is whether the United States ought to proactively rebuild a new regional order in its place, keeping in mind the very real limitations about what is actually possible. In principle, a responsible-competition approach could include retrenchment from the region or engagement with it. The case for retrenchment mirrors that of a sharing of power: engagement of all kinds have failed; if the United States becomes involved, it will pay a heavy price; and there are better places for the United States to invest its resources. While these are good arguments, there is a compelling reason for increased engagement in the Middle East: the implosion of a region as large as the Middle East would inevitably undermine the current liberal order in Europe and beyond.

The view that the United States should disengage from the Middle East typically rests on the claim that the region is in the throes of a great upheaval rooted in old rivalries that is likely to last for decades, akin to Europe's Thirty Years' War. There is little the United States can do to arrest this descent into conflict, so it should try to stay out and limit its exposure to it, or so the argument goes. But this view is deeply problematic. Imagine that its premise is correct—the Middle East is in the early stages of a catastrophic, decades-long conflict that could kill more than a quarter of the population of the affected states. Or even suppose it was not as bad, but still the worst war since World War II. Such a disaster would have immense implications for the global order. It would utterly devastate and transform the region, and have a major impact on Turkey and the European Union, possibly to the extent of ending the six-decades-old European project.

The question in the Middle East is not whether certain narrow interests—such as maintaining the supply of oil, preventing terrorist safe havens, and protecting the security of Israel—are currently affected. The question is where the trajectory is headed. If the answer is anywhere close to the worst-case scenarios, then the United States, as the world's only superpower and the leader of the international order, has an obligation to intercede, arrest the march of history, and help to achieve an equilibrium that may be imperfect but is far better than a decades-long conflict.

At this stage, it is impossible to say what such an equilibrium would be, much as it was impossible to predict in 1620 what the 1648 Peace of Westphalia would look like. But America's short-term goals are readily identifiable. The United States has a vital interest in stabilizing the region and halting the unraveling, to protect vital U.S. interests both in the region and further afield. Tempting as it is to focus exclusively on East Asia, Europe, and areas of greater economic opportunity, the crisis in the Middle East is not self-containing. It must be deliberately contained by U.S. policy.

There are no easy answers. Acknowledging that the United States should be engaged in the region diplomatically and militarily in order to seek a new equilibrium is itself a departure from America's Middle East policy from 2011 to 2016. Such a change in mindset ought to create the political space in Washington for initiatives across a wide range of areas, from gaining leverage in the Syrian civil war by putting pressure on Russia and Assad to working with partners in the region to improve governance. For it is important to realize that the United States is not doing a favor to its allies by being so engaged; it is looking out for its long-term interests.

The United States is better at certain things than others. A decade of war in Iraq and repeated interventions in the greater Middle East show that there are limits on what the United States can accomplish in reforming states internally. This is not to say that reform should not be attempted, but we must be humble in our expectations of what can be accomplished. Moreover, the United States tends to be better at traditional geopolitics, including reassurance, deterrence, and alliance management. These strategies have been lacking in recent years, and it is in this domain that there is the greatest scope for improvement. Geopolitical approaches can also be a critical component in stabilizing the sectarian-infused geopolitical struggle between Saudi Arabia and Iran.

The best prospect for restoring stability to the Middle East is to reengage with America's traditional Arab allies in the region. Yes, this approach has obvious flaws. These allies are much more problematic than America's allies in Europe and Asia. They are authoritarian and some led the suppression of the Arab Spring. Nevertheless, there are no good options and this is far better than the alternatives of further disengagement or aligning with Iran.

Reengaging with allies could begin with Saudi Arabia, where there are glimmers of reform for the first time in over half a century. The deputy crown prince, Mohammed bin Salman, is poised to be the next leader of Saudi Arabia and is driving a reform program to modernize the Saudi economy and take it off its reliance on oil by 2030.[13] The United States should back the Saudi government in this effort. Bruce Riedel, a former senior intelligence official on Saudi Arabia, has argued that the only time the United States ever succeeded in persuading Saudi Arabia to reform was in 1962 when two conditions were met. The first was that Crown Prince Faisal (later king) wanted to abolish slavery but faced domestic opposition. The second was that President Kennedy pressed him privately and made reform a condition for American cooperation—something Riedel says no president did before or has done since. This combination meant that the reform package passed. Hillary Clinton would have been well positioned to repeat this feat as president given her commitment to women's rights and the deputy crown prince's commitment to domestic reform. That moment has passed, but if President Trump, or more likely a future president, were to make reform in Saudi Arabia a priority, it may not be beyond reach.[14] On foreign policy, Washington should encourage Saudi Arabia to play a constructive role in the region, including with Israel where there has already been some informal behind-the-scenes cooperation. Having reestablished trust, the United States should work quietly to discourage the Saudis from imprudent actions, such as the ill-advised intervention in Yemen.

Egypt is, in many ways, the toughest case in the region for U.S. foreign policy. Abdel el-Fattah al-Sisi appears to have restored order to Egypt, but his suppression of the political opposition and reluctance to carry out far-reaching economic reform all but guarantee that Egypt will remain profoundly unstable and vulnerable to revolution. Moreover, if al-Sisi fails and Egypt descends into civil war or massive upheaval, the repercussions for the region would be severe. Ideally, the United States could make support for al-Sisi contingent on political reform, but it is abundantly clear that al-Sisi will not tolerate any role for the Muslim Brotherhood or political Islam more generally. The United States should avoid the temptation to unconditionally support al-Sisi. This would buy time but would make Egypt less stable over the long run. While political reform is out of reach for the time being, Washington should press al-Sisi hard on introducing economic reforms, linking their introduction to cooperation between the two countries. It should also make clear that the United States believes he should not serve more than two terms in office and it should engage with him on ensuring that the succession reflects the will of the Egyptian people.

Relations with Turkey plummeted after the attempted coup of 2016, for which Turkish President Recep Tayyip Erdoğan blamed the United States. Turkey remains a member of NATO and merits U.S. support. Toward this end, the United States should be more sensitive to Turkey's legitimate security concerns in Syria. But Turkey's NATO membership works both ways—NATO members are expected to adhere to democratic standards and the United States must hold Erdoğan to this.

A key part of reengaging with America's Arab and Muslim allies will be to balance against Iran. The United States should encourage greater cooperation, including formally, with Israel. This will require tough choices in the Arab world but it may also necessitate Israel's reengagement with the peace process to remove one of the reasons that Arab publics oppose overt cooperation. The balancing of Iran should primarily be diplomatic, though to be successful in such conditions, diplomacy must include a coercive element backed by military power and the potential use of force. The United States can also encourage greater military cooperation between Arab states as a way of containing Iran by attaching conditions to arms sales to individual Arab governments. These conditions would require Arab states to work with one another on operations such as joint radar and air defense.[15] In addition, the United States can push back against Iran by insisting on strict enforcement of the 2015 nuclear deal and by working with its partners to limit Iranian influence in the Gulf.

The United States should make clear to Tehran, however, that this balancing is a response to its aggressive and revisionist behavior. If Iran pursues a different and more cooperative course, the path will be open to greater engagement. It is containment with a view to engagement, not containment with a view to regime change. If this balancing strategy leads Iran to be more cooperative, the United States could work with Tehran on a negotiated federal settlement to the Syrian civil war and the tamping down of regional rivalries. If this diplomacy is fruitful it could continue with the long-term goal of a regional settlement that would both guarantee minority and majority rights within each state and establish the principle of non-interference by

Iran.[16] This endpoint is a very long way off and may never be achieved, but it could be explored if the conditions were right. From Iran's perspective, the incentive would be threefold: guaranteed rights, influence, and status for Shiite populations in Sunni states; regional stability; and the conditions for greater economic engagement with the Arab world and the West.

The geopolitical piece of the Middle East puzzle is not sufficient to stabilize the region, but it is a necessary component.

PROSPECTS FOR PROGRESS ON ESSENTIAL GLOBAL ISSUES

As the United States competes with Russia and China, and as it works to impose stability in the Middle East, it cannot lose sight of the many areas in which the United States must cooperate with its rivals out of a shared interest. Volatility in the global economy, climate change, counterterrorism, and nuclear proliferation are challenges for all major powers regardless of their geopolitical ambitions—and they are problems for which progress is extremely unlikely without sustained cooperation. The issue is whether it is possible to cooperate on these problems while competing on others.

In theory, the answer should be yes. After all, the United States worked closely with Putin's Russia to negotiate the nuclear deal with Iran even while the two countries were at loggerheads over Russia's aggression against Ukraine. The Paris Agreement on climate change, which included the United States, Russia, and China, came at a tense time in both Syria and the South China Sea. The United States must avoid the temptation to link negotiations on transnational issues to regional geopolitical competitions, for it is wise to try to keep all the rivals inside the tent when the stakes are universally high.

Nevertheless, it is easy to imagine that cooperation will become much more difficult over time. To take a small example, when Malaysia Airlines flight MH370 went missing in 2014, countries in the region refused to fully share sensitive radar and satellite data because they worried that these data would reveal their military capabilities to rivals. China was circumspect because its capabilities were very advanced, whereas India initially refused to discuss its data for precisely the opposite reason—it had limited capabilities and little to offer, a weakness it did not want to reveal to others.[17] Keep in mind that this was a Malaysian plane with 239 passengers, most of whom were Chinese. The interests of all parties should have been perfectly aligned, but the investigation was complicated by the shadow of future rivalry. Now think about how complex and difficult it would be to arrange a coordinated response to a new Asian financial crisis if it were to occur in the near future. China, and maybe Japan, would undoubtedly be thinking not just about how to end the crisis, but also how to do so in a way that would increase its own regional influence and possibly damage a rival.

There is no easy fix to this problem. The harsh truth is that Asian nations were not being paranoid to worry about revealing their radar capabilities in the search for MH370. They were right. Their vulnerabilities would have been noted and used against them by their competitors. It would be naïve and counterproductive to deny this basic fact, and it would be irresponsible to call on leaders to set those concerns aside. Countries will have to navigate these issues when they arise and they will need to remember that they have shared interests as well as conflicts of interest. They must adopt a balanced approach to relations with rivals, cooperating where possible and competing when necessary.

In this more geopolitically competitive world, the United States must think hard about how inclusive it wants the international order to be. Requiring the approval of Russia and China before acting could be a recipe for gridlock and failure. However, deliberately excluding them as a matter of principle would be equally foolhardy. Instead of following either of these paths, the United States should try to create an architecture of cooperation that works best if all countries participate but also functions adequately even if rival powers object. This means being able to fall back on coalitions of like-minded powers in the event that cooperation with Moscow or Beijing proves impossible.

It is important to remember that Russia and China have, by definition, an interest in effectively tackling shared challenges, especially climate change (more for China than Russia), nuclear proliferation, and terrorism. Linking geopolitical problems to transnational problems, then, could actually make cooperation on transnational problems less likely because it will give Russia and China an incentive to be obstructionist in the hope of making gains elsewhere. Compartmentalizing this cooperation can help. Nations should agree not to link these efforts to ongoing rivalries. As mentioned, it was right to keep Russia in the nuclear talks on Iran; it will also be necessary to engage Russia on other transnational challenges even if tensions are high over Ukraine or the Middle East. The most difficult problems will arise with China: because the levels of interdependence between China and the West are so high, China will be tempted to link issues. The West must be clear that it will not allow such linkages to be made and if they are, that Western nations are willing to pay the price of lower cooperation. Once that principle has been established, it is likely that the great powers will cooperate on these issues when it is in their interest to do so.

Cooperation with Russia and China on the global economy will be complicated by the fact that each country, including the United States, will be tempted to use for geopolitical purposes any leverage that it gains through engagement. If Russia is dependent on the United States for its banking system, an American president will be tempted to use that dependence in a time of crisis. No assurance given now can change that reality. Similarly, Russia would use any influence it has over the price of energy and China would use its economic influence over small countries and even over the United States, with which it is intertwined financially.

The United States should not allow itself or its allies to become dependent on geopolitical rivals except when absolutely necessary. In thinking this through, it is not enough to ask if both countries will benefit from the interaction. One must imagine the likely incentive structure at a time of heightened geopolitical tension. Would China be willing to take a hit financially to inflict pain on the United States? If the answer is yes or even if it is unclear, it may be a risky form of engagement. In practice, this means reducing U.S. exposure to China on U.S. Treasury holdings and other systemically important asset types. It also means helping U.S. allies to diversify in order to reduce their own dependencies on geopolitical rivals. Dependence can never be eliminated for smaller countries in the neighborhood of a geopolitical rival, but initiatives like the Trans-Pacific Partnership and Transatlantic Trade and Investment Partnership, or other forms of economic engagement, can provide some protection.

The United States must also be cognizant of, and somewhat sympathetic to, the fact that Russia, China, and Iran will look for ways to reduce their exposure to U.S.- and Western-dominated systems. This will reduce U.S. leverage but it may have the effect of stabilizing great-power relations. There is a parallel here to the Cold War. The United States and the Soviet Union took some time to realize that it was better for both of them if neither side could beat the other by using nuclear weapons first. If your rival had a survivable nuclear arsenal, it would be more secure and so less likely to preemptively use nuclear weapons. Today, Russia and China worry that a lopsided economic order could give the United States added incentives to take action against them.

Responsible competition is a comprehensive strategy for a more competitive but still interdependent world. It requires increased U.S. engagement in the three most strategically important regions, but it is focused in its efforts and offers clear guidance on how U.S. leaders can set priorities in foreign policy. The goal of this strategy is not to defeat or collapse U.S. competitors, as it was during World War II and the Cold War. Rather, it is to create a global situation of strength that incentivizes these competitors to become status quo powers. In the Middle East, its objective is to reestablish a favorable balance of power so as to provide the foundation for future progress.

EPILOGUE

Trumpism and the Global Order

In the alternative history novel *The Plot Against America*, Philip Roth imagines a world in which the aviator Charles Lindbergh wins the U.S. presidency in 1940, defeating Franklin Delano Roosevelt. Lindbergh was one of America's first celebrities, famous as the first man to fly across the Atlantic and for his child having been kidnapped in the "crime of the century." In the late 1930s, he led the America First movement—a pro-German, isolationist organization that sought to keep the United States out of World War II. In Roth's novel, President Lindbergh, elected thanks to his celebrity and the public's desire for peace, accepts Hitler's conquests in Europe and turns the United States into an anti-Semitic state.

In the real world, of course, Lindbergh did not stand for the nomination, and Roosevelt beat a Republican internationalist, Wendell Willkie. After Pearl Harbor, America First was discredited and was never spoken of again in polite company—until 2016, that is, when Donald Trump appropriated the term as his campaign slogan. Trump's knowledge of Lindbergh appears limited, but the America First label does convey something very important about his foreign policy. Trump is the first president who campaigned against the liberal international order that the United States created after World War II and has led ever since. Every other president accepted the parameters of postwar U.S. strategy, but Trump argued that American leadership of the order was hurting the United States.

This argument was not just something he plucked from thin air. Trump has a set of core beliefs about the world that date back thirty years to when he spent $95,000 to buy a full-page advertisement in the *New York Times*, the *Boston Globe*, and the *Washington Post* and used it to publish an open letter to the American people about his views on U.S. foreign policy.[1] Three beliefs stand out. Trump has been a staunch critic of America's security alliances since the 1987 letter and has demanded that U.S. allies transfer vast sums of money to the United States in exchange for protection. He has opposed every trade deal the United States has signed since World War II and advocated for the widespread use of tariffs. And he has a soft spot for authoritarian strongmen, particularly of the Russian variety. This appears to date back to 1990, when he visited Russia and came back deeply disillusioned with Mikhail Gorbachev and convinced that Moscow should have emulated China in repressing dissent, as China did in Tiananmen Square. Trump repeatedly raised these views in the campaign, even when it was politically costly to do so (as in his praise of Vladimir Putin).

At the time of writing (December 2016), we do not know if and how Trump's personal beliefs will affect U.S. foreign policy. It is likely that his administration will contain people with a variety of views—some probably with Trump's own America First perspective, some who want to fight a global and religiously infused war against radical Islam, and some who support traditional U.S. strategy—and Trump's core beliefs may be somewhat diluted. However, there is no doubt that the election of 2016 is a highly significant event for U.S. grand strategy. It demonstrates that American commitment to the order is not guaranteed. A significant constituency in the United States wants to do much less in the world and to define its interests narrowly rather than in terms of a healthy international order.

The liberal international order has been around for so long that we take it for granted—not just by assuming that it will survive but also by assuming that even if it goes away, we can still be assured of peace and prosperity. We may now be about to test that proposition. Four years of American nationalism will weaken the liberal order. The crisis of American leadership is merely the most dramatic example of rising populism and nationalism in the West. The year 2016 was truly an annus horribilis for internationalists. It has left the liberal order battered and bruised. Britain's vote to leave the European Union, Rodrigo Duterte's victory in the Philippines, and the defeat of the Italian referendum on constitutional reform were all manifestations of a revolt against the political order. We do not know whether the rise of populism and nationalism is a delayed but fleeting reaction to the financial crisis or something more lasting. But what we do know is that the new nationalists have a common purpose: blaming other nations for their country's problems and acting unilaterally to protect one's own interests, whether that involves immigration and refugee flows, banking debt, military commitments, or trade. And they have an impact greater than their electoral success. Few, if any, Western leaders are running on a platform of more globalization, more European integration, or more trade, as they did in the 1990s.

Not surprisingly, Russia and China are challenging the West to see where the true limits lie. Moscow and Beijing believe that the United States will remain a superpower for some time and do not buy the narrative of decline. But they also understand that the approach of broadly defining American interests to include a liberal international order has a soft underbelly—public opinion may not support costly action to defend places that American voters regard as peripheral. And they see great opportunities in Trump's rejection of the liberal international order. They will surely test the United States in the years to come, probing the regional orders in Europe, East Asia, and the Middle East. Even if the United States seeks a rapprochement with Russia, it will be temporary and will only serve to worsen geopolitical competition in Europe.

If the United States disengages from its traditional leadership of the international order, it will dramatically accelerate the shift away from convergence and toward a more nationalist and geopolitically competitive world, as described in this book. U.S. support for alliances, an open global economy, multilateral cooperation, and democracy are the foundation of international stability. Without it, everything will be in flux. Revisionists will be empowered because they will not worry so much about a U.S. response. Fragile democracies, particularly in Eastern Europe and parts of Southeast Asia, may flirt with authoritarianism. The global economy will be especially vulnerable to a new financial crisis and a trade war. The process of deglobalization described in Chapter 5 may rapidly accelerate. And the levels of international cooperation on common challenges will plummet. We have no idea where this will lead, but it is a good rule of thumb that the greater the U.S. disengagement, the greater the global problems.

Some will say that this turn of events is inevitable—that the West was already declining and would eventually give way to the will of emerging powers. But Russia is not a rising power and China no longer seems to be on a permanent upward trajectory. Other non-Western powers, like Brazil, India, and Indonesia, are not revisionist. And, most important of all, the United States is not in decline. In fact, when President Obama left office, the United States was more powerful than it was eight years earlier, just after the financial crisis. Its economy appears to be more resilient than Russia's or even China's. America's allies may have problems but they are still wealthy and capable countries that can determine their own destiny. And, crucially, what the United States has traditionally wanted—an open liberal order—is still what most of the rest of the world wants, thus giving Washington a crucial strategic advantage. Yes, America has vulnerabilities, just as its rivals do. But the future is not preordained. Raw metrics of GDP growth and military spending still matter, but they may be eclipsed by the strategic decisions that leaders make.

Clearly, the United States is highly unlikely to pursue responsible competition under a Trump presidency. But it is the strategy his successor should pursue. He or she will probably encounter a world in which the liberal international order has weakened further than it has already. The United States benefits hugely from a functioning and healthy international system. The liberal international order continues to function well both on its own terms and relative to the alternatives. It is capable of checking revisionist powers in Europe and Asia. An open global economy offers a much better prospect of shared prosperity than does a mercantilist system. And it alone is capable of generating increased levels of international cooperation to tackle common problems like nuclear proliferation and climate change. The specific actions described here—on Ukraine, Iran, the South China Sea, among others—may be overtaken by events, but the principles of responsible competition will endure. Ultimately, this strategy offers the best prospect of an order that is peaceful, prosperous, and just.

NOTES

Unless otherwise indicated, all websites mentioned in the Notes are current as of October 18, 2016.

CHAPTER 1. THE CONVERGENCE MYTH

1. As Fen Osler Hampson and David Gordon point out, convergence theory originated in the 1950s. They refer to convergence as being primarily oriented around democracy. The meaning of convergence is broader here. It includes governance type, but it also includes the liberal international order, which countries could be a part of even if they were not democratic. See Fen Osler Hampson and David Gordon, "The Enduring Myth of Democratic Convergence," *Diplomat Online,* September 27, 2015, http://diplomatonline.com/mag/2015/09/the-enduring-myth-of-democratic-convergence/.

2. The end of history thesis was that liberal democracy offered the only pathway to modernization. There would still be struggles, crises, and war, but they would not be fought over what it means to be modern. In the last chapter of *The End of History and the Last Man,* Fukuyama predicted that nations would rebel against peace and prosperity if necessary because the need to struggle is intrinsic to human nature. See Francis Fukuyama, *The End of History and the Last Man* (New York: Avon Books, 1992).

3. G. John Ikenberry, ed., *America Unrivaled: The Future of the Balance of Power* (Ithaca, NY: Cornell University Press, 2002).

4. The literature on balancing is vast. Good entry points are Stephen Walt, *The Origin of Alliances* (Ithaca, NY: Cornell University Press,

1990); and John Mearsheimer, *The Tragedy of Great Power Politics* (Ithaca, NY: Cornell University Press, 2001).

5. Ikenberry, *America Unrivaled.*

6. Charles Krauthammer, "The Unipolar Moment," *Foreign Affairs* (Winter 1990/1991): 23–33.

7. William Wohlforth, "The Stability of a Unipolar World," *International Security* 24, no. 1 (Summer 1999): 7.

8. G. John Ikenberry, *Liberal Leviathan: The Origins, Crisis, and Transformation of the American World Order* (Princeton, NJ: Princeton University Press, 2011).

9. Thomas Friedman, *The Lexus and the Olive Tree,* 2nd ed. (New York: Farrar, Straus and Giroux, 2000), Kindle edition, location 42.

10. Michael Mandelbaum, *The Ideas That Conquered the World* (New York: Public Affairs, 2004), p. 1.

11. Ibid., p. 4.

12. G. John Ikenberry, "The Logic of Order: Westphalia, Liberalism, and the Evolution of International Order in the Modern Era," in Ikenberry, *Power, Order, and Change in World Politics* (Cambridge, UK: Cambridge University Press, 2014), pp. 83–106.

13. The case for primacy was made in early drafts of the *Defense Planning Guidance,* written by Wolfowitz and his staff and leaked to the press. The White House subsequently distanced itself from the notion of primacy as a strategic objective. See Justin Vaisse, *Neoconservatism: The Biography of a Movement* (Cambridge, MA: Harvard University Press, 2010), pp. 224–225.

14. See Anthony Lake, "From Containment to Enlargement," speech, Johns Hopkins University School of Advanced International Studies, Washington, DC, September 21, 1993, https://www.mtholyoke.edu/acad/intrel/lakedoc.html.

15. Quoted in Derek Chollet and James Goldgeier, *America between the Wars: From 11/9 to 9/11* (New York: Public Affairs, 2008), p. 151.

16. In this passage, Clinton is partially quoting and endorsing Strobe Talbott's assessment of his Russia policy. See Bill Clinton, *My Life* (New York: Vintage Books, 2004), Kindle edition, location 10272.

17. Ibid., location 16210.

18. Ibid.

19. Ibid., location 19446.

20. Ibid., location 19431.

21. Quoted in Chollet and Goldgeier, *America between the Wars*, p. 247.

22. President George W. Bush, Graduation Speech at West Point, June 1, 2002, https://georgewbush-whitehouse.archives.gov/news/releases/2002/06/20020601-3.html.

23. Office of the President, *The National Security Strategy of the United States*, September 2002, p. 2, http://georgewbush-whitehouse.archives.gov/nsc/nss/2002/.

24. Fukuyama, *End of History and the Last Man*.

25. Robert Zoellick, "Whither China: From Membership to Responsibility," speech, National Committee on US-China Relations, New York City, September 21, 2005, http://2001–2009.state.gov/s/d/former/zoellick/rem/53682.htm.

26. Condoleezza Rice, *No Greater Honor: A Memoir of My Years in Washington* (New York: Crown, 2011), pp. 436–440.

27. For instance, see G. John Ikenberry and Anne-Marie Slaughter, "Forging a World of Liberty under Law," final report of the Princeton Project on National Security (Princeton, NJ: Woodrow Wilson School of Public and International Affairs, Princeton University, 2006); and Anne-Marie Slaughter et al., *Strategic Leadership: Framework for a 21st Century National Security Strategy*, a Phoenix Initiative Report (Washington, DC: Center for a New American Security, 2008), https://www.brookings.edu/research/strategic-leadership-framework-for-a-21st-century-national-security-strategy/.

28. Joe Biden, "Remarks by Vice President Biden in Ukraine," speech, Ukraine House, Kyiv, Ukraine, July 22, 2009, http://www.whitehouse.gov/the_press_office/Remarks-By-Vice-President-Biden-In-Ukraine/.

29. Oleg Schedrov and Matt Spetalnick, "Obama, Medvedev to Reset Ties with Arms Pact," *Reuters*, April 1, 2009, http://www.reuters.com/article/idUSL1949256200090401.

30. Helene Cooper, "On the World Stage, Obama Issues an Overture," *New York Times*, April 2, 2009, http://www.nytimes.com/2009/04/03/world/europe/03assess.html.

31. Barack Obama, "A New Beginning," speech, Cairo University, Cairo, Egypt, June 4, 2009, https://www.whitehouse.gov/the-press-office/remarks-president-cairo-university-6-04-09.

32. Emile Nakhleh, *A Necessary Engagement: Reinventing America's Relations with the Muslim World* (Princeton, NJ: Princeton University Press, 2008).

33. Jeffrey Goldberg, "The Obama Doctrine," *Atlantic* (April 2016), http://www.theatlantic.com/magazine/archive/2016/04/the-obama-doctrine/471525/.

34. James Goldgeier, "Stop Blaming NATO for Putin's Provocations," *New Republic,* April 17, 2014, https://newrepublic.com/article/117423/nato-not-blame-putins-actions.

35. Joe Biden, "Vice President Biden's Remarks at Moscow State University," speech, Moscow State University, Moscow, Russia, March 10, 2011, https://www.whitehouse.gov/the-press-office/2011/03/10/vice-president-bidens-remarks-moscow-state-university.

36. Kenneth Lieberthal and Wang Jisi, "Addressing US-China Strategic Distrust," John L. Thornton China Center Monograph Series, no. 4, Brookings Institution, March 30, 2012, pp. 8–11, http://www.brookings.edu/~/media/research/files/papers/2012/3/30-us-china-lieberthal/0330_china_lieberthal.pdf.

37. World Bank Dataset, http://data.worldbank.org, accessed July 23, 2016.

38. Strobe Talbott, *The Russia Hand: A Memoir of Presidential Diplomacy* (2002; New York: Random House, 2003), pp. 7–8.

39. Robert Kagan, *The Return of History and the End of Dreams* (New York: First Vintage Books, 2008), p. 1.

40. Quoted in Angela Stent, *The Limits of Partnership* (Princeton, NJ: Princeton University Press, 2014), pp. 138–139.

41. Vladimir Putin, "Putin's Prepared Remarks at 43rd Munich Conference on Security Policy," speech, Munich, Germany, February 2007, *Washington Post,* http://www.washingtonpost.com/wp-dyn/content/article/2007/02/12/AR2007021200555.html.

42. Ron Asmus, *A Little War That Shook the World: Georgia, Russia and the Future of the West* (New York: St. Martin's, 2010).

43. Samuel Charap, "Beyond the Reset to Russia," *National Interest* (July–August 2013).

44. Presentation by Philip Gordon, former assistant secretary for Europe, U.S. Department of State, 2009–2013, at the German Marshall Fund, September 21, 2015.

45. Quoted in Mike Dorning, "Obama Saw Too Late That Putin's Return Would Undermine the Reset," *Bloomberg*, February 19, 2015, http://www.bloomberg.com/news/articles/2015-02-19/obama-putin.

46. Stephen Lee Myers, *The New Tsar: The Rise and Reign of Vladimir Putin* (New York: Knopf, 2015), Kindle edition, locations 7922, 7930.

47. Ibid., location 7954.

48. Dorning, "Obama Saw Too Late."

49. David Kang, *China Rising: Peace, Power, and Prosperity in East Asia* (New York: Columbia University Press, 2009).

50. Joshua Kurlantzick, "China's Charm Offensive in Southeast Asia," *Carnegie Endowment for International Peace*, September 1, 2006, http://carnegieendowment.org/2006/09/01/china-s-charm-offensive-in-southeast-asia/35wf.

51. Thomas Wright, "Strategic Engagement's Track Record," *Washington Quarterly* 33, no. 3 (July 2010): 35–60.

52. Jeffrey Bader, *Obama and China's Rise: An Insider's Account of America's Asia Strategy* (Washington, DC: Brookings Institution Press, 2010), p. 80. For the case that Chinese assertiveness was not new, see Alastair Iain Johnston, "How New and Assertive Is China's New Assertiveness?" *International Security* 37, no. 4 (Spring 2013): 7–48. Johnston does acknowledge, though, that China became more assertive in the maritime domain.

53. Andrew Nathan and Andrew Scobell, *China's Search for Security*, 2nd ed. (Ithaca, NY: Columbia University Press, 2012), Kindle edition, pp. 98–99.

54. Jeffrey Bader, "How Xi Jinping Sees the World . . . And Why," *Asia Working Group Paper*, Brookings Institution, February 2016, http://www.brookings.edu/~/media/Research/Files/Papers/2016/02/xi-jinping-worldview-bader/xi_jinping_worldview_bader.pdf?la=en.

55. President George W. Bush, *Remarks at the 20th Anniversary of the National Endowment for Democracy*, Chamber of Commerce, Washington, DC, November 6, 2003, http://www.ned.org/remarks-by-president-george-w-bush-at-the-20th-anniversary/.

56. President Obama, 2016 State of the Union Address, January 13, 2016, https://www.whitehouse.gov/the-press-office/2016/01/12/remarks-president-barack-obama-%E2%80%93-prepared-delivery-state-union-address.

57. Barry Eichengreen and Kevin O'Rourke, "A Tale of Two Depressions: What Does the New Data Tell Us?" *VoxEu*, March 8, 2010, http://www.voxeu.org/article/tale-two-depressions-what-do-new-data-tell-us-february-2010-update#jun09.

58. Jonathan Kirshner, *American Power after the Financial Crisis* (Ithaca, NY: Cornell University Press, 2014).

59. Raghuram Rajan, *Faultlines: How Hidden Fractures Still Threaten the World Economy* (Princeton, NJ: Princeton University Press, 2010), p. 4.

60. Michael Mandelbaum, *Mission Failure: America and the World in the Post–Cold War Era* (New York: Oxford University Press, 2016), Kindle edition, location 246.

CHAPTER 2. EUROPE'S MULTIPLE CRISES

1. *A Secure Europe in a Better World: European Security Strategy*, Brussels, December 12, 2003, http://www.consilium.europa.eu/uedocs/cmsUpload/78367.pdf.

2. See, for instance, Mark Leonard, *Why Europe Will Run the Twenty-First Century* (New York: Public Affairs, 2006); T. R. Reid, *The United States of Europe: The New Superpower and the End of American Supremacy* (New York: Penguin Press, 2004); Charles Kupchan, *End of the American Era: US Foreign Policy and the Geopolitics of the Twenty-First Century* (New York: Vintage Press, 2003).

3. Richard Haass, "Why Europe No Longer Matters," *Washington Post*, June 17, 2011, https://www.washingtonpost.com/opinions/why-europe-no-longer-matters/2011/06/15/AG7eCCZH_story.html.

4. "Unromantic" was the word Jeffrey Goldberg used to sum up President Obama's view on Europe based on extensive conversations with him. See Jeffrey Goldberg, "The Obama Doctrine," *Atlantic* (April 2016), http://www.theatlantic.com/magazine/archive/2016/04/the-obama-doctrine/471525/.

5. David Marsh, *Europe's Deadlock: How the Euro Crisis Could Be Solved—and Why It Won't Happen* (New Haven: Yale University Press, 2008), Kindle edition, location 232.

6. Ambrose Evans Pritchard, "Financial Crisis: U.S. Will Lose Superpower Status, Claims German Minister," *Daily Telegraph*, September 25, 2008, http://www.telegraph.co.uk/finance/financialcrisis/3081909/Financial-Crisis-US-will-lose-superpower-status-claims-German-minister.html.

7. Ten-year bond yields for these countries are available from www.tradingeconomics.com. See http://www.tradingeconomics.com/germany/government-bond-yield; http://www.tradingeconomics.com/portugal/government-bond-yield; http://www.tradingeconomics.com/ireland/government-bond-yield; and http://www.tradingeconomics.com/greece/government-bond-yield.

8. Quoted in Carlo Bastasin, *Saving Europe: How National Politics Nearly Destroyed the Euro* (Washington, DC: Brookings Institution Press, 2012), p. 17.

9. German structural reforms took place at a time of global economic growth, a mild domestic recession, and low debt. These conditions limited or offset the contractionary effect of structural reform. They do not apply today. See Martin Wolf, "Germany's Strange Parallel Universe," *Financial Times,* September 24, 2013, https://www.ft.com/content/b3faf9b0-2489-11e3-8905-00144feab7de.

10. Wolfgang Schäuble, "Europe at a Crossroads (Again): A Conversation with Wolfgang Schäuble," *Brookings Institution,* Washington, DC, April 16,2015,http://www.brookings.edu/~/media/events/2015/04/16-wolfgang-schauble-eurozone-crossroads/20150416_germany_eurozone_schauble_transcript.pdf.

11. Barry Eichengreen, "The Break-Up of the Euro Area," in Alberto Alesina and Francesco Giavazzi, eds., *Europe and the Euro* (Chicago: University of Chicago Press, 2010), pp. 11–51.

12. On Greece, see David Gordon and Thomas Wright, "No Exit: Why Greece and Europe Will Stay Attached," *Foreign Affairs,* June 30, 2015, https://www.foreignaffairs.com/articles/greece/2015-06-30/no-exit.

13. George Soros and Gregor Peter Schmitz, "The EU Is on the Verge of Collapse—An Interview," *New York Review of Books,* February 11, 2016, http://www.nybooks.com/articles/2016/02/11/europe-verge-collapse-interview/.

14. Author interview with a former senior EU official, Washington, DC, March 15, 2016.

15. Oil fell from $140 a barrel in 2008, just before the financial crisis, to $31 per barrel in 2016.

16. Vladimir Putin, "Meeting with Heads of Leading International News Agencies," press conference, Saint Petersburg, May 24, 2014, http://en.kremlin.ru/events/president/news/21090.

17. Fiona Hill and Clifford Gaddy, *Mr. Putin: Operative in the Kremlin* (2013; Washington, DC: Brookings Institution Press, 2015), pp. 318–319.

18. Angela Stent, *The Limits of Partnership: US-Russian Relations in the Twenty-First Century* (Princeton, NJ: Princeton University Press, 2014), pp. 238–241.

19. Valery Gerasimov, "The Value of Science in Forecasting: New Challenges Require a Rethinking of the Forms and Methods of Warfare," speech to the AVN (Military Sciences Academy) in late January 2013. Translation provided to author by Clifford Gaddy.

20. Ibid.

21. Ibid.

22. *Army Modernization: Hearing before the Subcommittee on Airland of the Armed Services Committee, U.S. Senate,* 114th Cong., 2016 (joint testimony from Lieutenant Generals Michael Williamson, Joseph Anderson, Herbert R. McMaster, and John Murray), http://www. armed-services.senate.gov/hearings/15-04-14-army-modernization.

23. Gustav Gressel, *Russia's Quiet Military Revolution and What It Means for Europe* (London: European Council on Foreign Relations, 2015), p. 3.

24. Mark Galeotti, "Hybrid, Ambiguous, and Non-Linear? How New Is Russia's 'New Way of War'?," *Small Wars and Insurgencies* 27, no. 2 (March 2016): 282–301.

25. Vladimir Putin, "Address by President of the Russian Federation," press conference, The Kremlin, Moscow, March 18, 2014, http:// en.kremlin.ru/events/president/news/20603.

26. Hill and Gaddy, *Mr. Putin*, p. 320.

27. For an excellent overview of Russian nuclear doctrine, see Elbridge Colby, "Russia's Evolving Nuclear Doctrine and Its Implications," Fondation pour la Recherche Stratégique, January 12, 2016, http:// www.frstrategie.org/publications/notes/russia-s-evolving-nuclear-doctrine-and-its-implications-2016–01.

28. Zachary Keck, "Russia's Military Begins Massive Nuclear War Drill," *Diplomat,*March29,2014,http://thediplomat.com/2014/03/russias-military-begins-massive-nuclear-war-drill/.

29. For more on how domestic insecurity is driving Putin's aggressive foreign policy, see Michael McFaul and Kathryn Stoner, "Who Lost Russia (This Time)? Vladimir Putin," *Washington Quarterly* 38, no. 2 (2015): 167–187.

30. Quoted in Henry Kissinger, *World Order* (New York: Penguin Press, 2014), p. 52.

31. Ibid., p. 56.

32. Quoted in Robert Jervis, *Perception and Misperception in International Politics* (Princeton, NJ: Princeton University Press, 1976), Kindle edition, p. 63.

33. The UN special envoy in Syria said in April 2016 that the Syrian war had killed 400,000. In February, estimates by a Syrian non-governmental organization put the number at 470,000. See John Hudson, "UN Envoy Revises Syria Death Toll to 400,000," *Foreign Policy*, April 22 ,2016, http://foreignpolicy.com/2016/04/22/u-n-envoy-revises-syria-death-toll-to-400000/.

34. Deena Zaru, "Donald Trump Says US Should 'Possibly' Accept Refugees," *CNN*, September 4, 2015, http://www.cnn.com/2015/09/04/politics/donald-trump-refugee-migrant-crisis-syria/.

35. International Organization for Migration, *Over 3,770 Migrants Have Died Trying to Cross the Mediterranean to Europe in 2015,* December 31, 2015, http://www.iom.int/news/over-3770-migrants-have-died-trying-cross-mediterranean-europe-2015.

36. See Andrea Thomas, "Record Number of Asylum Seekers Flood Germany," *Wall Street Journal*, January 6, 2016, http://www.wsj.com/articles/germany-records-rise-in-asylum-seekers-to-postwar-high-1452081246.

37. Author interviews with German officials, Washington, DC, January 2016.

38. Olivier Roy, "France's Oedipal Islamist Complex," *Foreign Policy,* January7,2016,http://foreignpolicy.com/2016/01/07/frances-oedipal-islamist-complex-charlie-hebdo-islamic-state-isis/.

39. "Cologne Assaults: Police Report Outlines 'Chaotic and Shameful' New Year's Eve," *Der Spiegel,* January 7, 2016, http://www.spiegel.de/international/germany/cologne-attacks-on-new-years-produced-chaos-say-police-a-1070894.html.

40. Author interviews with EU and German officials, March 2016.

41. Patrick Collinson, "Bookies Got EU Vote Wrong, Ladbrokes Says," *Guardian*, June 24, 2016, https://www.theguardian.com/business/2016/jun/24/bookies-got-eu-vote-wrong-ladbrokes-says.

42. This section draws not just on the Goldberg article, but also on conversations with several individuals who have spoken with President Obama at length on Europe.

43. Vladimir Putin, "Meeting of the Valdai International Discussion Club," press conference, Valdai International Discussion Club, Sochi, October 22, 2015, http://en.kremlin.ru/events/president/news/50548.

44. Natalie Nougayrède, "Europe Is in Crisis: Once More, America Will Have to Step in to Save Us," *Guardian,* January 23, 2016, http://www.theguardian.com/commentisfree/2016/jan/23/europe-crisis-america-save-us-again-refugees-security-brexit.

CHAPTER 3. CHINA'S EAST ASIA CHALLENGE

1. Ely Ratner, "Learning the Lessons of Scarborough Reef," *National Interest,* November 21, 2013, accessed May 8, 2016, http://nationalinterest.org/commentary/learning-the-lessons-scarborough-reef-9442.

2. Ibid.

3. Former senior U.S. official at off-the-record roundtable, Washington, DC, 2014.

4. Ratner, "Learning the Lessons of Scarborough Reef."

5. Ryan D. Martinson, "China's Second Navy," *Proceedings Magazine* (April 2015), http://www.usni.org/magazines/proceedings/2015–04–0/chinas-second-navy.

6. Andrew Erickson and Kevin Bond, "Dredging under the Radar: China Expands South China Sea Footprint," *National Interest,* August 25, 2015, http://nationalinterest.org/feature/dredging-under-the-radar-china-expands-south-sea-foothold-13701.

7. Quoted in Andrew Erickson, "Doctrinal Sea Change, Making Real Waves: Examining the Naval Dimension of Strategy," in Joe McReynolds, ed., *China's Evolving Military Strategy,* prepublication edition (Washington, DC: Jameston Foundation, 2016), p. 113.

8. Fu Ying, "The US World Order Is a Suit That No Longer Fits," *Financial Times,* January 6, 2016, http://www.ft.com/intl/cms/s/0/c09cbcb6-b3cb-11e5-b147-e5e5bba42e51.html#axzz40ulHNBNw.

9. G. John Ikenberry, *Liberal Leviathan: The Origins, Crisis, and Transformation of the American World Order* (Princeton, NJ: Princeton University Press, 2011).

10. Thomas Christensen, *The China Challenge: Shaping the Choices of a Rising Power* (New York: W. W. Norton, 2015), p. xv.

11. Ibid., p. 115.

12. Jeffrey Bader, "Changing China Policy: Are We in Search of Enemies?" *Order from Chaos* (blog), Brookings Institution, June 22, 2015,http://www.brookings.edu/blogs/up-front/posts/2015/06/22-changing-china-policy-bader.

13. Robert Hartmann, "China Rising: Back to the Future," *Asia Times,* March 16, 2007, http://www.atimes.com/atimes/China/IC16Ad01.html.

14. Andrew J. Nathan and Andrew Scobell, *China's Search for Security* (New York: Columbia University Press, 2012), p. 5.

15. Andrew Small, *The China-Pakistan Axis: Asia's New Geopolitics* (New York: Oxford University Press), p. 164.

16. Ibid., p. 178.

17. Ibid., p. 179.

18. Yinhong Shi, director, Center on American Studies, Renmin University, in discussion with the author, October 2015.

19. Yinhong Shi, director, Center on American Studies, Renmin University, in discussion with the author, March 2016.

20. Some Chinese strategists have argued that China ought to emulate Russia and be willing to use force to advance its interests, but this is very much a minority position. The most prominent Chinese advocate of this position is Zhang Wenmu, a professor at Beihang University. For an analysis of his views see Lyle Goldstein, "Get Ready: China Could Pull a Crimea in Asia," *National Interest,* April 11, 2015, http://nationalinterest.org/feature/get-ready-will-china-pull-crimea-asia-12605.

21. "US Pacific Command and US Forces Korea, before the Senate Armed Services Committee," statement of Admiral Harry Harris, Jr., commander, U.S. Pacific Command, 114th Cong. (February 23, 2016). The hegemony remark was made in the questions and answers. For access to Admiral Harris's testimony and video of the exchange, see: http://www.armed-services.senate.gov/hearings/16–02–23-us-pacific-command-and-us-forces-korea.

22. Andrew S. Erickson and Conor M. Kennedy, "China's Island Builders: The People's War at Sea," *Foreign Affairs,* April 9, 2015, https://www.foreignaffairs.com/articles/east-asia/2015–04–09/china-s-island-builders.

23. Megha Rajagopalan, "China Trains 'Fishing Militia' to Go into Disputed Waters," *Reuters*, April 30, 2016, http://www.reuters.com/article/us-southchinasea-china-fishingboats-idUSKCN0XS0RS.

24. Manuel Mogato, "Exclusive: Philippines Reinforcing Rusting Ship on Spratly Reef Outpost," *Reuters*, July 13, 2015, accessed on May 8, 2016, http://www.reuters.com/article/us-southchinasea-philippines-shoal-exclu-idUSKCN0PN2HN20150714.

25. "America's Security Role in the South China Sea, before the House Committee on Foreign Affairs Subcommittee on Asia and the Pacific," statement of Patrick Cronin, senior adviser and senior director, Asia-Pacific Security Program, Center for a New American Security, 114th Cong. (July 23, 2015), https://foreignaffairs.house.gov/hearing/subcommittee-hearing-americas-security-role-in-the-south-china-sea/.

26. The most dramatic example of China using its coast guard to bully its neighbors occurred in the Scarborough Reef in 2012, though this was not an isolated incident. China used new fishing regulations to take action against Philippine and Vietnamese ships. In addition, China placed and protected a China National Offshore Oil Company (CNOOC) deep-water oil rig (called HD-981) in the Parcel Islands close to the Vietnam coast in May of 2014. See Patrick M. Cronin et al., *Tailored Coercion: Competition and Risk in Maritime Asia* (Washington, DC: Center for a New America Security, March 2014).

27. Ashton Carter, "A Security Architecture Where Everyone Rises," speech, The Shangri-la Dialogue, Singapore, May 30, 2015.

28. U.S. Department of Defense, *The Asia Pacific Maritime Security Strategy: Achieving US National Security Objectives in a Changing Environment* (Washington, DC: U.S. Department of Defense, July 27, 2015), p. 16, accessed May 8, 2016, http://www.defense.gov/Portals/1/Documents/pubs/NDAA%20A-P_Maritime_SecuritY_Strategy-08142015–1300-FINALFORMAT.PDF.

29. Ibid., p. 5.

30. Ibid., p. 1.

31. This is the Japanese government's official count for the period between September 1, 2012, and February 16, 2016. See *Current Japan-China Relations*, briefing document (Japanese Ministry of Foreign Affairs, February 2016), p. 8.

32. Franz Stefan Gady, "Japan's Fighter Jets Intercepted Chinese Aircraft 571 Times in 2015," *Diplomat,* April 26, 2016, http://thediplomat. com/2016/04/japans-fighter-jets-intercepted-chinese-aircraft-571- times-in-2015/.

33. *China's Recent Air and Maritime Activities in East China Sea* (Tokyo: Japanese Ministry for Foreign Affairs, February 2016), p. 4.

34. Author interview with senior Japanese official no. 2, Tokyo, March 4, 2016.

35. Author interviews with Chinese policy experts in Beijing, October 11–14, 2015.

36. Caitlin Campbell et al., "China's 'Core Interests' and the East China Sea," *US-China Economic and Security Review Commission Staff Research Backgrounder,* May 20, 2013, http://origin.www.uscc.gov/sites/default/ files/Research/China's%20Core%20Interests%20and%20the%20 East%20China%20Sea.pdf.

37. Hillary Clinton, "Closing Remarks for U.S.-China Strategic and Economic Dialogue," speech, U.S.-China Strategic and Economic Dialogue, Washington, DC, July 28, 2009, http://www.state.gov/ secretary/20092013clinton/rm/2009a/july/126599.htm.

38. Campbell et al., "China's 'Core Interests,'" p. 4.

39. Edward Wong, "China's Security Law Suggests a Broadening of China's 'Core Interests,'" *New York Times,* July 2, 2015, http://www. nytimes.com/2015/07/03/world/asia/security-law-suggests-a- broadening-of-chinas-core-interests.html?_r=0.

40. Cui Tiankai and Pang Hanzhao, "China-US Relations in China's Overall Diplomacy in the New Era," in *Chinese International Strategy Review, 2012* (San Francisco: Long River Press, 2013). Also available from the Embassy of the People's Republic of China in Malaysia, http://my.china-embassy.org/eng/zgxw/ t954784.htm.

41. Author interviews, Beijing, October 11–14, 2015.

42. Quoted in Edward Wong, "Beijing Warns US about South China Sea Disputes," *New York Times,* June 22, 2011, http://www.nytimes. com/2011/06/23/world/asia/23china.html?_r=0.

43. Cui Tiankai, "China and America: Stay Focused on What Really Matters," *National Interest,* August 26, 2015.

44. Author interview with Japanese official, Tokyo, March 4, 2016.

45. President Barack Obama, "Remarks by President Obama to the Australian Parliament," speech, Parliament House, Canberra, Australia, November 17, 2011, https://www.whitehouse.gov/the-press-office/2011/11/17/remarks-president-obama-australian-parliament. See also Secretary of Defense Ashton Carter, "Remarks on the Next Phase of the US Rebalance to the Asia-Pacific," speech, The McCain Institute, Arizona State University, Tempe, AZ, April 6, 2015, http://www.defense.gov/News/Speeches/Speech-View/Article/606660. For a comprehensive analysis of the strategy by one of its chief architects, see Kurt Campbell, *The Pivot: The Future of American Statecraft in Asia* (New York: Twelve Books, 2016).

46. Nina Silove, "The Pivot before the Pivot: U.S. Strategy to Preserve the Power Balance in Asia," *International Security* 40, no. 4 (Spring 2016): 45–88.

47. For instance, see the congressionally mandated report by CSIS on the future of the rebalance: Michael Green, Kathleen Hicks, and Mark Cancian, *Asia-Pacific Rebalance, 2025: Capabilities, Presence, and Partnerships; an Independent Review of US Defense Strategy in the Asia Pacific,* report (Washington, DC: Center for Strategic and International Studies, January 2016).

48. President Barack Obama, "The TPP Would Let America, Not China, Lead the Way on Global Trade," *Washington Post,* May 2, 2016, https://www.washingtonpost.com/opinions/president-obama-the-tpp-would-let-america-not-china-lead-the-way-on-global-trade/2016/05/02/680540e4-0fd0-11e6-93ae-50921721165d_story.html?utm_term=.79b4ed3f369f.

49. Yuka Hayashi, "For Japan's Shinzo Abe, Unfinished Family Business," *Wall Street Journal,* December 11, 2014, http://www.wsj.com/articles/for-japans-shinzo-abe-unfinished-family-business-1418354470.

50. For a description of Abe's strategy, see Michael Auslin, "Japan's New Realism," *Foreign Affairs* (March/April 2016), https://www.foreignaffairs.com/articles/japan/japans-new-realism.

51. Author interview with senior Japanese naval officer, Tokyo, March 1, 2016.

52. Opinion polls by Yomiuri, Asahi, and Nikkei in January 2016 all showed 46 percent opposed to the revision of the constitution, with 36 percent, 33 percent, and 34 percent supportive (respectively).

53. Author interview, senior Japanese naval officer, Tokyo, March 1, 2016.

54. Author interview with senior Japanese official no. 2, Tokyo, March 3, 2016.

55. Patrick M. Cronin et al., *The Emerging Asia Power Web: The Rise of Bilateral Intra Asia Security Ties,* report (Washington, DC: Center for a New American Security, June 2013), https://www.cnas.org/publications/reports/the-emerging-asia-power-web-the-rise-of-bilateral-intra-asian-security-ties.

56. Edward Luttwak, *The Rise of China versus the Logic of Strategy* (Cambridge, MA: Belknap Press, 2012), p. 66.

57. Minxin Pei, *China's Crony Capitalism: The Dynamics of Regime Decay* (Cambridge, MA: Harvard University Press, 2016).

58. David Shambaugh, "The Coming Chinese Crackup," *Wall Street Journal,* March 6, 2015, http://www.wsj.com/articles/the-coming-chinese-crack-up-1425659198.

59. Ruchir Sharma, "How China Fell off the Miracle Path," *New York Times,* June 3, 2016, http://www.nytimes.com/2016/06/05/opinion/sunday/how-china-fell-off-the-miracle-path.html.

60. See Dale Copeland, *The Origins of Major War* (Ithaca, NY: Cornell University Press, 2001).

CHAPTER 4. GEOPOLITICS AND CONTAGION IN THE MIDDLE EAST

1. Tamara Wittes, "Remarks at Princeton University Conference on Global Governance," Princeton, NJ, May 14, 2016.

2. Quoted in Ryan Lizza, "The Consequentialist: How the Arab Spring Remade Obama's Foreign Policy," *New Yorker,* May 2, 2011.

3. Shadi Hamid, "Islamism, the Arab Spring, and the Failure of America's Do-Nothing Policy in the Middle East," *Atlantic,* October 9, 2015, http://www.theatlantic.com/international/archive/2015/10/middle-east-egypt-us-policy/409537/.

4. Robert F. Worth, *A Rage for Order: The Middle East in Turmoil: From Tahrir Square to ISIS* (New York: Farrar, Straus and Giroux, 2016), Kindle edition, location 104.

5. Ibid.

6. Jeffrey Goldberg, "The Obama Doctrine," *Atlantic,* April 22, 2016.

7. Emma Sky, "Who Lost Iraq?" *Foreign Affairs,* June 24, 2014, https://www.foreignaffairs.com/articles/iraq/2014–06–24/who-lost-iraq.

8. Emma Sky, *The Unraveling: High Hopes and Missed Opportunities in Iraq* (New York: Public Affairs, 2015), p. 338.

9. Quoted in Deter Filkins, "The Shadow Commander," *New Yorker*, September 30, 2013, http://www.newyorker.com/magazine/2013/09/30/the-shadow-commander.

10. Sky, "Who Lost Iraq?"

11. Lizza, "The Consequentialist."

12. Marc Lynch, "Obama and the Middle East: Rightsizing the US Role," *Foreign Affairs* (September/October 2015), https://www.foreignaffairs.com/articles/middle-east/obama-and-middle-east.

13. Dennis Ross, "Why Middle Eastern Leaders Are Talking to Putin, Not Obama," *Politico Magazine*, May 8, 2016, http://www.politico.com/magazine/story/2016/05/putin-obama-middle-east-leaders-213867.

14. Quoted in Michael Grunwald, "Ben Rhodes and the Tough Sell of Obama's Foreign Policy," *Politico Magazine*, May 10, 2016.

15. President Barack Obama, "Remarks to the UN General Assembly," September 24, 2013, https://www.whitehouse.gov/the-press-office/2013/09/24/remarks-president-obama-address-united-nations-general-assembly.

16. For instance, see Steven Simon and Benjamin Stevenson, "The End of Pax Americana," *Foreign Affairs* (November/December 2015), https://www.foreignaffairs.com/articles/middle-east/end-pax-americana.

17. President Barack Obama, *The State of the Union*, January 13, 2016, https://www.whitehouse.gov/the-press-office/2016/01/12/remarks-president-barack-obama-%E2%80%93-prepared-delivery-state-union-address.

18. Philip Gordon, "The Middle East Is Falling Apart. The US Is Not to Blame. There Is No Easy Fix," *Politico*, June 4, 2015, http://www.politico.com/magazine/story/2015/06/america-not-to-blame-for-middle-east-falling-apart-118611#ixzz3zWF3y2Ap.

19. David Crist, *The Twilight War: The Secret History of America's Thirty-Year Conflict with Iran* (New York: Penguin Books, 2013), chapter 27 and epilogue.

20. Frederic Wehrey et al., *Saudi-Iranian Relations since the Fall of Saddam: Rivalry, Cooperation, and Implications for US Policy* (Arlington, VA: RAND Corporation, 2009).

21. F. Gregory Gause III, "Beyond Sectarianism: The New Middle East Cold War," *Brookings Doha Center Analysis Paper*, no. 11, July 2014, p. 8.

22. Ibid., p. 19.

23. Olivier Roy, "The Sunni-Shia Divide: Where Religion Masks Geo-Strategy," in Luigi Narbone and Martin Lestra, *The Gulf Monarchies beyond the Arab Spring: Changes and Challenges* (Florence: European University Institute, 2015).

24. Gregory Gause, *The Gulf States and Iran: Two Misunderstandings and One Possible Game Changer,* James A. Baker Institute for Public Policy of Rice University, Houston, 2016.

25. Gause, "Beyond Sectarianism."

26. "Transcript: Interview with Muhammad bin Salman," *Economist,* January 6, 2016, http://www.economist.com/saudi_interview.

27. Robin Wright, "Iran and Saudi Arabia: The Showdown between Islam's Rival Powers," *New Yorker,* January 4, 2016, http://www.newyorker.com/news/news-desk/iran-and-saudi-arabia-the-showdown-between-islams-rival-powers.

28. Afshon Ostovar, *Vanguard of the Imam: Religion, Politics, and Iran's Revolutionary Guard* (New York: Oxford University Press, 2016), Kindle edition, locations 4278, 4290.

29. Ibid., location 4323–4362.

30. Ibid., location 4623.

31. Crist, *Twilight War.*

32. For an account of the Syrian civil war, see Emile Hokeyam, *Syria Uprising and the Fracturing of the Levant* (London: Routledge Press, 2013), and Charles Lister, *The Syrian Jihad, Al-Qaeda, The Islamic State, and the Evolution of an Insurgency* (New York: Oxford University Press, 2013).

33. Quoted in Ostovar, *Vanguard of the Imam,* location 4661.

34. Ibid., location 4731–4749.

35. For a good summary of the academic literature on this topic, see Max Fischer, "Syria's Paradox: Why the War Only Ever Seems to Get Worse," *New York Times,* August 26, 2016, http://www.nytimes.com/2016/08/27/world/middleeast/syria-civil-war-why-get-worse.html.

36. I am grateful to Bruce Jones for this point.

37. Ivan Krastev, "Putin Looks for Regime Change in Turkey," *Bloomberg View,* January 14, 2016, https://www.bloomberg.com/view/articles/2016-01-14/putin-looks-for-regime-change-in-turkey.

38. Ostovar, *Vanguard of the Imam,* location 4971–5212; David Ignatius, "Iran Overplays Its Hand," *Washington Post,* July 3, 2014, https://www.

washingtonpost.com/opinions/david-ignatius-iran-overplays-its-hand-in-iraq-and-syria/2014/07/03/132e1630-02db-11e4-8572-4b1b969b6322_story.html?utm_term=.051ce1e75108.

39. Jeremy Shapiro and Laura Daniels, "The US Plan to Counter Russia in Syria," *Brookings Order from Chaos* (blog), November 17, 2015, http://www.brookings.edu/blogs/order-from-chaos/posts/2015/11/17-us-plan-to-counter-russia-shapiro-daniels.

40. David Remnick, "Going the Distance: On and Off the Road with Barack Obama," *New Yorker,* January 27, 2014, http://www.newyorker.com/magazine/2014/01/27/going-the-distance-david-remnick.

41. That this is Obama's view was the central point made by Jeffrey Goldberg after interviewing him for hours on the topic. See Jeffrey Goldberg, "The Obama Doctrine," *Atlantic,* April 2016, http://www.theatlantic.com/magazine/archive/2016/04/the-obama-doctrine/471525/.

42. Vladimir Putin, "Address to the United Nations General Assembly," September 28, 2015, http://en.kremlin.ru/events/president/news/50385.

43. Dmitri Trenin, "Russia in the Middle East: Moscow's Objectives, Priorities, and Policy Drivers," Task Force White Paper, Carnegie Endowment for International Peace, Washington, DC, April 5, 2016, http://carnegie.ru/2016/04/05/russia-in-middle-east-moscow-s-objectives-priorities-and-policy-drivers/iwni.

44. Michael Singh, "China's Middle East Tour," *Foreign Affairs Snapshot,* January 24, 2016, https://www.foreignaffairs.com/articles/china/2016–01–24/chinas-middle-east-tour.

45. "China Issues Arab Policy Paper," *China Daily,* January 13, 2016, http://www.china.org.cn/world/2016-01/13/content_37569936.htm.

46. Li Xiaokun, "Syrian Opposition Leader to Start 4 Day Beijing Visit," *China Daily,* January 5, 2016, http://www.chinadailyasia.com/nation/2016-01/05/content_15367342.html.

47. Off-the-record discussion with Chinese Middle East expert, March 7, 2016. See also Xue Li and Zheng Yuwen, "The Future of China's Diplomacy in the Middle East," *Diplomat,* July 26, 2016, http://thediplomat.com/2016/07/the-future-of-chinas-diplomacy-in-the-middle-east/.

CHAPTER 5. INTERDEPENDENT COMPETITION

1. Nicholas Lambert, *Planning Armageddon: British Economic Warfare and the First World War* (Cambridge, MA: Harvard University Press, 2012).

2. There is a robust debate in international relations theory on this topic. For a broad overview, see Edward Mansfield and Brian M. Pollins, *Economic Interdependence and International Conflict: New Perspectives on an Enduring Debate* (Ann Arbor: University of Michigan Press, 2003).

3. Albert O. Hirschman, *National Power and the Structure of Foreign Trade* (Berkeley: University of California Press, 1945).

4. Jeremy Adelman, *Worldly Philosopher: The Odyssey of Albert O. Hirschman* (Princeton, NJ: Princeton University Press, 2013).

5. World Bank, *World Development Indicators*, accessed September 16, 2015, http://data.worldbank.org/data-catalog/world-development-indicators.

6. OECD, "Measuring Globalization: Better Data for Better Policy," agenda, FDI Statistics Workshop, Paris, March 20, 2014, p. 1, http://www.oecd.org/daf/inv/2014-FDI-Statistics-Workshop-Agenda.pdf.

7. Mark Leonard, *Weaponising Interdependence*, European Council on Foreign Relations, January 20, 2016, http://www.ecfr.eu/publications/summary/connectivity_wars_5064.

8. Ibid.

9. This was originally said by French president Giscard D'Estaing, who meant it as an insult.

10. Benn Steil, "Taper Trouble: The International Consequences of the Fed's Policies," *Foreign Affairs* (July–August 2015), https://www.foreignaffairs.com/articles/united-states/2014–06–04/taper-trouble.

11. Ian Bremmer and Cliff Kupchan, "Top Risks 2015," Eurasia Group, January 5, 2015, https://www.eurasiagroup.net/media/eurasia-group-publishes-top-risks-2015.

12. Juan Zarate, *Treasury's War: The Unleashing of a New Era of Financial Warfare* (New York: Public Affairs, 2013), Kindle edition, location 154.

13. Jack Lew, "Remarks of Secretary Lew at CSIS," speech, Center for Strategic and International Studies, Washington, DC, June 2, 2014, https://www.treasury.gov/press-center/press-releases/Pages/jl2414.aspx.

14. Zarate, *Treasury's War*, location 6667.

15. Walter R. Mead, "Russia Threatens SWIFT," *American Interest*, January 26, 2015, http://www.the-american-interest.com/2015/01/26/russia-threatens-swift/.

16. International Monetary Fund, *World Economic Outlook Database*, Washington, DC, http://www.imf.org/external/pubs/ft/weo/2016/02/weodata/index.aspx.

17. The U.S. sanctions are detailed at https://www.treasury.gov/resource-center/sanctions/Programs/Pages/ukraine.aspx.

18. Kathrin Hille and Martin Arnold, "Sberbank Says Sanctions Hit Global Financial System," *Financial Times*, August 1, 2014, https://www.ft.com/content/190a5378-1958-11e4-9745-00144feabdc0.

19. Jarosław Cwiek-Karpowicz and Stanislav Secrieru, eds., *Sanctions and Russia* (Warsaw: Polish Institute of International Affairs, 2015), pp. 21–32, http://www.pism.pl/files/?id_plik=19045.

20. "Russia—Trade—European Commission," *European Commission*, last modified March 10, 2016, http://ec.europa.eu/trade/policy/countries-and-regions/countries/russia/.

21. "US-Russian Trade Relationship? There Isn't Really One," *Fortune*, March 18, 2014, http://fortune.com/2014/03/18/u-s-russian-trade-relationship-there-really-isnt-one/.

22. Peter Spiegel and Geoff Dyer, "EU and US Present United Front with Tough Sanctions on Russia," *Financial Times*, July 29, 2014, https://www.ft.com/content/1905aac0-1738-11e4-87c0-00144feabdc0.

23. Barack Obama, "Statement by the President on Ukraine," speech, White House, Washington, DC, July 29, 2014, https://www.white house.gov/the-press-office/2014/07/29/statement-president-ukraine.

24. It subsequently recovered to 50 to 1 in May 2015, only to fall back to 69 to 1 in August 2015. See http://www.bloomberg.com/quote/USDRUB:CUR.

25. Anna Andrianova, "Russian GDP Plunges 4.6%," *Bloomberg*, August 10, 2015, http://www.bloomberg.com/news/articles/2015–08–10/russian-economy-shrinks-4-6-as-oil-slump-risks-deeper-recession.

26. "Update 2—Russian Economy Stagnates as Capital Flight Hits $75 Billion," *Reuters*, July 9, 2014, http://www.reuters.com/article/ukraine-crisis-russia-money-idUSL6N0PK43020140709.

27. Alice Ross, Chris Bryant, and Camilla Hall, "Russian Crisis Already Taking Toll on Western Businesses," *Financial Times*, July 31, 2014, https://www.ft.com/content/494e088e-18ce-11e4-80da-00144feabdc0?siteedition=uk.

28. "Russian Inflation Rate, 1991–2016," *Trading Economics*, accessed September 8, 2015, http://www.tradingeconomics.com/russia/inflation-cpi.

29. Sabrina Tavernise, "Inflation Robs Russians of Buying Power," *New York Times*, August 18, 2015, http://www.nytimes.com/2015/08/19/world/europe/russians-feel-rubles-fall-but-putin-remains-mostly-unscathed.html.

30. Fiona Hill and Clifford G. Gaddy, *Mr. Putin: Operative in the Kremlin* (Washington, DC: Brookings Institution Press, 2013), pp. 222–225.

31. Quoted in Clifford G. Gaddy and Barry W. Ickes, "Putin's Third Way," *National Interest* (January–February 2009), http://nationalinterest.org/article/putins-third-way-2958.

32. "Western Sanctions See Russia Looking to China for Military, Aerospace Components," *Sputnik News*, June 8, 2014, http://sputniknews.com/military/20140806/191767747/Western-Sanctions-See-Russia-Looking-to-China-for-Military.html.

33. Vladimir Putin, "Security Council Meeting," remarks at Security Council meeting, Kremlin, Moscow, July 22, 2014, http://en.kremlin.ru/events/president/news/46305.

34. Jonathan Kirshner, *American Power after the Financial Crisis* (Ithaca, NY: Cornell University Press, 2014), p. 107.

35. David Barboza, "Billions in Hidden Riches for Family of Chinese Leader," *New York Times*, October 25, 2012, http://www.nytimes.com/2012/10/26/business/global/family-of-wen-jiabao-holds-a-hidden-fortune-in-china.html.

36. Edward Wong, "Bloomberg News Is Said to Curb Articles That May Anger China," *New York Times*, November 8, 2013, http://www.nytimes.com/2013/11/09/world/asia/bloomberg-news-is-said-to-curb-articles-that-might-anger-china.html.

37. David Brunnstrom, "US Warns China Not to Attempt Crimea-Style Action in Asia," *Reuters*, April 4, 2014, http://uk.reuters.com/article/uk-usa-china-crimea-asia-idUKBREA3300020140404.

38. Philippe le Corre and Alain Sepulchre, *China's Offensive in Europe* (Washington, DC: Brookings Institution Press, 2016).

39. Stuart Gottlieb and Eric Lorber, "The Dark Side of Interdependence," *Foreign Affairs*, August 5, 2014, https://www.foreignaffairs.com/articles/russian-federation/2014–08–05/dark-side-interdependence.

40. Ed Crooks and Jack Farchy, "Exxon Considers Its Course after Sanctions Hit Russian Ambitions," *Financial Times,* September 30, 2014, https://www.ft.com/content/586ae5c0-487c-11e4-ad19-00144feab7de.

41. Hille and Arnold, "Sberbank Says Sanctions Hit Global Financial System."

42. Anne Applebaum, "Russia's Corrupt Chokehold on Europe," *Slate,* July 25, 2014, http://www.slate.com/articles/news_and_politics/foreigners/2014/07/russia_s_corrupt_control_of_europe_how_vladimir_putin_keeps_the_continent.html.

43. For analysis of the New Silk Road see James McBride, "The New Silk Road," *Council on Foreign Relations,* May 15, 2015, http://www.cfr.org/asia-and-pacific/building-new-silk-road/p36573.

44. Xi Jinping, "Promote Friendship between Our People and Work Together to Build a Bright Future," speech, Nazarbayev University, Astana, Kazakhstan, September 7, 2013, http://www.fmprc.gov.cn/ce/cebel/eng/zxxx/t1078088.htm.

45. Gabriel Wildau, "New BRICS Bank in Shanghai to Challenge Major Institutions," *Financial Times,* July 21, 2015, https://www.ft.com/content/d8e26216-2f8d-11e5-8873-775ba7c2ea3d.

46. Gillian Tett and Jack Farchy, "Russian Banker Warns West over SWIFT," *Financial Times,* January 23, 2015, https://www.ft.com/content/7020c50c-a30a-11e4-9c06-00144feab7de.

47. Kathrin Hille, "Sanction-Scarred Russian Groups Eye BRIC Finance Options," *Financial Times,* July 7, 2015, https://www.ft.com/content/20275444-24ec-11e5-9c4e-a775d2b173ca.

48. Di Dongsheng, "The Renminbi's Rise and Chinese Politics," in Alan Wheatley, ed., *Power of Currencies and the Currencies of Power* (London: International Institute for Strategic Studies, 2013), chapter 6.

49. Krishna Guha, "Paulson Claims Russia Tried to Foment Fannie-Freddie Crisis," *Financial Times,* January 29, 2010, https://www.ft.com/content/ffd950c4-0d0a-11df-a2dc-00144feabdc0.

50. The raw data of foreign holdings of U.S. debt can be found at U.S. Treasury Department, "Major Foreign Holders of Treasury Securities," http://www.treasury.gov/resource-center/data-chart-center/tic/Documents/mfh.txt; Marc Labonte and Jared Nagel, *Foreign Holdings of*

US Debt, CRS Report RS33251 (Washington, DC: CRS, June 24, 2013), http://www.fas.org/sgp/crs/misc/RS22331.pdf. The statement that foreign holdings are at a record high referred to the number for December 2012, but it still applies because the figure for May 2013 was larger still.

51. There is a large drop to third place, which is held by a collection of oil exporters with a total of $266 trillion. See U.S. Treasury Department, "Major Foreign Holders of Treasury Securities."

52. For example, "China Must Punish US for Taiwan Arm Sales with 'Financial Weapon,'" *People's Daily,* August 8, 2011, http://english.people.com.cn/90780/91342/7562776.html.

53. For example, see Daniel Drezner, "Bad Debts: Assessing China's Financial Influence in Great Power Politics," *International Security* 34, no. 2 (Fall 2009): 7–45.

54. James Reilly, "China's Unilateral Sanctions," *Washington Quarterly* 35, no. 4 (2012): 121–133.

55. See Peter Singer and Allan Friedman, *Cybersecurity and Cyberwar: What Everyone Needs to Know* (New York: Oxford University Press, 2014), p. 138.

56. Ibid., p. 141.

57. Ibid., p. 142.

58. Joe Davidson, "OPM Hackers Are More Likely to Get Counterintelligence Action Than Criminal Charges, Report Says," *Washington Post,* July 28, 2015, https://www.washingtonpost.com/news/federal-eye/wp/2015/07/28/opm-hackers-are-more-likely-to-get-counterintelligence-measures-than-charges-report-says/.

59. Ellen Nakashima, "With a Series of Major Hacks, China Builds a Database on Americans," *Washington Post,* June 5, 2015, https://www.washingtonpost.com/world/national-security/in-a-series-of-hacks-china-appears-to-building-a-database-on-americans/2015/06/05/d2af51fa-0ba3-11e5-95fd-d580f1c5d44e_story.html.

60. Julianne Pepitone, "China Is the 'Leading Suspect' in OPM Hacks Says US Intelligence Chief James Clapper," NBC News, June 25, 2015, http://www.nbcnews.com/tech/security/clapper-china-leading-suspect-opm-hack-n381881.

61. Ankit Panda, "Former US Spymaster: China Could Use OPM Data to Recruit Spies," *Diplomat,* June 17, 2015, http://thediplomat.

com/2015/06/former-us-spymaster-china-could-use-opm-data-to-recruit-spies/.

62. This section draws on my 2013 article on interdependence. See Thomas Wright, "Sifting Through Interdependence," *Washington Quarterly* 36, no. 4 (Fall 2013): 12–13.

63. Christopher Joye, "Transcript: Interview with former CIA, NSA Chief Michael V. Hayden," *Australian Financial Review,* July 19, 2013, http://genius.com/Michael-hayden-interview-regarding-edward-snowden-cyber-security-and-transparency-annotated.

64. Permanent Select Committee on Intelligence, U.S. House of Representatives, *Investigative Report on the U.S. National Security Issues Posed by Chinese Telecommunications Companies Huawei and ZTE,* 112th Congress, October 8, 2012, http://intelligence.house.gov/sites/intelligence.house.gov/files/Huawei-ZTE%20Investigative%20Report%20(FINAL).pdf.

65. See Shelley Shan, "National Security Concerns Leads to Parts Ban," *Taipei Times,* June 30, 2011, http://www.taipeitimes.com/News/taiwan/archives/2011/06/30/2003507055; Maggie Lu Yueyang, "Australia Bans Huawei from Broadband Project," *New York Times,* March 26, 2012, http://www.nytimes.com/2012/03/27/technology/australia-bars-huawei-from-broadband-project.html?_r=0; Ray Le Maistre, "Huawei Denied German Bid," *Light Reading,* October 5, 2012, http://www.lightreading.com/author.asp?section_id=210&doc_id=695791.

66. Daniel Thomas, Jim Pickard, and James Blitz, "Cameron Reaffirms Support for Huawei," *Financial Times,* October 19, 2012, https://www.ft.com/content/ad81935a-19ea-11e2-a179-00144feabdc0; Kalyan Parbat, "Government Shuts Out Top Global Network Vendors from Rs 21,000 Crore Fibre Optic Venture," *Economic Times,* January 19, 2013, http://economictimes.indiatimes.com/industry/telecom/government-shuts-out-top-global-network-vendors-from-rs-21000-crore-fibre-optic-venture/articleshow/18086110.cms.

67. James Kynge and Lucy Hornby, "Hinkley Decision Threatens UK 'Golden Era' with China," *Financial Times,* July 31, 2016, https://www.ft.com/content/d087a126-572d-11e6-9f70-badea1b336d4.

68. Jamie Smyth, "Australia Moves to Block a $10 Billion Power Grid Sale to Chinese," *Financial Times,* August 11, 2016, https://www.ft.com/content/918980ce-5f8f-11e6-ae3f-77baadeb1c93.

CHAPTER 6. DEVISING A STRATEGY

1. U.S. National Security Council, *NSC 68: United States Objectives and Programs for National Security; A Report to the President Pursuant to the President's Directive of January 31, 1950* (Washington, DC: National Security Council, 1950), quoted in Ernest May, ed., *American Cold War Strategy: Interpreting NSC-68* (New York: St. Martin's Press, 1993).

2. For a detailed account of the liberal order, see G. John Ikenberry, *Liberal Leviathan: The Origins, Crisis, and Transformation of the American World Order* (Princeton, NJ: Princeton University Press, 2011).

3. Reinhold Niebuhr, *The Irony of American History* (Chicago: University of Chicago Press, 1952), p. 1.

4. Dean Acheson, *Present at the Creation: My Years at the State Department* (New York: Norton, 1969).

5. See Jason Davidson, *The Origins of Revisionist and Status-Quo States* (New York: Palgrave Macmillan, 2006).

6. Andrew Kydd, "Sheep in Sheep's Clothing: Why Security Seekers Do Not Fight Each Other," *Security Studies* 7, no. 1 (Autumn 1997): 114–154; John H. Herz, "Idealist Internationalism and the Security Dilemma," *World Politics* 2, no. 2 (January 1950): 157–180.

7. Randall L. Schweller, "Neorealism's Status Quo Bias: What Security Dilemma?" *Security Studies* 5, no. 3 (1996): 98–101.

8. Davidson, *Origins of Revisionist and Status-Quo States*, pp. 12–14.

9. The only major power that really flirted with revisionism after 1990 was, ironically, the United States, which expanded NATO and the U.S. alliance system in Asia, and sought to remake the Middle East. Yet it is important to note one crucial distinction between revisionism by the United States in Europe and Asia and past revisionists: the states that joined the U.S. alliance system did so by choice and to protect themselves against troublesome neighbors.

10. For an excellent analysis of modern revisionism see Jakub Grygiel and Wess Mitchell, *The Unquiet Frontier: Rising Rivals, Vulnerable Allies, and the Crisis of American Power* (Princeton, NJ: Princeton University Press, 2016).

11. Paul Kennedy, *Strategy and Diplomacy, 1870–1945: Eight Studies*, 2nd ed. (London: Fontana Press, 1989), chapter 2.

12. W. Averell Harriman and Elie Abel, *Special Envoy to Churchill and Stalin, 1941–1946* (New York: Random House, 1975), 236.

13. The literature on this is vast. For the case that America is not in decline, see Bruce Jones, *Still Ours to Lead: America, Rising Powers, and the Tension between Rivalry and Restraint* (Washington, DC: Brookings Institution Press, 2014). For the case that the United States is in decline, see Christopher Layne, "This Time It's Real: The End of Unipolarity and the Pax Americana," *International Studies Quarterly* 56, no. 1 (March 2012): 203–213.

14. This passage draws on Thomas Wright, "Review Essay on American Decline," *Orbis* 54, no. 3 (2010): 479–488.

15. Quoted in William Wohlforth, *The Elusive Balance: Power and Perceptions during the Cold War* (Ithaca, NY: Cornell University Press, 1993), p. 9.

16. William Wohlforth and Stephen Brooks, "The Once and Future Superpower: Why China Won't Overtake the United States," *Foreign Affairs* (May–June 2016): 93.

17. Ibid.

18. Daniel Yergin, *Shattered Peace: The Origins of the Cold War* (Cambridge, MA: Harvard University Press, 1977), p. 13.

19. Henry Kissinger, *Problems of National Strategy: A Book of Readings* (New York: Praeger, 1965), p. 7.

20. Barry Posen, *Sources of Military Doctrine* (Ithaca, NY: Cornell University Press, 1983), p. 13.

21. Stephen Sestanovich, *Maximalist: America in the World from Truman to Obama* (New York: Vintage Press, 2014).

22. Jeffrey Goldberg, "The Obama Doctrine," *Atlantic,* April 2016, http://www.theatlantic.com/magazine/archive/2016/04/the-obama-doctrine/471525/.

23. Ibid.

24. Ibid.

25. Nina Hachigian and David Shorr, "The Responsibility Doctrine," *Washington Quarterly* (Winter 2013): 73–91, http://csis.org/files/publication/TWQ_13Winter_HachigianShorr.pdf.

26. Goldberg, "Obama Doctrine."

27. Ibid.

28. David B. Larter, "White House Tells the Pentagon to Quit Talking about Competition with China," *Navy Times,* September 26, 2016, https://www.navytimes.com/articles/white-house-tells-the-pentagon-to-quit-talking-about-competition-with-china.

29. John Mearsheimer and Stephen Walt, "The Case for Offshore Balancing: A Superior US Grand Strategy," *Foreign Affairs* (July–August 2016), https://www.foreignaffairs.com/articles/united-states/2016–06–13/case-offshore-balancing.

30. Barry Posen, *Restraint: A New Foundation for U.S. Grand Strategy* (Ithaca, NY: Cornell University Press, 2015).

31. Ian Bremmer, *Superpower: Three Choices for America's Role in the World* (New York: Penguin, 2015).

32. Thomas Wright, "Donald Trump's 19th Century Foreign Policy," *Politico*, January 20, 2016. http://www.politico.com/magazine/story/2016/01/donald-trump-foreign-policy-213546.

33. John Kerry, "Remarks on US Policy in the Western Hemisphere," speech, Organization of American States, Washington, DC, November 18, 2013, accessed May 7, 2016, http://www.state.gov/secretary/remarks/2013/11/217680.htm.

34. George H. W. Bush, "Remarks to the Citizens in Mainz," speech, Rheingoldhalle, Mainz, Federal Republic of Germany, May 31, 1989, accessed May 7, 2016, http://www.presidency.ucsb.edu/ws/?pid=17085.

35. Hugh White, "Need to Face the Facts in Asia," *East Asia Forum*, April 18, 2016, accessed May 7, 2016, http://www.eastasiaforum.org/2016/04/18/need-to-face-the-facts-in-asia/. See also Michael Swaine, "The Real Challenge in the Pacific," *Foreign Affairs* (May–June 2015), https://www.foreignaffairs.com/articles/asia/2015–04–20/real-challenge-pacific.

36. Hugh White, *The China Choice: Why America Should Share Power* (Collingwood, Australia: Black, 2012), Kindle edition, location 117.

37. Lyle Goldstein, *Meeting China Halfway: How to Defuse the Emerging U.S.-China Rivalry* (Washington, DC: Georgetown University Press, 2015), pp. 211, 244.

38. Samuel Charap and Jeremy Shapiro, "How to Avoid a New Cold War," *Current History* (October 2014): 265–271.

39. Samuel Charap and Jeremy Shapiro, "Consequences of a New Cold War," *Survival* 57, no. 2 (April–May 2015).

CHAPTER 7. RESPONSIBLE COMPETITION

1. I am grateful to Stephen Hadley for this point.

2. Robert Kagan, "Superpowers Don't Get to Retire," *New Republic*, May 26, 2014, https://newrepublic.com/article/117859/superpowers-dont-get-retire.

3. Richard Haass, *Foreign Policy Begins at Home: The Case for Putting America's House in Order* (New York: Basic Books, 2013); Thomas Friedman and Michael Mandelbau, *That Used to Be Us: How America Fell Behind in the World It Invented and How We Can Come Back* (New York: Picador Books, 2012).

4. Stephen Peter Rosen, "Competitive Strategies: Theoretical Foundations, Limitations, and Extensions," in Thomas Mahnken, ed., *Competitive Strategies for the 21st Century: Theory, History, and Practice* (Stanford, CA: Stanford Security Studies, 2012), p. 12.

5. Henry Kissinger, *The Troubled Partnership* (New York: Anchor Books, 1966).

6. Tyler Cowen, *The Great Stagnation: How America Ate All the Low-Hanging Fruit of Modern History, Got Sick, and Will (Eventually) Feel Better* (New York: Penguin Press, 2011).

7. Lawrence Summers, "What's Behind the Revolt against Global Integration?" *Washington Post*, April 10, 2016, https://www. washingtonpost.com/opinions/whats-behind-the-revolt-against-global-integration/2016/04/10/b4c09cb6-fdbb-11e5-80e4-c381214de1a3_story.html?utm_term=.72aaa0ad7d17.

8. Tamara Wittes, "Remarks at Princeton University Conference on Global Governance," lecture, Princeton University Conference on Global Governance, Princeton, NJ, May 14, 2016.

9. Andrew Shearer, *Australia-Japan-US Maritime Cooperation: Creating Federated Capabilities for the Asia Pacific,* draft report (Washington, DC: Center for Strategic and International Studies, March 23, 2016), 27.

10. Jeffrey Goldberg, "The Obama Doctrine," *Atlantic,* April 2016, http://www.theatlantic.com/magazine/archive/2016/04/the-obama-doctrine/471525/.

11. Robert Blackwill and Jennifer Harris, *War by Other Means: Geoeconomics and Statecraft* (Cambridge, MA: Belknap Press, 2016), pp. 229–231.

12. Shearer, *Australia-Japan-US Maritime Cooperation*, p. 5.

13. See *Saudi Vision 2030,* http://vision2030.gov.sa/en.

14. Bruce Riedel, *Kings and Presidents: Saudi Arabia and America since FDR* (Washington, DC: Brookings Institution Press, forthcoming).

15. I am grateful to Matthew Spence for this point.

16. The case for hard-headed engagement with Iran to stabilize the Middle East is made in Zalmay Khalizad, "The Neo-Conservative Case

for Negotiating with Iran," *Politico Magazine*, March 28, 2016, http://www.politico.com/magazine/story/2016/03/iran-negotiation-foreign-policy-middle-east-213772?paginate=false.

17. Edward Wong, "Search for Lost Jet Is Complicated by Geopolitics and Rivalries," *New York Times*, March 26, 2014, http://www.nytimes.com/2014/03/27/world/asia/geopolitical-rivalries-jet.html.

EPILOGUE

1. Thomas Wright, "Donald Trump's 19th Century Foreign Policy," *Politico*, January 20, 2016, http://www.politico.com/magazine/story/2016/01/donald-trump-foreign-policy-213546.

INDEX

203–206; use of term, 2. *See also* balance of power

Baltic states, 34, 63, 179–180, 183, 197, 205–206

Bataclan Theater terrorist attack, 56

Biden, Joseph, 13, 17, 104, 105

Bloomberg, 139

Bond, Kevin, 69

Boston Globe, 224

Brazil, 6, 19, 31, 227. *See also* BRICS

Bremmer, Ian, 178

Brexit, 58–61, 63, 66, 200, 202

BRICS (Brazil, Russia, India, China, and South Africa), 49, 51, 137, 144

British Empire, use of accommodation strategy, 160

Brooks, Stephen, 165, 166

Bush administration (George H. W. Bush), 9, 63

Bush administration (George W. Bush): and convergence, 11–13, 15, 21–22, 28; and European integration, 63; and Middle East, 13, 28; spy plane incident in China (2001), 3; and terrorism, 15, 20

Cambodia, 92

Cameron, David, 59–60, 152

Campbell, Kurt, 68–69

Carter, Ashton, 81, 173

Catherine the Great, 52

Charap, Samuel, 182

Charlie Hebdo massacre, 55–56

chemical weapons, 106–107

Cheney, Dick, 22

China, 67–98; and balance of power, 196; balancing against, in East Asia, 87–96, 97–98, 206–212; Clinton administration and, 10; conflict avoidance strategy, 77, 79–80, 84, 207, 239n20; convergence and the threat of democratization, 16–18; cooperation on global issues, 33–34, 70, 98, 220–221; core interests of, 84–85; cyberwarfare operations, 148–149; domestic problems, 96–97; and East China Sea, 78, 82, 87, 146, 208–209; economic growth in, 19–20; and European Union, 140; fears of U.S. sanctions, 139–140; and flow of information, 138–139; foreign policy change to assertive, 25–27; and George W. Bush administration, 3, 12; and interdependence, 138–141, 143–145; investment in U.S. and U.K. companies, 151–152; linkages to U.S. economy, 140–141; and the Middle East, 123–125; and nationalism, 26–27, 97, 206; and North Korea, 211–212; and Obama administration, 14, 173; One Belt, One Road initiative, 124; possibility of crisis or decline

China (continued)
in, 97; power assessment of,
167, 168; regional challenges
to the power and influence of,
74–76; and Russia, 136–137;
and sharing East Asia with
U.S., 83–86, 181–182; and
South China Sea, 25, 68–71,
78–82, 208–210, 246n26;
strategic goals of (overview),
76–78; as threat to U.S. global
order, 71–74; and U.S.
accommodation strategy,
181–182; as U.S. competitor,
190, 191–192; and U.S. debt,
146–147; use of sanctions by,
147. *See also* BRICS
Christensen, Thomas, 72–73
Churchill, Winston, 206
Clapper, James, 149
Clark, Wesley, 3
Clinton, Hillary, 150, 215
Clinton administration (Bill
Clinton), 6, 8–11, 20, 63
Cold War: balancing during, 2–3,
4; Clinton on, 10; and
instability, xi; and nuclear
weapons, 155, 222; and
proxy wars, 117; sanctions,
128; and trade, 130
competitive strategy school of
thought, 190–191
connectivity wars, 130
convergence, 1–34; during George
W. Bush administration,
11–13, 15, 21–22, 28; and
China, 16–18, 25–27; during

Clinton administration, 8–11;
concept of, 1–2, 229n1; end
of, ix–x, 20–21; financial crisis
of 2008 and, 29–31; flaws of,
16–20; globalization and
market democracy and, 5–7;
and global vs. regional issues,
33–34; as independent of U.S.
primacy, 7–8, 13–14; and lack
of balancing against U.S., 2–8;
and the Middle East, 27–29;
during Obama administration,
13–15, 23–27, 28–29; post-
Cold War, ix–x; and Russia,
16–18, 21–24; shared threats
and interests and, 7, 11–12,
13–14; successes and failures
of, 31–32
Coordinating Committee for
Multilateral Export Controls
(CoCom), 128
Cowen, Tyler, 194–195
Crimea, 47–50, 96, 133–135, 139
Cronin, Patrick, 80
Cui Tiankai, 84, 85
cyber attacks, 51, 147–151,
205–206

Dai Bingguo, 84
Demirtas, Selahattin, 118
democracy: European Union and,
38; in Japan, 91–92; in the
Middle East, 20, 28, 99, 100,
102, 122 (*see also* Arab
Awakening / Arab Spring); as
optimal way, 6, 12, 226;
Russia's and China's fears of,

and, 18, 57–58, 117–118, 122–123; responsible competition strategy in, 212–218; rise of ISIS in, 100–101, 105, 118–120, 121; risks of chaos in, 125–126, 213–214; Saudi Arabia–Iran cold war (*see* Saudi Arabia–Iran cold war); Shia-Sunni divide, 100, 104, 105, 111–112, 114, 118–119, 123, 125, 126, 197; signs of hope in, 126; U.S. engagement vs. disengagement in, 120–122, 126, 163, 212–214. *See also specific countries*

military power, 166–167

Mission Failure (Mandelbaum), 31

Mitterrand, François, 38, 63

Mohammed bin Nayef, crown prince of Saudi Arabia, 113

Mohammed bin Salman, deputy crown prince of Saudi Arabia, 113, 215

Morsi, Mohamed, 111

Moscow Conference (1943), 163–164

Mubarak, Hosni, 102, 109–110, 113, 115, 194

multilateralism: as basic to international order, x, 192–193; China and, 3, 25–26, 80, 86; Obama administration and, 172–173

multipolarity, 13–14

Munich Security Conference (2007), 22

Muslim Brotherhood, 102, 111, 216

Myers, Stephen Lee, 24

Nathan, Andrew, 27, 75

nationalism: East Asia and, 26–27, 74, 83, 92, 97, 206; European Union and, 64; nations in decline and, 97; new era of, ix, x, xii, 31, 36–37, 65, 161–164, 205, 225, 226; Putin regime and, 36, 51–52, 195; Trump and America First, ix, 178, 223–224

National Power and the Structure of Foreign Trade (Hirschman), 129–130

National Security Strategy (European Union, 2003), 35

NATO: expansion, 9, 10, 16, 17, 19, 21, 23, 63, 181; Putin and, 17, 21, 23, 43, 44–45, 48, 50, 117, 133, 179, 200, 203; and responsible competition strategy, 204–205, 216–217; and restraint strategy, 177, 178, 179; Trump and, 37, 64; and U.S.-Russia power-sharing strategy, 182

Nazi Germany, 3, 128, 129, 159

neo-isolationism, 177–179, 180

New Development Bank (NDB), 144

New Silk Road, 143–144

New Year's Eve sexual assaults (Germany), 57

New Yorker, 101, 119–120

Union and NATO, 17, 21, 23,
43–52, 64–65, 117, 133,
200–201, 203–206; invasion
of Georgia, 22–23; and the
Middle East, 18, 57–58,
117–118, 122–123; and
Obama administration, 14,
23–24, 43, 133–135, 150, 173,
182; power assessment of,
167, 168; proposed dumping
of U.S. bonds, 145–146;
protests against, 43; sanctions
against, 49, 133–135,
141–143, 204; strategy of
reserves and self-reliance,
135–138, 144; Trump and,
224; and Ukraine crisis and
annexation of Crimea, 45,
47–50, 117, 133–135, 173;
and U.S. accommodation
strategy, 182–183, 184; as
U.S. competitor, 190,
191–192; use of hard
power, 50; and U.S. war
on terrorism, 20–21

Qaddafi, Muammar, 105
Qatar, 111

Rajan, Raghuram, 30
RAND corporation, 110
Ratner, Ely, 68–69
realist foreign policy (offshore
balancing), 176–177
refugee crisis (2015), 53–55,
57–58, 61–62
relative power, 165–166

Remnick, David, 119–120
renminbi internationalization,
144–145
reset with Russia, 14, 23–24, 43
Responsibility Doctrine, 172
responsible competition, 187–222;
and China, 206–212; vs.
competitive strategy school of
thought, 190–191; competitive
vs. noncompetitive
relationships, 188–189;
defined, 188–189; and free-
riding alliances, 197–199;
goals of, 221–222; importance
of balance of power in,
196–197; importance of liberal
values in, 192–196; and the
Middle East, 212–218;
promotion of, in Europe
(balancing Russia), 199–206;
vs. restraint/retrenchment
strategy, 170–171; vs. shared
global interests, 218–222;
two components of, 191–192;
and U.S. engagement in
Europe, 66
Restraint (Posen), 177–178
restraint/retrenchment, 170–186;
accommodation strategy,
180–186; vs. maximalist
strategies, 170–171; neo-
isolationism, 177–179; Obama
doctrine of, 171–176; offshore
balancing (realist foreign
policy), 176–177
retrenchment. *See* restraint/
retrenchment